Democratic Commitments

Democratic Commitments

LEGISLATURES AND
INTERNATIONAL COOPERATION

Lisa L. Martin

PRINCETON UNIVERSITY PRESS
PRINCETON, NEW JERSEY

Copyright © 2000 by Princeton University Press
Published by Princeton University Press, 41 William Street,
Princeton, New Jersey 08540
In the United Kingdom: Princeton University Press, Chichester, West Sussex

Library of Congress Cataloging-in-Publication Data

Martin, Lisa L., 1961–
Democratic commitments : legislatures and international cooperation / Lisa L. Martin.
p.   cm.
Includes bibliographical references and index.
ISBN 0-691-00923-6 (cl : alk. paper) — ISBN 0-691-00924-4 (pb : alk. paper)
1. Legislative bodies.   2. International cooperation.   3. Legislative bodies—European
Union countries.   4. United States. Congress.   I. Title.
JF511 .M37 2000
328.73'0746—dc21   99-049295

This book has been composed in Times Roman

The paper used in this publication meets the minimum requirements
of ANSI/NISO Z39.48-1992 (R1997) (*Permanence of Paper*)

www.pup.princeton.edu

Printed in the United States of America
10 9 8 7 6 5 4 3 2 1
10 9 8 7 6 5 4 3 2 1
(Pbk.)

Contents

Preface   vii

CHAPTER 1
Introduction   3

CHAPTER 2
Theoretical Framework: Legislatures, Executives, and Commitment   21

CHAPTER 3
Institutions and Influence: Executive Agreements and Treaties   53

CHAPTER 4
Economic Sanctions: Domestic Conflict of Interest
and International Cooperation   81

CHAPTER 5
U.S. Food-Aid Policy: The Politics of Delegation and Linkage   112

CHAPTER 6
National Parliaments and European Integration:
Institutional Choice in EU Member States   147

CHAPTER 7
Implementing the EU's Internal Market: The Influence
of National Parliaments   164

CHAPTER 8
Conclusion   190

References   203

Index   221

Preface

THIS BOOK has been a long time coming, and along the way has benefited from extraordinarily generous and insightful advice from colleagues. The general question asked is whether legislatures have an impact on the credibility of state commitments. The answer I find is yes; and I also find that the impact of organized legislative participation is positive overall. Both claims—the latter more than the former, I believe—are controversial within the field of international relations. Just as controversial is the general approach that led me to these conclusions. This general approach begins from the presumption that domestic and international politics are not creatures that inhabit different universes, but fields to which we can apply similar concepts and models. This presumption challenges decades (at least) of teaching and writing in international relations, where the assumption that international relations is different, not operating according to the same laws of political life as domestic politics, is strongly held.

The empirical puzzle that motivated this book, as well as my other work, is the problem of international cooperation and how cooperation is related to the demand for credibility. My previous book, *Coercive Cooperation,* also centered on the problems of cooperation and credibility. There, I concentrated on systemic sources of credibility. I found that international institutions contributed to the credibility of state commitments when they followed policies of imposing economic sanctions.

The desire to deepen my understanding of how institutions worked, and in particular how they might resolve credibility problems, led me to the study of domestic institutions. Modern work on domestic institutions is often framed around problems of credibility and collective action. This is especially true for the literature on legislative organization and legislative-executive interaction. Thus, I spent several years studying these literatures, developing a general sense of institutional dynamics and how they changed the parameters of credibility. These years were allowed and encouraged by the financial support of the University of California, San Diego; the National Fellows Program at the Hoover Institution at Stanford University, the MacArthur Foundation; and the Social Science Research Council. For this support, and for the opportunity to interact with faculty in the political science department and Graduate School of Business at Stanford, I am deeply grateful.

My study of the literature on domestic institutions both informed my understanding of international institutions and gave rise to the project that has resulted in this book. In learning about legislatures and how political scientists today conceive of their activities and organization, I realized that the way in which nearly all studies of international politics and foreign policy treated legislatures diverged substantially from the literature on domestic politics. While foreign-policy studies tended to see legislative activity as an impediment and hindrance to a successful foreign policy, the domestic-politics literature suggested ways in which legislatures could learn, influence policy in a productive manner, and make consistent commitments to policies. With studies of international cooperation increasingly turning to the domestic level, bringing these new understandings of legislative capacities to the problem of international credibility and cooperation was a natural step.

This project began as a more narrowly focused study of foreign-aid policy, which is still reflected in chapter 5 of this book. However, during my first couple of years in the Harvard government department, I decided to broaden my sights, considering a wider range of issue-areas. The environment of the government department has been, as all find it, a challenging and stimulating one, where colleagues and students, as well as a vast assortment of visitors, encourage bold thinking.

First and foremost in my personal thanks, as always, is Bob Keohane. As a friend, colleague, and mentor, no one could possibly offer more support and constructive yet penetrating criticism. Jeff Frieden has for years provided a sounding board, critical ear, and willingness to spend time reading and talking whose value is difficult to calculate. Other individuals have given generously of their time and thoughts: Karen Alter, Bob Axelrod, Marc Busch, Randy Calvert, Dan Drezner, Geoff Garrett, Stanley Hoffmann, Peter Katzenstein, Dan Keleman, Jeff Legro, Gary Marks, Walter Mattli, Tim McKeown, Andy Moravcsik, Andy Rutten, Duncan Snidal, and Amy Verdun. While not all agree with the arguments of this book as it has evolved, all have prodded me to think critically in ways that I value highly. I have also benefited enormously from the comments of seminar participants at Stanford, the Olin Institute at Harvard, UCSD, NYU, the University of Colorado-Boulder, the European University Institute, Yale, UNC, Columbia, UC Irvine, and the University of Washington. Finally, I am grateful for the superb research assistance of Mary Kwak, Liliana Botcheva, and Lawrence Hamlet.

Lexington, Massachusetts
April 1999

Democratic Commitments

CHAPTER 1

Introduction

CREDIBILITY of commitments is a persistent problem in international politics. The forms of international cooperation that offer states the highest benefits require them to make credible commitments to one another. States that lack the capacity for commitment cannot achieve many potential gains from economic exchange. They find it difficult to keep the peace and to reestablish peace after wars. Without commitment, mutual distrust confines cooperative endeavors to the most shallow and least risky, as states will be reluctant to undertake actions that involve any degree of irreversibility or sunk costs. Commitment is the keystone of international politics, as it is of all social relations that contain the potential for both conflict and mutual benefit (i.e., in any relationship based on exchange). But because states exist in an international system that does not provide the social context that allows for mutual trust among individuals in other social settings, states face special challenges in making the commitments necessary to promote deep cooperation.

This book approaches the problem of international credibility by examining the domestic sources of commitments. In particular, it concentrates on the role of national legislatures in established democracies. It addresses two central questions: do legislatures matter; and if so, so what? The first question involves the degree of influence that legislatures have on processes of international cooperation in stable democracies. The second turns to the consequences of legislative influence, asking how it affects the credibility of states' commitments to one another and therefore patterns of international cooperation.

The answers provided in this book challenge much of our conventional understanding about Congress in the United States and parliaments in Western Europe. First, I find that the degree of legislative influence on international cooperation, in both presidential and parliamentary systems, exceeds usual estimates. Because legislative influence is often exercised in indirect ways (especially in parliamentary systems), it is easy to underestimate its extent. Second, legislative influence and the domestic institutions through which it is channeled vary systematically and predictably in response to conflicts of interest between the executive and legislature. Turning to the question of the consequences of legislative influence, I again challenge the mainstream viewpoint held in studies of U.S. foreign policy and European integration. I argue that institutionalized legislative participation in international cooperation enhances the credibility of states' commitments, thus leading to more stable and deeper patterns of international cooperation.

I come to these conclusions via an analysis of modern theories of legislative organization and their application to areas of international cooperation that have not previously been studied using these approaches. Existing metaphors for legislative-executive interaction stress the zero-sum, competitive nature of a battle for influence between the branches: executive or legislative "dominance," or a "struggle for power." These metaphors are misleading when applied to the problem of international cooperation, because they fail to take into account the branches' mutual interest in being able to make credible commitments to other states. Instead, I offer the metaphor of an exchange relationship between political actors, in which elements of competition coexist with the pursuit of mutually beneficial deals. The exchange image draws our attention to the institutions that structure legislative-executive interaction and the credibility of state commitments.

Prominent instances of international cooperation at the end of the millennium show the demand for credibility. Examples run from expansion of NATO to enlargement and deepening of regional trade arrangements to European Monetary Union (EMU). In all cases, concerns for the credibility of partners' commitments permeate the process of cooperation. Rules of cooperation are designed so as to force states to demonstrate their commitment to particular policies. Concerns about credibility make the process of enlarging and deepening cooperative arrangements long and laborious. Without the capacity to make credible commitments, states can find themselves excluded from modern forms of international cooperation.

States' attempts to cooperate, and our attempts to explain successes and failures of international cooperation, are complicated by the fact that states are not unitary actors. The state is not an individual that makes and puts into practice its own decisions. It is a complex organizational and social structure. Internal structure may account for patterns of cooperation beyond those defined by the constraints of the international system. We find it difficult to believe that authoritarian dictatorships face the same commitment dilemmas as open, stable democracies. In individual instances of failed or successful attempts to cooperate, we often appeal to the nature of domestic political arrangements for explanation. Yet we lack a systematic understanding of how these domestic factors matter, or even which domestic structures deserve our closest attention. This book finds that, for democracies, the role of the legislature is a crucial explanatory variable.

As another democratic wave brings massive changes in state regimes throughout the world (Huntington 1991), it becomes vitally important that we attempt to understand the implications of democracy for states' international behavior. Our current state of knowledge is muddled. On the one hand, most foreign-policy analysis highlights the difficulties of democracy, with its complex procedures for making decisions, its transparency, and its lack of insulation from public pressure. The tradition of deploring the effect of democracy on ability to conduct foreign policy has illustrious roots, going back at least to Tocqueville (1945, 243). On the other hand, we usually believe that we would all be safer in a world of democracies, and would prefer to have democracies as partners in international economic and security relationships. Democracy is valuable not only as an end in itself but also has beneficial implications for behavior in the international realm. In spite of the pessimistic projections of foreign-policy analysis, political leaders and most others believe a world of democracies would be safer and richer than a world of non-democracies. Somehow democracies seem able to overcome their supposed handicaps to deal successfully with the demands of interdependence, even if we do not yet have a good understanding of how they do so (Waltz 1967).

No doubt foreign-policy analysts are correct in noting that legislators who care about the state's external behavior can make life difficult for international negotiators, adding complexity to an already messy process. It is not surprising that diplomats and heads of government find themselves frustrated by legislative constraints, since these constraints are sometimes painful and force negotiators to take a broader range of preferences into account. However, concentrating only on bargaining difficulties obscures more important patterns of international life, such as the actual level of cooperation achieved. Unconstrained executive-branch actors can indeed bargain more flexibly. But such apparently powerful negotiators can find it difficult to put into effect the agreements they reach with such ease at the international table. Their lack of *ex ante* domestic constraints also gives them the capacity to act arbitrarily, making them unreliable partners in international cooperation in spite of their apparently enviable freedom of maneuver. To understand how legislatures influence the course of international cooperation, we must ask two kinds of questions. First, we need to develop an understanding of the nature of legislative influence on processes of international cooperation and how that influence changes over time and across issues. With this in hand, we can turn to consider how legislative engagement affects democracies' ability to cooperate.

LEGISLATURES AND COOPERATION

In the United States, studies of foreign policy frequently focus on the question of how much influence Congress has, and whether congressional influence undermines the coherence of U.S. policy. Textbooks and surveys of foreign policy devote substantial attention to the role of Congress (for example, see Nathan and Oliver 1994). Numerous books focus specifically on the congressional role in foreign policy or legislative-executive battles over it (see Lindsay 1994a; Crabb and Holt 1992; Peterson 1994a; Destler 1986; Hinckley 1994; Pastor 1980). From the level of attention it receives, one would suspect that Congress must be an important foreign-policy actor, as I will argue in this book it is. However, despite the number of pages devoted to the study of Congress, most students of U.S. foreign policy conclude in their surveys that the president dominates policymaking. While Congress may show increased activism on foreign affairs in the last twenty years, at least relative to the early cold-war era, few analysts find that this activism has meant any fundamental change in the president's ability to get his way on foreign-policy issues.

The reasons that analysts provide for presidential dominance on foreign policy are legion. Going back at least to the authors of the *Federalist Papers,* analysts have held an assumption that foreign relations require a level of expertise and secrecy that precludes legislators from properly or consistently taking an active part. The electoral system encourages members of Congress (MCs) to focus on parochial, district-specific concerns, leaving them only intermittently interested in foreign-policy issues. When MCs do become interested, they are responding to media coverage or some other source of publicity, and the contribution they can make to effective foreign policy is minimal, according to this assumption. At best, they have no effect; at worst, they undermine the centralized, rational policy that could follow from leaving decisions in the hands of the executive. Executive dominance does not follow from specific constitutional provisions, since the Constitution is surprisingly, sometimes frustratingly, silent on the assigned powers of the branches on foreign policy. It follows instead from the logic of electoral concerns and the necessity of having a strong state to cope with the demands of international relations.

The executive-dominance view of policymaking is widely, though not universally, accepted. While most authors admit that Congress on occasion influences foreign policy, they see such instances as rare and inconsequential enough to pose no serious challenge to the basic executive-dominance logic. Nathan and Oliver, for example, note that Congress became more active on foreign policy during the 1970s as the bipartisan cold-war consensus broke down, but conclude that "Congress remained an essentially reactive participant" (1994, 239). Lack of consensus did lead Congress to block presidential actions at times, but the result was only to create deadlock, not to contribute to an effective foreign policy. Thus, while the imperial-presidency model may not be fully accurate today, Congress has little constructive role to play; the United States may in fact have been better off with executive dominance.

Peterson similarly notes that Congress became more active in foreign policy in the 1970s and 1980s, but concludes that "the primary locus of decision making remained in presidential hands. . . . The presidency continued to be the dominant foreign policy-making institution. For all of Capitol Hill's increased involvement, it still remained a secondary political player" (1994c, 217). Sharpe (1988) argues that the Cold War created a system of executive dominance in foreign policy that legislators tried to change after Vietnam, but that their attempts have had little sustained success. Studies of the domestic politics of U.S. foreign policy have reached a consensus that Congress remains a marginal player in spite of its increased activity. Some find increased activity a problem for U.S. foreign policy; others find it less threatening, noting that it has restrained executive excesses in Vietnam and other controversial uses of U.S. power abroad. Lindsay (1994a), in contrast to this widely held view, draws more heavily on recent studies of the internal organization and functioning of Congress and comes to a more optimistic conclusion about congressional influence and contribution to foreign policy, moving in the direction that this book follows.

An image of legislative lack of influence once characterized much writing on domestic policy as well, but has been seriously challenged in the last fifteen years. Studies of legislative organization and legislative-executive interaction, summarized in the next chapter, show that legislators can use procedural powers to influence the shape of policy outcomes even if they delegate authority to the executive branch and do not pass a great deal of substantive legislation. These new approaches to understanding legislative incentives and mechanisms of influence have been applied to trade policy (O'Halloran 1994; Lohmann and O'Halloran 1994), and on occasion to other areas of foreign policy (Milner 1997; Lindsay 1994b). These applications suggest that new understandings of how legislatures exercise influence are relevant in foreign policy as well as domestic, and that the potential of this literature to enhance our understanding of the domestic politics of foreign policy in democracies is vast.

One of the key lessons of modern theories of legislative institutions is that we must be especially careful to distinguish between action and influence, and not to infer one from observing the other. Arguments that Congress has little influence on foreign policy often start by noting that the president and his appointees actually *do* foreign policy: they negotiate, sign agreements, send troops abroad, spend money, and so on. The substantive activities of Congress, in contrast, appear quite inconsequential. Congress approves appropriations for foreign-policy purposes, and often writes into appropriation bills limitations on the use of these funds, but also usually leaves loopholes such as grants of executive discretion for purposes of "national security." Congress occasionally imposes economic sanctions, but not with the same frequency that the president does (see chapter 4 below). Congress approves some candidates for important foreign-policy posts within the administration, but rarely turns down a candidate nominated by the president. The vast majority of international agreements negotiated by the president today take the form of executive agreements rather than treaties (see chapter 3), limiting the participation of Congress. If we equate activity with influence, we would easily conclude that executive-branch influence far outweighs that of Congress.

Yet such an inference would constitute a fundamental and misleading logical error. Influence and activity are not identical, nor are they even necessarily highly correlated with one another. The most powerful actors, meaning those who exercise the most influence over outcomes, may be those who need to take the fewest actions. To illustrate this logic, consider a naive *legislative-*

dominance perspective. One of the constitutional tools with which the president in the United States can influence legislation is the veto, which can only be overridden by a two-thirds majority vote in both houses of Congress. Yet, we see that presidents in the United States rarely exercise vetoes. Do we conclude from this observation that the veto provides presidents with no leverage over legislation? No, since we understand that presidents only use the veto if they have failed sufficiently to influence legislation at some earlier stage in the process. Because Congress can anticipate the probability of a presidential veto, legislators will take presidential preferences into account at a point in the legislative process prior to actual exercise of the veto. Accumulating a frequency count of the use of presidential vetoes might tell us some interesting things, perhaps about the cooperative or conflictual nature of executive-legislative relations or the value of taking public stands on various issues. But it would tell us nothing about the leverage presidents have on legislation. In fact, it is natural to assume that when presidents are the most active in the use of the veto is when they have most profoundly failed to have their preferences reflected in legislation.

Equating lack of legislative activity on foreign policy with lack of legislative influence may lead us into a similar logical trap, leading us to misunderstand how and when foreign policy reflects legislators' preferences. But if we cannot use legislative activity as an indicator of legislative influence, the implications for empirical research may at first look less than promising. Models of executive dominance may predict little legislative activity, for reasons of lack of interest and capacity; models that allow for legislative influence may also predict little legislative activity. How can we distinguish between the two, empirically? One might conclude that modern models of legislative institutions, allowing for indirect mechanisms of influence and recognizing the role of anticipated reactions, are not refutable and so refuse to take them seriously.

However, things are not so grim. Alternative models of legislative influence are not observationally equivalent, unless one is sloppy about devising tests of legislative influence. Developing appropriate tests requires that we concentrate on deriving observable implications of alternative models that provide the greatest possible discrimination between their predictions. In particular, if we wish to develop empirical propositions that allow us to distinguish between models, we generally need to devote more attention to studying *outcomes,* less to studying *processes.*

For example, if we are wondering whether legislative preferences had any impact on a specific set of trade negotiations, it would not be sufficient to see whether Congress put explicit legislative limits on the negotiations, or how many legislative representatives were included in the delegation to the negotiations. Such pieces of information may be useful, but if the actors in our models are sophisticated they are unlikely to allow us to distinguish between executive-dominance and legislative-influence models. An appropriate test of legislative influence would lie in examining the outcome of trade negotiations, to determine whether negotiators made concessions to legislative preferences. Since determining the connection between outcomes and preferences in an individual instance is difficult, the most persuasive tests of legislative influence consist of observing how outcomes vary as a function of changes in key legislative variables, such as party control of relevant congressional committees. If substantial changes in these legislative variables give rise to changes in outcomes, we can infer that legislators have indeed managed to exercise influence.[1] We may also consider outcome variables other than the characteristics of agreements reached, such as the institutional framework chosen to structure negotiations or the conditions under which agreements are implemented efficiently. Influence, defined as the ability of an actor to bring outcomes close to his or her preferred position, is best measured by looking at patterns of outcomes, asking whether they covary with characteristics of the legislative environment. Studies of activity alone are insufficient for testing claims about influence; patterns of outcomes will be more revealing.

I have kept the necessity of examining outcomes in mind throughout the empirical material in this book. We also need at times to consider processes, in order to identify the indirect mechanisms through which legislatures can influence processes of international cooperation. In general, the outcome of international cooperation is a major dependent variable, and I look for patterns that link the level of cooperation to legislative structures. In chapter 7, for example, I find that cooperation in the process of European integration depends on domestic provisions for legislative-executive interaction. In chapter 4, I find that cooperation on economic sanctions depends on party control of the branches of government. These are patterns that are consistent with models that allow for legislative influence, but that are not consistent with executive-dominance models.

Alternative models are not, luckily for empirical researchers and those who are developing theories of legislative organization, observationally equivalent if one is careful about collecting the right kind of evidence. However, the tests that allow us to distinguish among models of legislative influence are sometimes more indirect than standard empirical work on foreign policy. Activity is relatively easy to observe directly. Measuring influence—or, even more difficult, credibility—requires more subtle, indirect tests. As argued below, legislators often exercise influence through the mechanism of anticipated reactions. If executives accurately anticipate legislative constraints, much of the action of influence takes place behind the scenes. Thus we will have little luck finding overt, public expressions of influence. Instead, we must follow King, Keohane, and Verba's (1994) advice to generate as many observable implications of any

---

[1] Rueschemeyer, Stephens, and Stephens (1992, 33) similarly argue that process-oriented studies, while appropriate for examining some causal claims, are not well designed for testing structural theories, such as theories about the impact of domestic institutional arrangements.

proposition as possible. Some of these implications may be rather indirect, not addressing the problem of influence or credibility in as immediate a fashion as is usual in studies of foreign policy. For example, rather than looking for statements by negotiating partners that they believe a particular commitment to be credible, we might ask about the overall pattern of implementation of international agreements, or about the form of agreement used under different circumstances. While such tests lack immediacy, they are a more discriminating test of propositions about influence or credibility than the most obvious, direct observations of activity or beliefs. In fact, if arguments about behind-the-scenes influence and anticipated reactions are correct, these indirect tests tell us much more about actual influence than the more obvious approaches that fall under the catch-all phrase "process tracing."

I argue that executive-dominance models do not tell us what we need to know about legislative influence on international cooperation, nor do descriptive analyses of the rise and decline of one branch or the other. I draw on models of legislative delegation to the executive to develop expectations about variation in legislative engagement on foreign policy and the scope of executive discretion. However, I do not intend to argue in favor of anything like a legislative-dominance model. Instead, I suggest that we should conceive of legislative-executive relations as an exchange relationship. The exchange metaphor is useful because it draws our attention to the fact that well-designed domestic institutions can benefit *both* the executive and the legislature. Lack of appropriate institutional arrangements can leave executives unable to make commitments to other states and legislatures with little power except to frustrate and delay policy. Both branches therefore have an interest in finding ways to work with one another to pursue goals that can only be achieved through international cooperation. In an interdependent international economy and polity, legislators would be foolish to ignore the implications of other states' actions for their constituents' well-being. Likewise, executives would be foolish to ignore the legitimate interest of legislators in these issues and their potential to undermine executive-driven foreign policies.

An exchange model of legislative-executive interaction, built on the insights of U.S. policy on food aid as well as the other cases examined in this book, is spelled out most fully in chapter 5. Arguing about whether the legislature or the executive "dominates" foreign policy, in contrast to an exchange model, neglects the scope for arrangements that benefit both branches, portraying instead a purely competitive, distributional approach to interbranch relations. For example, consider the fast-track procedures that have been used to approve many international trade agreements in the 1980s and 1990s, including NAFTA. These procedures allow the president to make more certain commitments to other countries, since they make transparent the American ratification process and severely limit congressional power to amend international agreements. At the same time, they provide for an explicit legislative role in negotiations and a legislative vote at the end. How do we interpret fast-track procedures, therefore—as a triumph for the executive or for the legislature? Neither, I would argue, and the question itself misses central elements of the logic of domestic institutions. Such arrangements can enhance U.S. credibility, credibility that under at least some configurations of preferences would otherwise be quite questionable. They therefore benefit both branches.

The central questions about legislative-executive interaction, I would venture, are how the nature of legislative participation in processes of international cooperation varies and how it influences the outcomes of international cooperation.[2] Whether the executive or the legislature is "winning" on any particular issue is of secondary importance, not to mention nearly impossible to measure with any confidence. Thus the conventional wisdom that executive-legislative interaction on foreign policy is a "struggle for power" (Corwin 1940, 200) is misguided, since it assumes that these actors are playing a zero-sum game. Instead, well-designed institutional arrangements have the potential to benefit both branches.

Studies of legislative organization that model indirect, subtle mechanisms of legislative influence have focused on Congress, as has my discussion thus far. One of the central questions in the study of legislatures, as well as of democracy and international cooperation, is whether these models give us insight into only one specific institution—i.e., Congress—or whether they can be extended to others, particularly to parliamentary systems. The mechanisms of executive accountability and the ways in which the legislature organizes itself and interacts with the executive vary greatly between presidential and parliamentary systems; they also vary greatly among parliamentary systems. The most fundamental difference is that in parliamentary systems, the executive—i.e., the Prime Minister and other cabinet ministers—is chosen from and directly responsible to the legislature. Parliamentary systems are characterized by a lack of separation of powers between the executive and legislative. One might expect that such a system would produce less executive discretion than presidents enjoy, with their independent base of electoral support.

However, the logic of parliamentary institutions does not support such a view. Yes, parliament can overturn the government by a vote of "no confidence." Yet, unless parliament can replace the government with one more to its liking, the power to remove the incumbent is of little practical importance (Laver and Shepsle 1994, 291). The mechanisms of parliamentary democracy produce a more intimate relationship between the legislature and executive than we find in the United States. This intimacy creates a mutual dependence that in

---

[2] These questions are basically the same as those Shepsle (1986) poses about "equilibrium institutions" and "institutional equilibrium," respectively.

turn generates significant executive discretion. In particular, strong parties have arisen to mediate relations among politicians in parliamentary systems (Cox 1987). A parliament that rejects a government is putting itself at risk, since such a move often requires new elections. Votes of no confidence, even if they do not lead to general elections that put the seats of all incumbent members of parliament (MPs) on the line, undermine the value of the party label that is so essential to the functioning of parliamentary government. As a result of the mutual dependence of backbenchers and the government, as well as strong party discipline, analysts uniformly agree that the executive has more discretion to make policy in parliamentary than presidential systems. In particular, the executive has significantly more control over setting the legislative agenda in parliamentary systems than in the United States (Laver and Shepsle 1994, 295).

In spite of these vital differences between presidential and parliamentary government, analysts have begun applying related models of legislative-executive relations to both, extending the sort of anticipated-reaction logic of legislative influence outlined above (Huber 1992, 1996; Reinhardt 1994; Milner and Rosendorff 1995). While the mechanisms of executive accountability vary across systems, they continue to exist. While the scope of executive discretion may vary, we can understand how it varies using models of delegation rather than starting from completely different points in studying various types of democracy. In this book, I hypothesize that legislative mechanisms of influence on international cooperation exist in parliamentary systems as well as in the United States, and examine this hypothesis in the context of the European Union.[3] Parties may play a more important role in Europe than in the United States (although I find significant party effects in the United States as well), and executives may be less tightly constrained in Europe. But these differences do not imply that the role of the legislature is irrelevant to understanding how parliamentary systems make commitments to other states; at least the proposition that it is irrelevant should be treated as a hypothesis subject to the same constraints of logical inference as in presidential systems. Once we think of executive-legislative relations as an exchange relationship rather than a battle that one side must lose, the potential for treating presidential and parliamentary systems within a unified analytical framework, one that allows for and explains variation in legislative influence, becomes promising.

If democracies are in fact able to establish credible commitments in international relations, one of the obvious places to begin exploring the sources of credibility lies in the legislative institutions of democracy. Political scientists are now well placed to begin such an investigation, since our understanding of how legislatures are organized, how they operate, and how they interact with the executive has improved immensely over the last couple of decades. This

---

[3] Within the EU, the executive's supposed power of agenda control may in fact be significantly attenuated as policymaking authority on many issues is shifted to Brussels.

study explores the propositions that legislatures have substantial, consistent influence on foreign policy, and that legislative involvement in international cooperation enhances the capacity of democracies to make credible commitments and therefore engage in cooperation.

ARGUMENT AND APPROACH

This book addresses two questions: how to explain variation in legislative influence on foreign policy, and how legislative participation affects stable democracies' ability to make commitments to other states. The models from which I draw hypotheses and the general structure of the argument are outlined in the next chapter. Specific hypotheses are then developed and tested in the following empirical chapters. The basic logic underlying the two central propositions is the following. First, legislative influence is greater than generally appreciated because legislatures retain multiple mechanisms for frustrating implementation of international agreements. Thus, executives that care about implementing agreements will take legislative preferences and powers into account during negotiations. Second, institutionalized legislative participation in processes of international cooperation enhances the credibility of commitments through a number of mechanisms, relying on signaling and commitment dynamics. Institutionalized legislative participation provides executives and other states with better information about legislative and societal preferences, reducing the chances of reneging. It also creates institutional obstacles to changing policy, enhancing the stability of policies. Enhanced credibility in turn leads to greater levels of international cooperation.

The three central outcome variables I am interested in explaining are influence, credibility, and cooperation. *Influence* has been defined above, referring simply to an actor's ability to achieve outcomes close to those he or she prefers. I define *cooperation* in the now standard way found in the literature on international cooperation, relying on Robert O. Keohane's definition of cooperation as the mutual adjustment of state policies (Keohane 1984, 49–52). While cooperation improves the expected welfare of the cooperating states relative to the status quo *ex ante,* it is not necessarily a Pareto-improving (mutually beneficial) move for the world as a whole.

Defining *credibility* turns out to be a more difficult and controversial issue. While the term is used with great frequency both in studies of international relations and of domestic politics, authors rarely offer an explicit definition. The lack of specificity matters, because two different notions of credibility are used in these literatures. Many authors implicitly think of credibility as a matter of *beliefs:* commitments are credible if other players believe that an actor will do what he or she says. Other authors use the term credibility to refer to a characteristic of a *strategy* rather than of a belief: a commitment is credible if the structure of the game makes it rational for actors to do what they say they will (i.e., a strategy is credible if it is subgame-perfect).[4]

These two ways of thinking about credibility are distinct, and the way in which beliefs and strategies are related to one another depends on one's analytical framework. In a rational-choice framework, beliefs and strategies are intimately linked. Actors update their beliefs about a player's type, and therefore his likely behavior, throughout the course of a game. A belief about whether a player will behave in a certain manner depends on whether this strategy is, in fact, subgame perfect. Therefore, within a rational-choice setting, the decision about whether to define credibility in terms of beliefs or strategies is not all that consequential. Because the two move in tandem, evaluating beliefs is essentially the same as evaluating strategies. Direct evidence on beliefs is for all practical purposes interchangeable with behavioral evidence on strategies.

If we were to adopt a nonrational-choice framework, such as one that focused on cognitive or affective limitations on actors' ability to update beliefs (Mercer 1996), the choice between beliefs and strategies as a definition of credibility would become more important. If actors do not update their beliefs in the Bayesian manner assumed in rationalist models of games of incomplete information, the link between beliefs and strategies becomes considerably weaker. We may find that an actor is playing a subgame-perfect (i.e., credible) strategy, but that cognitive constraints prevent partners from appreciating this fact. Therefore the actor would lack credibility defined in terms of beliefs, but would have credibility defined in terms of strategies.

I adopt a rationalist framework in this book, and find it most useful to think about credibility defined in terms of strategies. This choice of definition means that the primary evidence I present to test claims about credibility asks whether states actually implement international agreements as they promise that they will. Evidence on implementation seems to be the most direct measure of credibility defined in terms of strategies. I also present occasional anecdotal evidence about actors' beliefs, but find this less powerful and convincing than the more objective measures of what states actually do. This approach to defining and measuring credibility may be unsatisfying to those who reject rationalist frameworks and who define credibility solely in terms of beliefs. But it should pose no problem to those working within a rationalist framework, where beliefs and strategies are intimately linked, or to those working outside a rationalist framework who are willing to think about credibility defined in terms of state behavior rather than beliefs. I am primarily interested in whether states do what they say they are going to do, and how legislatures influence this outcome variable. This seems to be an important question regardless of one's stance on the value of rational-choice theorizing.

---

[4] A subgame-perfect strategy is one that is an equilibrium in a proper subgame. That is, subgame-perfect strategies are those where an actor has no incentive to unilaterally deviate and follow some other course of action.

The states I study in this book are the United States and the member states of the EU. In order to develop a more general understanding of the legislative role in international cooperation, I do not focus on just one issue but examine a diverse group of cases. The role of legislatures in international trade, an important type of international cooperation, has received substantial attention in books and articles by political scientists and economists (Milner 1997), so I do not focus on this issue here (although it does relate to the discussion of European integration in chapters 6 and 7). Instead, I look at cases that allow us to examine the outcome of attempts to cooperate with other states and to consider the legislative role in areas where it may not be quite as obvious as when Congress votes on trade agreements.

A few words are in order on case selection. As mentioned, since we have available numerous studies on legislatures and trade, I have stayed away from the trade issue. My major desiderata for empirical research were that it push the study of legislatures and international cooperation into new issue-areas and beyond the borders of the United States; and that it provide clear tests of alternative hypotheses about legislative influence and credibility. These criteria led me to include European integration as a subject of study, and to focus on issues where good data are available about legislative institutions, implementation, and cooperation.

Thus, overall case selection was determined by a search for an intersection of inherently interesting and new issues with the availability of discriminating evidence. This is not to say that I ignored standard criteria for case selection, such as maximizing variation on the explanatory variables and controlling for alternative hypotheses. The demands of scientific inference are met by selection of observations within each broad issue studied. Thus, for example, while the procedure of selecting paired, controlled cases did not determine the choice of issues examined in the book as a whole, it did determine the choice of cases for deeper study within the issue-areas of food aid or economic sanctions.

The four issues I study are executive agreements and treaties in the United States; the domestic politics of economic sanctions in the United States; U.S. foreign assistance in the form of food aid; and the creation of the single internal market in the EU. In all these cases, we see variations in the level and type of legislative engagement and of international cooperation within the issue that demand explanation. Developing explanations allows us to test alternative models of legislative-executive interaction. The study of executive agreements and treaties concentrates on the form of international agreements, showing that the president cannot simply choose informal agreements as a way to circumvent legislative influence. It also shows that divided government leads to a decreased ability to reach agreements with other states. The chapter on the domestic politics of economic sanctions in the United States shows how legislative-executive interaction influences the credibility of U.S. commitments and thus the level of cooperation achieved. The discussion of food aid considers both the level of legislative participation and the level of cooperation achieved with recipient states. The two chapters on the EU consider in particular the problem of completing the single market and how parliamentary participation has influenced this process and the trajectory of European integration overall.

Chapter 2 develops my theoretical framework. I discuss three related bodies of literature that provide a coherent way of thinking about the role of legislatures: on legislative organization; on legislative-executive relations; and on institutions as commitment devices. These literatures have in common assumptions of rationality on the part of legislators and executives, and the assumption that these political actors design institutions that will constrain them in the future. Institutions are thus chosen by political actors at the same time that they provide the context within which these actors go about their business. Institutions do not change without effort or cost, so once actors make decisions about institutional design they will be forced to work within these constraints for some period of time. Chapter 2 introduces the important concepts and models that will be used in the empirical studies and develops in general terms the book's major hypotheses about legislative participation, credibility, and international cooperation. More specific testable hypotheses, sensitive to the contexts of various issue-areas, are developed in later chapters.

Chapter 3 begins the empirical examination by considering the use of executive agreements and treaties in the United States. Ratification procedures, such as deciding whether a particular agreement will be informal or have to undergo the rigors of treaty ratification, are one of the most important domestic institutions with the potential to influence patterns of international cooperation. Therefore, we are driven to ask what explains the choice of these domestic procedures, which is the question I address in chapter 3. I find evidence that the choice of procedures is driven not just by executive strategies to escape legislative constraints, as most literature on this subject argues. Instead, I find that legislators continue to have the capacity to influence even informal agreements. Therefore, executives are forced to consider the implications of choosing a particular procedure for the credibility of any international agreements they reach, leading to a pattern in the choice of institutional form different than a purely domestic perspective would predict. This study provides an important piece of evidence for this book, as it shows how legislatures can exercise indirect means of influence and that domestic institutions vary systematically. It tests the general hypotheses about variation in legislative institutions and resulting levels of cooperation. It also makes a contribution to the study of the use of executive agreements in the United States, by arguing that they are not the effective evasive devices that most authors assume.

Chapters 4 and 5 focus on the United States and analyze both the variation in the role of Congress and the effects of this variation. Chapter 4 turns to the domestic politics of economic sanctions. Sanctions are a popular foreign-policy tool, especially in the United States, in spite of persistent questions about their utility. The end of the Cold War has, if anything, increased governments' willingness to impose sanctions. One of the reasons analysts question sanctions' effectiveness is the necessity of generating international support if sanctions are to be effective. This support is difficult to achieve. Explaining when sanctions gain international support is thus an important practical as well as theoretical question. Chapter 4 finds that the level of international cooperation achieved is a function of domestic as well as systemic variables. In particular, we find an intriguing interaction between the branch of government responsible for initiating sanctions and party control of government. Legislative willingness to take the initiative of imposing sanctions depends on relations with the executive branch. Success in generating international support for sanctions does as well. The general hypotheses tested here again involve variation in legislative institutions and their impact on patterns of international cooperation.

Chapter 5 considers U.S. foreign assistance, particularly food aid. Here, we ask about both the level of executive discretion to use assistance without congressional constraints and the effects of such discretion on the success of efforts to use food aid as a foreign-policy tool. The level of executive discretion on food aid is quite high, presenting the central puzzle addressed in this chapter. I argue that Congress has allowed such a high level of discretion because food aid is a program MCs support strongly, in contrast to other foreign-assistance programs. But within this overall high level of executive discretion, intriguing patterns of variation remain that are accounted for by factors similar to those we see in other chapters. I also find that presidential attempts to use food aid as a foreign-policy tool are not substantially enhanced by having a great deal of discretion. Unless presidents can demonstrate congressional support for their foreign-policy goals or institutionalize a linkage between aid and foreign policy, their attempts to generate leverage with the aid weapon do not meet with much success. Even on a program with such a high level of executive discretion, international outcomes depend heavily on legislative preferences and domestic institutions. Variation in legislative institutions and resulting levels of international cooperation again serve as dependent variables here.

In chapters 6 and 7 I shift gears, turning attention from the U.S. Congress to national parliaments in EU member states. Doing so makes this book more than a study of U.S. foreign policy, but requires some justification. As the following chapter will show, most of the theoretical literature on which I draw to develop propositions about legislatures and international cooperation has been developed in the American context. The United States is characterized by division of powers, with the executive and legislative branches being elected separately. Divided government is a common phenomenon. Europe, in contrast, is characterized by parliamentary government. The executive is directly responsible to the legislature and not elected separately (except in the case of semipresidential systems like France; but even here the prime minister is powerful). Many scholars of foreign policy are skeptical that models can be transported from one context to another. Thus, they would argue against testing the same general propositions about delegation, credibility, and cooperation in the two contexts.

I argue that, while the specifics of legislative-executive interaction differ in the two types of systems, the logic of legislative influence on foreign policy holds in both systems. Like Congress, parliaments have to decide how to organize themselves internally so as to achieve their objectives most successfully. They must decide how tightly to constrain executives in international negotiations. They must appropriate funds, and can cause real difficulties for international cooperation if they refuse to implement international agreements. Often their incentives for taking disruptive steps will be different from those found in Congress, because of the closer linkages between legislature and executive. However, in both systems party loyalties matter substantially (as I shall show) and in both legislatures have tools they can use to inflict costs on the executive, if they choose to use them. I propose that similar hypotheses about influence, credibility, and cooperation can be applied to the United States and the EU, if we are sensitive to how to operationalize and test these hypotheses in different contexts. To some extent, the proof is in the pudding—whether hypotheses can be transported across democratic political systems is an empirical question. I leave it to the reader to decide whether the evidence offered in this book supports my proposition.

Chapters 6 and 7 consider the impact of domestic institutions on credibility by looking at the creation of the internal market in the EU. Chapter 6 takes on the argument that national parliaments have been irrelevant to the course of European integration, since they lack the capacity and interest to exercise control over executives. I find that the degree to which parliaments have organized to constrain governments is in fact a variable that varies systematically, not a constant. When conflict over the course of integration rises, national parliaments organize themselves to oversee the executive and exercise more control over the implementation of EU-level agreements. Variation in legislative institutions is the key question in this chapter.

In chapter 7, I ask about the consequences of such parliamentary organization. I find strong evidence that organized legislative involvement in international cooperation is not an impediment to international cooperation. In fact, we see just the opposite: that where legislatures are well integrated in the process of international cooperation, the process of implementing agreements proceeds most predictably. As argued above, international cooperation does not end at the bargaining table. If agreements are not implemented, and the necessary policies changed, no cooperation has taken place. So it is essential that we consider implementation of international agreements if we are to understand patterns of international cooperation. This study suggests that, contrary to most of the literature on European integration, national parliaments are important actors in the process; and their role can be constructive, not just an impediment to efficient integration. We do not have to conceive of democracy and efficiency as in a zero-sum battle with one another. Chapter 7 thus provides the most direct test of hypotheses about credibility in this book, although evidence about credibility is found throughout the empirical work.

Research agendas on international cooperation and on domestic institutions come together when we ask about the factors that explain democracies' abilities to make commitments to other states. Without the capacity to make commitments, states will be confined to minimal levels of cooperation and find it difficult to cope with conditions of international interdependence. A long tradition in political theory worries that the institutions of democratic government, with their dispersal of power and openness to public influence, are destructive of the capacity to make credible commitments. Applications of such logic to U.S. foreign policy, for example, have argued that unless the executive effectively closes Congress out of the foreign-policy process, the foreign policies of the United States will be incoherent and ineffective. Studies of European integration have come to much the same conclusion about national parliaments.

By applying modern theories of legislative organization and legislative-executive interaction, I challenge these views. Legislatures do influence international cooperation, often through indirect and nonobvious mechanisms; and their influence can enhance the credibility of states' commitments. Rather than focusing our analyses on which branch of government has "the most" influence or wins ongoing struggles for power, we should think of legislative-executive relations as an exchange relationship in which distributive, competitive elements coexist with the potential for both parties to gain from well-designed institutions. The legislative role in foreign policy needs to be reconceptualized, along lines similar to the reconceptualization of legislative institutions in domestic policy. We also need to reconceptualize our approach to international cooperation. Too much of the work on international cooperation focuses on the initial bargaining process, asking whether states are able to reach agreements and the distribution of benefits in these agreements. However, this is only the beginning of international cooperation. Implementation of agreements is key, since this is when state policies actually change. When we consider implementation, we gain a better understanding both of international cooperation and of the ways that legislatures exert influence on it.

What is the extent and effect of legislative influence on international cooperation? We can only come to persuasive answers, I argue, by considering these questions through the lens of credible commitments. When we do so, we find powerful evidence for the following propositions, some of them sure to be controversial. Legislatures will institutionalize their participation in international cooperation when there is greater conflict of interest between the executive and legislature. A related proposition is that executives are unable to manipulate structures of legislative participation in such as way as to evade legislative influence on international cooperation. Turning to the effects of legislatures, we find that institutionalized legislative participation in international cooperation leads to greater credibility of international commitments, and therefore to higher levels of international cooperation.

CHAPTER 2

Theoretical Framework: Legislatures, Executives, and Commitment

PROCESSES of representation and policymaking in democracies engage organized legislatures. But on foreign-policy issues, executives rather than legislators directly negotiate with other countries. The degree to which legislatures can, or should, influence such negotiations remains the subject of deep controversy. This study is designed to explain variation in legislative influence and its effects on international cooperation, via the mechanism of credibility. Drawing on modern treatments of legislative organization, legislative-executive relations, and institutions as commitment devices, as well as the empirical work in this book, I make a twofold argument. First, theory and evidence suggest that legislative influence on international bargaining and cooperation is deep and subtle. The scope of discretion left to executives in the United States and the EU varies in predictable ways. Analyses of the "resurgence of Congress" or the "decline of parliaments" that observe apparent independent swings in legislative activity over time miss many of these more regular patterns of influence.

Second, I consider the consequences of legislative influence. Democracies are often thought handicapped by their distinctive system of representation, at least when it comes to international interactions. Legislative influence impairs efforts to "speak with one voice" on foreign affairs, and politics often do not stop at the water's edge. However, the experience of the twentieth century promotes little confidence in pessimistic generalizations about democracies' capacity to cope with international relations. Democracies are able to avoid wars with one another (Russett 1993); when they do get involved in militarized conflict, they generally win (Dassel 1998, 33). They are able to participate in deeply beneficial forms of international cooperation, such as the creation of free-trade areas. If we look at cooperative outcomes rather than solely the processes of international bargaining, the supposed handicaps facing democracies disappear, replaced by consistent successes. Institutionalized legislative participation in bargaining allows democracies to make credible commitments to other states, increasing the scope of mutual confidence (see Cowhey 1993; Keohane 1984, 117). Proposals to evade or minimize legislative participation in the interest of "efficiency" are thus misguided. In fact, it is precisely when executives try to circumvent legislatures that democracies face their most significant foreign-policy crises.

Developing these two lines of argument—about legislative influence, and about commitment—requires that we understand institutionalist models of legislative organization, legislative-executive interaction, and credible commitments. This chapter introduces those models and applies them to the problem of international cooperation. I turn first to the question of the scope of discretion available to the executive branch and how it varies. Analysts have often studied executive freedom from legislative constraints by considering problems of delegation, drawing on models of principal-agent interactions. These models suggest ways in which legislators can constrain, directly or indirectly, the activities of the executive branch. They also suggest ways in which the executive branch can attempt to maximize its freedom of action. I use the agency perspective to clarify mechanisms of legislative influence that have not consistently been considered in studies of foreign policy and to specify factors that can lead to regular variation in the scope of executive flexibility.

Institutionalist models of legislatures also bring to the forefront the problem of commitment. Policymakers face the challenge of establishing credible commitments to policies, commitments that are necessary if they wish policies to have the intended effect on political and economic outcomes. In international relations, the problem of commitment is omnipresent. International cooperation involves mutual adjustment of policies. Unless states can persuade one another that they will in fact carry out commitments to such mutual policy adjustment, the benefits available from international interaction will be shallow. Studies of international cooperation have repeatedly suggested that credibility depends on domestic politics, without specifying what it is about domestic politics that allows for credible commitments or impedes them. I focus on the way in which legislatures are integrated into the process of international cooperation, arguing that in democracies institutionalized legislative integration is a key determinant of the credibility of commitments.

Reviewing these literatures leads me to an analytical framework that emphasizes the following points. First, legislatures can delegate negotiating authority to the executive yet retain the capacity to reclaim this authority or to refuse to implement international agreements. Second, legislatures can exercise substantial influence through indirect mechanisms of control, including the refusal to appropriate funds or the delay and obstruction of implementing legislation for international agreements. Executives that accurately anticipate such legislative responses will take legislative preferences into account. Thus, legislatures can have substantial influence without the appearance of high levels of legislative activity. While these points are developed primarily with reference to theoretical work on the U.S. Congress, later in the book I test whether they provide explanatory leverage when applied to parliamentary systems as well. Parliaments have different incentives when interacting with executives than does Congress, but they possess many of the same tools of influence—if they choose to exercise them. Similar propositions about the conditions under which legislatures exercise influence, and how this applies to international cooperation, should hold in both the U.S. and European contexts of stable democracies.

Putting together modern theories of legislative organization with theories of international cooperation and commitment leads me to suggest that legislative-executive relations should be conceptualized as an exchange relationship, rather than as a question of who dominates. While having elements of distributional tension, this relationship is also about finding institutions that allow both branches to benefit from international cooperation. They can only do so if they can make credible commitments to uphold international agreements. Based on these insights, this chapter develops in general terms the hypotheses that will be studied in more concrete, context-specific ways in the rest of the book. These expectations have to do with legislative influence (the Influence and Delegation Hypotheses), the credibility of commitments (the Credibility Hypothesis), and the level of international cooperation achieved (the Cooperation Hypothesis).

LEGISLATIVE INFLUENCE

Legislators care about policy outcomes. They wish to exercise influence over the course of policy, both domestic and international. It is not necessary to assume that legislators care *only* about policies; they of course have other goals, such as distributing private benefits, claiming credit, raising money for reelection, and so on (Arnold 1990). But many of these activities are influenced by, and have an influence on, policy positions. Since this book considers variation in policies, rather than claiming to develop a more complete model of legislative activity, I concentrate on the policy dimension of legislators' activities.

Legislators care about foreign policies as well as domestic policies. In this era of international interdependence, the well-being of their constituents often depends as heavily on interaction with other states as on purely domestic policies. The effects of foreign-policy decisions can be immediate, as when calculating winners and losers from trade policies. In other cases, they are more indirect. Preferences for foreign policies may also be traced to the constraints of party membership or ideology, although these immediate influences also have electoral roots. The intensity with which legislators favor a particular policy can vary, and provides an important explanatory variable for the outcomes of interest in this study. The effects of some policies—say, imposing economic sanctions on China—may be quite diffuse. This fact does not imply that legislators will have no preferences over the outcome of a debate about sanctions. But it does suggest that if sanctions against China are somehow linked to other issues, legislators may be willing to give up their preferred policy on sanctions in exchange for benefits on these other, linked issues. Consideration of policy preferences, often analyzed using spatial models (Enelow and Hinich 1984), and of policymaking as an exchange process, are central to the theoretical framework used in this study.

If legislators care about foreign-policy outcomes, they need to consider how to influence the activities of other countries. This problem of influence constitutes one of the fundamental differences—perhaps *the* fundamental difference—between domestic and foreign policy. Making one's constituents better off, or pursuing a general preference for, say, democracy in other states, requires finding a mechanism through which to shape other states' behavior. It is difficult for legislators to exercise international influence on their own. Constitutionally and functionally, executives are better placed to exercise such influence than are legislative branches of government. Executives have responsibility for negotiating with other states. Their capacity for acquiring information about the rest of the world exceeds that of legislatures, although with the professionalization of legislatures in the twentieth century this informational distinction is less substantial than it once was. Developing an understanding of legislative influence on international cooperation thus requires that we have an understanding of legislative-executive interaction. Legislators can most effectively influence the international system by working with the executive. When attempts to do so fail, legislatures may attempt to make foreign policy on their own, leading to complaints of "micro-management" and overstepping the bounds of legislative prerogatives.

The initial task of this study is to understand variation in patterns of legislative-executive interaction on international bargaining. At times, executives seem to behave as if they were nearly unconstrained by legislators. At others, legislators exercise a veto over international bargains or put explicit constraints on executive activities. Legislators may even, in extreme instances, attempt to take matters into their own hands. Descriptions of changes in behavior are common, for example in discussions of a "swinging pendulum" of congressional activism on foreign affairs or of the "decline of parliaments." The next sections of this chapter suggest ways that we can explain such variation, rather than simply describing it. These explanations are applied and tested in the empirical chapters of this book.

Legislative Institutions

Over the last fifteen years, our understanding of legislative organization and behavior has undergone a revolution. The source of this revolution was the application of models of institutions and of principal-agent relations to problems faced by legislators.[1] The application of economic models was motivated in part by a desire to respond to more descriptive work that claimed to find declining legislative power. In the United States, analysts worried about (or sometimes championed) the advent of the "imperial presidency" and the "abdication" of policymaking authority to the executive branch of government

---

[1] These approaches can be called part of the "new institutionalism." However, since this term has taken on so many different meanings, I refrain from using it. By institutional models of legislatures, I refer to models that assume rationality on the part of legislators and their constituents and that see legislative institutions as solutions to recurrent problems faced by legislators. The institutional approach has its roots in theories of industrial organization.

(Sundquist 1981; Schlesinger 1989; Friedberg 1991). These concerns arose in studies of West European democracies as well, where analysts increasingly saw parliaments as irrelevant to policymaking (Rose 1989; Garrett 1992; Lenman 1992; Clarke 1992).

Since one intention of the institutional literature was to respond to concerns about executive dominance, there arose a natural tendency to emphasize the ways in which legislatures could in fact continue to exercise influence, even in the absence of traditional lawmaking activity. These studies emphasized the point that delegation of policymaking authority does not always lead to abdication (Lupia and McCubbins 1992). Legislatures can delegate to executives but still maintain influence over policy outcomes without "controlling" the government. Because of its emphasis on the capacity to retain influence, the institutional literature has been misleadingly labeled the "congressional dominance" approach (Moe 1990). Some works indeed have a congressional-dominance character, presenting nonrefutable claims of consistent legislative influence. But approached carefully, the modern literature on legislative organization specifies mechanisms of legislative influence that give rise to expectations about the conditions under which legislatures tightly constrain policies and when, in contrast, they exert little influence.

One body of theorizing about legislative organization focuses on the distributional incentives facing legislators. Legislators care about the benefits they can bring home to their own district. But in order to provide any benefits, they must put together a majority vote to support a particular package of policies. Assuming distributional conflict—the benefits going to one district do not accrue to others, which however bear some of the costs of policies—gaining majority approval of policies is problematic. Why should any legislator vote for a measure that will impose some costs on his district but provide benefits only to others? Achieving majority approval of distributive legislation involves organizing package deals that provide benefits to a majority of legislators.

However, the process of putting together packages of legislation creates its own difficulties. One solution could be to deal with all policies in omnibus bills, pulling together in one vote a wide range of issues. But such massive logrolls could prove highly inefficient (Baron 1991). Another solution, identified by Weingast and Marshall (1988), is provided by the committee system in the U.S. Congress. In Congress, committees are made up of legislators with particularly strong interests in a specific kind of legislation: agricultural policy, foreign assistance, etc. The legislation that emerges from committees is designed to provide benefits to their members' intensely interested constituents on the issues where the committee has jurisdiction. However, legislation must also gain majority approval on the floor, including votes from legislators who have little interest in the specific issues in any bill. The committee system, in the distributional perspective, is organized to allow legislators to exchange votes and make credible commitments to provide support on the floor for bills that emerge from committees. Because committees have gatekeeping power, deals forged there will not be torn apart on the floor of the legislature. Thus, one of the central insights about legislative organization that has emerged from the application of institutional models is that the committee structure of Congress is designed to enforce bargains among legislators that would not be credible in a decentralized, unorganized system.

An implication of models of legislative organization is that the delegation of authority, such as gatekeeping power, to congressional committees is of great importance and presents the means with which to test alternative theories. Theorists now focus on the problem of delegation, to legislative committees and to members of the executive branch (Epstein and O'Halloran 1997). Different patterns of delegation provide evidence in support of one or another model of legislative organization. The distributional approach just outlined has been amplified and developed over time, with more details of institutional structure included in the models and interpreted (see Shepsle 1986; Baron and Ferejohn 1989; Shepsle and Weingast 1995).

A major alternative to the distributional approach has also emerged: a perspective focusing on the informational problems legislators confront (Krehbiel 1991). Like the distributional approach, informational models of legislative organization assume rational, self-interested legislators interacting in a setting where they need to gain majority approval of bills in order to provide benefits to their constituency. However, the informational approach focuses on the uncertainty surrounding policymaking rather than the need to construct package deals.

Gilligan and Krehbiel (1989, 1990) consider a specific, but common, informational problem: the uncertainty that intervenes between adoption of a policy and realization of outcomes. They build a theory of legislative organization that sees institutions as the solution to such informational dilemmas. Legislators do not know with certainty the outcome that will result from adopting a particular piece of legislation, such as air-pollution controls. But they care only about outcomes, such as air quality, not about the policies themselves. Thus, gaining policy-relevant information, which can be thought of as information about causal relationships between policies and outcomes, is valuable. Becoming an expert, however, requires a major investment of time and effort that few legislators can afford. They face the problem of encouraging someone to make the necessary investment, and then hoping that person will reliably reveal the information gained in such a way that legislators can use it to make policy. For Gilligan and Krehbiel, this informational problem gives rise to the committee system in Congress. As in the distributional approach, they see delegation of authority to committees as something of fundamental importance. However, the motivation for delegation lies in the need to acquire information rather than to provide credible commitments to complex cross-issue bargains.

For our purposes, this debate about legislative organization—of which I have touched on just a few examples—is worth mention for a few reasons. First, it shows how institutional analysis can be used to understand political behavior. Legislators confront certain basic problems; they construct institutions that allow them to resolve these problems. I adopt this approach to develop explanations of how legislative engagement in international bargaining varies. Second, the literature on legislative organization draws our attention to the problem of delegation. There are a number of reasons why legislators might choose to delegate authority. These "logics of delegation" generate propositions about how the level of delegation varies, as further elaborated below. Finally, models of legislative organization drive home the point that delegation is not abdication. Legislators do not allow committees to become powerful with the knowledge that they will then be closed out from the policymaking process. Instead, legislators allow committees to gain powers that will make legislators better off in the long run by allowing them to make commitments to certain procedures or to gain information. This fundamental problem—how legislators can benefit from delegation and the kinds of influence they retain—is at the heart of legislative influence over international cooperation.

Another branch of theorizing about institutions and legislatures concentrates more directly on legislative-executive interaction. These models challenge the notion that the bureaucratization of government has resulted in a system where policy effectively is made by administrators, not by legislators. They concentrate on the mechanisms that legislators can use to maintain influence over administrative actions, some of which will play a central role in the empirical studies that follow. These studies focus on how structure and process allow legislatures to exercise influence over executive activities (Fiorina 1977).

Weingast and Moran (1983) develop a model of legislative influence on executive-branch activities that allows them to test whether bureaucracies, in this case the Federal Trade Commission (FTC), operate independently of the legislature or are responsive to congressional preferences. They find substantial evidence that indirect mechanisms of congressional influence over bureaucratic outputs are at work, even though one may observe few direct legislative activities designed to constrain bureaucrats. In particular, Weingast and Moran find that the activities of the FTC change when the membership of key congressional committees does. They point to the budgetary process, oversight of errant agencies, and appointment of agents as important mechanisms of congressional influence (Weingast and Moran 1983, 769). These factors—the power of the purse, the threat of open and embarrassing legislative oversight, and procedural controls on executive-branch activity—will prove to be central in the operation of foreign as well as domestic policy. Far from being nonfalsifiable, the hypothesis that legislators can delegate but maintain influence, using delegation to achieve their objectives, gives rise to clear comparative-statics predictions about policy outputs.

If legislators are to control agencies' activities, they must be able to learn about what those agencies are doing. The problem of learning is a classic problem of principal-agent analysis, and students of Congress have considered it in some depth. McCubbins and Schwartz (1984), in an important contribution, differentiate "police patrol" oversight from "fire alarms." Observers who believe that Congress lacks the capacity to control agency activities tend to focus on the infrequency of explicit, overt oversight activities. McCubbins and Schwartz label such traditional actions police-patrol oversight, and argue that it is of lesser importance than generally assumed. Fire-alarm oversight, in contrast, relies on interested groups to warn legislators when agencies are behaving in inappropriate ways. Fire alarms might generate less noise than police patrols when working properly, and so are easy to overlook. But they would also constitute a more efficient use of legislators' time and provide an effective mechanism for exerting control over agencies' activities. Later contributions (Lupia and McCubbins 1994a, 1994b, 1995) have extended the oversight models, specifying the conditions for effective use of various mechanisms.

Besides oversight, legislators use other tools to maintain influence over the activities of those to whom they delegate. The power of the purse is one important mechanism. Agencies that operate in ways not desired by Congress can anticipate having their budgets cut during the next budgetary cycle. The power of the purse is sometimes even more immediate in foreign policy. In a particularly notable example, Congress effectively terminated U.S. military involvement in Vietnam and Cambodia by eliminating funding for these operations. On foreign assistance, Congress must approve a level of funding and frequently attaches conditions to aid-expenditures or even mandates an end to aid to particular countries. According to one analysis, "the power of the purse has become, by necessity and preference, a key congressional counterweight to presidential initiative" (Banks and Raven-Hansen 1994, 3). In the empirical studies in this book, particularly those on foreign assistance and on economic sanctions, we will see frequent use of spending power as a mechanism by which legislators influence foreign policy.

As on domestic policy, legislators can establish procedures for agencies on foreign policy that effectively limit the scope of agency discretion. One recent example of such activity is the creation of an independent agency to decide which military bases should be closed (Mayer 1995). By specifying a particular process, with input from specified groups, Congress constrained the activities of the base-closing commission.

One additional, general mechanism for legislative influence lies in the process of implementing international agreements. When states reach such agreements, they may formally attain the status of law without explicit legislative ratification. However, even self-executing agreements often require changes in some preexisting domestic legislation. By exercising control over the implementation phase, legislators have de facto influence over the process of negotiation itself. The Influence Hypothesis, elaborated below, states this proposition more formally. In general, an executive that rationally anticipates legislative reaction to his initiatives will in fact incorporate legislative preferences into bargains with other countries. Thus, legislative preferences have an influence on international cooperation.

Models of legislative control over executive activities have developed over time, becoming more sophisticated and adding factors that may frustrate legislative influence, such as incomplete information. McCubbins, Noll, and Weingast (1989) elaborate the ways in which procedural constraints on agencies allow the realization of legislative preferences, applying their model to changes in environmental legislation. Ferejohn and Shipan (1990) add the features of an independent judiciary and a presidential veto. Banks and Weingast (1992) consider problems of uncertainty about the impact of policy. Assuming that interest groups can provide such information, Banks and Weingast introduce them as actors in the policymaking process. These models have moved beyond the initial stage of demonstrating merely that legislators have tools with which they can influence the behavior of executive-branch actors. They now provide a set of tools that allows us to develop expectations about the variation in such influence, specifying factors that provide for high levels of executive responsiveness to legislative preferences as well as those that keep legislators from maintaining tight control.

Logics of Delegation

Institutional perspectives on legislatures draw our attention to the phenomenon of delegation: how legislators use it to pursue their interests and attempt to resolve the dilemmas it presents. Delegation to committees within legislatures and to the executive provides solutions to many of the common, recurrent problems faced by politicians dealing with complexity and uncertainty. For the purposes of this book, the delegation of most interest is substantive delegation to the executive branch. We are concerned with understanding how much discretion the executive has to make commitments and agreements with other nations in the course of international bargaining. In order to understand variation in the scope of substantive discretion, we first need to consider the reasons that legislators might decide to delegate. These logics of delegation give rise to expectations about the tightness of the constraints on the executive.

A fundamental reason for delegation, and perhaps the most common, is complexity. Given the vast range of issues dealt with on a daily basis by modern politicians, it is simply impossible for them to function except with significant delegation. Gary Cox, in an influential study of the rise of cabinet government in England, argues that increasing complexity forced Parliament to delegate most policymaking authority to the Cabinet, leaving backbenchers with very little control over policy (Cox 1987). Simple considerations of efficiency, which is promoted by division of labor, lead legislators to delegate to specialized bodies (McCubbins and Page 1987).

Legislators also delegate to establish credible commitments. The logic of doing so was spelled out in the discussion above of distributional theories of legislative organization. To achieve their goals, legislators need to find ways to commit to supporting one anothers' favored bills. The committee system of the U.S. Congress provides such a commitment mechanism. This specific model of distributional benefits illustrates a more general phenomenon, the need to resolve collective-action problems. In the distributional-theory case, legislators face the collective problem of committing to vote for one anothers' bills. But collective-action problems more generally are a persistent feature of politics, including legislative politics. For example, decisions about spending and budgets present politicians with collective dilemmas. On the one hand, they prefer to maximize the level of benefits flowing to their own districts. On the other, if all districts receive high levels of targeted benefits, either taxes or budget deficits will increase substantially, leaving everyone worse off than if they could control spending by committing themselves to exercise restraint in channeling benefits to their own districts. Attempts to resolve collective-action problems could involve leadership by political parties (Kiewiet and McCubbins 1991; Cox and McCubbins 1993). Alternatively, legislators could delegate to an independent agency, as when they are deciding which military bases to close (Mayer 1995); or to the executive branch, as in trade policy (Lohmann and O'Halloran 1994; Destler 1994; Haggard 1988; O'Halloran 1994; Pastor 1980).

Collective-action problems form one large class of commitment dilemmas legislators confront. Politicians also face commitment problems that arise from issues of time inconsistency. Frequently, adopting a course of policy that will benefit everyone in the long run involves forgoing immediate benefits today. Pursuing long-term benefits thus requires that politicians find a way to tie their own hands, i.e., a way to avoid the immediate temptations of manipulating policy today to achieve high payoffs, thereby postponing even higher costs to the future. The logic of time inconsistency and delegation has been explored most systematically in the context of independent central banks and inflation (Barro and Gordon 1983; Rogoff 1985; Lohmann 1992). Politicians, focusing on immediate electoral benefits, are tempted to take steps like raising government spending to create rapid economic growth. However, consistently using economic stimuli to provide political benefits has the negative consequence of increasing inflation, leaving everyone worse off than if politicians had been able to avoid the temptation of short-term spending boosts. A prominent solution to this dilemma of time-inconsistent preferences is to delegate monetary authority to an independent central bank, one that will not be tempted to manipulate spending for political benefits. The central-bank logic illustrates how delegation can allow politicians to achieve goals they could not otherwise attain. In such circumstances, interpreting delegation as somehow decreasing politicians' power is misleading. Instead, delegation is a tool that they use to pursue political goals, goals that sometimes require politicians to refrain from manipulating policy for short-term advantages.

As discussed above, one major alternative to distributional theories of legislative organization lies in consideration of informational demands. The informational perspective suggests an alternative logic of delegation. Particularly in foreign affairs, understanding the relationship between policies adopted and outcomes realized requires a high degree of expertise about particular issues. Delegation to those with expertise while maintaining a veto over implementation of the policies they propose can in some circumstances provide an effective mechanism for acquiring policy-relevant information while exercising influence over the particular policy chosen. To some extent, the informational logic of delegation is related to the complexity explanation. While complexity generally refers to the number of issues on the political table, another type of complexity might lie in the causal relationships specific to a particular issue. Acquiring causal knowledge may require legislators to delegate authority, but again such delegation should be understood as a tool, not as abdication.

One final logic of delegation to the executive is more specific to international interactions, not following directly from analysis of domestic policies. In foreign affairs, pursuit of economic or political goals requires strategic interaction with other states (Oye 1986a). The effect of any particular policy will depend on how other states, and possibly other international actors such as multinational firms and nongovernmental organizations, react to it. Outcomes are the result of a complex mix of policies and strategies. Effective foreign policy requires that states be able to anticipate the character of international strategic interaction. Governments need to be able to play the international game, which requires the capacity to act strategically. This logic underlies the notion that states need to "speak with one voice" in foreign affairs, and that foreign policy is properly a bipartisan issue, not subject to the usual domestic political debates. Putting such observations into the context of our revised understanding of legislative organization and incentives to delegate authority, they suggest that sometimes delegation may be necessary to allow a state to achieve its objectives on issues that involve interaction with other countries. The more that favorable outcomes depend on an ability to behave strategically—i.e., the capacity to bargain skillfully with others—the more we would expect to see legislators realize that they can only achieve their goals through delegation. However, using the mechanisms that have been discussed here and will be further elaborated in the next chapters, it is possible for legislators to delegate but maintain influence on processes of international cooperation.

Variation in Delegation

The various logics of delegation just discussed suggest why legislators might choose to transfer conditional authority for policymaking to other actors, particularly to the executive branch of government when we are considering international relations. But appreciating that delegation is often a rational response to the realities of politics, and that it is not equivalent to abdication, is only the beginning of an attempt to gain an understanding of legislative influence. The real challenge is to understand how incentives to delegate vary and to use this understanding to develop expectations about variation in the level of legislative engagement in processes of international cooperation. The next step is to move from an abstract level of theorizing to develop testable expectations. In particular, we need to consider observable variables that will provide some explanatory leverage in the empirical studies that follow. In this section, I discuss two sets of variables that prove most fruitful for explaining patterns of legislative engagement in the cases considered here: legislative preferences and partisan politics.

Models of delegation tell us something intuitively obvious: legislators should be most willing to delegate to an agent who has preferences similar to their own. There are exceptions to this general rule. For example, in the case of independent central banks discussed above, politicians would usually do best by delegating to a central banker with a slightly (but not drastically) lower preference for inflation than their own. Such transfer of authority constitutes the most efficient solution to the problem of removing temptations to inflate, since the logic of the market pulls realized inflation rates above the planner's target. As another example of delegation to those with different preferences, some distributional models of legislative organization predict delegation to committees of "preference outliers," legislators who are the most intensely interested in a particular issue.

In informational models, it is important to delegate to agents who can gain expertise at the lowest cost. This consideration may sometimes lead to a willingness to delegate to individuals with preferences somewhat different than one's own (Krehbiel 1991, 124). For example, representatives from agricultural districts may be the best placed to specialize in food policy. However, they are also likely to have preferences over food policy that differ from those of the median member of Congress. Legislators must then trade off the benefits of efficient specialization versus the losses that derive from delegating to an "outlier" committee, one with preferences that diverge significantly from the median. But holding constant the costs of specialization, informational models predict delegation to those with "median preferences," rather than to the preference outliers predicted by distributional models.

When thinking about the problem of delegation to the executive of authority to negotiate with other states, models that predict delegation to those with similar preferences seem the most appropriate. As discussed, one of the primary motivations to delegate in foreign affairs lies in the complexity of these issues and need to specialize. If so, informational models are appropriate, with their prediction of delegation to agents with similar preferences. Distributional models that focus on delegation to committees as a way to enforce legislative bargains seem less relevant to the problems we are interested in here. All else equal, we should expect to see legislatures willing to delegate more authority to the executive when the executive's preferences over outcomes are expected to be closer to those of the swing voter in the legislature. The intuition behind this expectation is fairly obvious, and does not require a great deal of elaboration. Through delegation, legislators increase the influence the executive will have on the nature of deals struck with other states. If they expect that the executive prefers a very different set of outcomes than they do, they will be less willing to provide the executive with such leverage. On the other hand, delegation to an executive with preferences similar to their own is an efficient way to pursue their goals.

Fundamentally, we should expect to see legislatures willing to transfer more authority to the executive when they are able to trust the executive to carry out policies in line with their own preferences. This proposition is formalized as the Delegation Hypothesis below. Legislative intervention in foreign policy should be lowest when the legislature has preferences in line with those of the executive. A number of more specific implications follow from this general expectation. For one, it provides some leverage on distinctions between presidential and parliamentary systems. In parliamentary systems, the executive is chosen directly by the legislature and responsible to it. All else equal, therefore, we should expect a lower level of legislative management of foreign policy in parliaments than in presidential systems like the United States, where the preferences of the two branches frequently diverge substantially.

Laver and Shepsle (1994) find that cabinets in parliamentary systems do indeed have a great deal of discretion and influence over policy. For example, cabinets have generally gained agenda-setting power, allowing them to control the flow of business through parliament. But they also note that the intersection of parties and the legislature forces cabinets to optimize under constraints, strategizing rather than simply choosing whatever policies they like. As discussed in chapter 6, there is substantial variation in the degree to which the legislature retains influence over what the executive does on foreign policy even within parliamentary systems. Just to give one example, some foreign-policy problems produce deep splits within parties, perhaps even deeper than those between parties. Policy toward the EU in Britain has this character. When parties face such internal splits, the level of conflict will be high and the level of delegation relatively low. Cabinets facing deep conflicts within their own parties will be more constrained than those who have unified party support. Variation in parliamentary participation in foreign policy leads to intriguing patterns of international bargaining and cooperation, as explored in chapter 7.

Within the United States, consideration of the similarity of preferences of the two branches leads us to expect that we should see the most legislative activism on foreign affairs when Congress believes that it cannot trust the executive. Such a situation might arise under conditions of divided government, which will be further considered momentarily. Another recurrent source of distrust lies in the activities of the executive branch. One of the more common stories about changing delegation on foreign policy follows from revelation of executive abuse of delegated authority. Executives are sometimes revealed to have gone beyond the bounds of legislative delegation, to have concealed information, or even to have purposefully circumvented explicit legislative constraints. Such revelations give rise to dramatic changes in legislative delegation.

One of the most discussed of such instances, addressed at length in analyses of U.S. foreign policy, involves the Nixon administration. The Nixon administration's policies in Southeast Asia convinced many legislators not only that their preferences diverged from the executive's substantially but that the executive was prone to abuse any delegated authority. This impression was exacerbated by the simultaneous Watergate revelations and general administrative disdain for Congress. It led to a revolution in legislative structure, not only reclaiming foreign-policy authority from the executive but from the congressional committees concerned with foreign affairs as well. The logic of delegation that has emerged from modern studies of legislatures helps us to understand the nature of this legislative reaction, and to see it as part of a more general pattern of variation in patterns of delegation dependent on the policy preferences of executives and legislators.

Preferences influence legislators' role in international cooperation through another path, one considered in some detail in chapter 5. When we analyze multidimensional issues, or linked issues, we need to consider preference intensities as well as the potential difference between branches in ideal points on each issue dimension. Preference intensities refer to the relative importance actors put on various issues. For example, a member of Congress from Kansas may have preferences over both agricultural subsidies and economic sanctions against Haiti, meaning that she could identify an ideal policy point on each dimension. However, it is likely that her preferences over subsidies will be held much more intensely. In the language of spatial models, this means that a small change in policy on subsidies will lead to a large change in this member's utility, while a large change in policy toward Haiti would lead to only a small change in utility. Under these conditions, if the legislative process somehow links agricultural subsidies and Haiti, the member from Kansas will be willing to make compromises on Haiti in exchange for benefits on subsidies. When the legislature bargains with the executive branch, a similar logic applies. Legislators, responding to a more narrowly defined constituency than the executive branch, may very well hold different preference intensities than the executive. Considering the intensity of preferences gives us some clue about the issues on which Congress is willing to allow the executive freedom of maneuver, as detailed when we examine U.S. food aid. This process allows us to flesh out the idea of legislative-executive relations as an exchange process, as discussed above.

Legislators are more willing to take a hands-off approach to foreign affairs, allowing the executive to take the initiative, when they believe that their policy goals are basically the same as those of the executive. In practice, one way in which to operationalize similarity in preferences is by asking about party control of government. Parties perform at least two separable sets of functions (Aldrich 1995). First, they aggregate politicians of similar ideologies and views about policies. For this reason, measuring party control of government provides one proxy for measuring preferences. So we ask about divided government in the United States, and about minority or coalition government in parliamentary systems. However, parties also perform functions that we could consider under the broad heading of "party discipline." Parties do not only aggregate individual preference functions, they add something to how these individual politicians actually behave. In particular, they provide a mechanism for overcoming collective-action problems that face individual, unorganized legislators. Party leaders disperse favors and set standards of behavior that allow for cooperative solutions to collective-action problems, allowing the members of their party to make longer-term commitments than they could otherwise, to specialize, and generally to take steps that unorganized individual politicians could not. In most parliamentary systems, these functions of parties have become institutionalized to the extent that party discipline is very high (Laver and Shepsle 1994). Yet it varies more than many realize, suggesting that party discipline does not make the preferences of backbenchers irrelevant to the framing of policy (Martin 1997).

In the United States, party discipline is generally understood to be low compared to parliamentary systems, and nearly absent since the early 1970s.[2] However, recent works on the role of parties in Congress are calling this view into question. Kiewiet and McCubbins (1991) consider the role of parties in the complex process of appropriations in Congress. They see party leaders as a solution to collective-action problems; in the appropriations case, in particular, as providing a cooperative solution to a repeated Prisoners' Dilemma facing individual party members. They explore the methods that party leaders can use to enforce discipline in the ranks, such as committee assignment and dispensation of favors, many of which are far more effective than the explicit imposition of sanctions. Cox and McCubbins (1993) further explore the logic of party government in the U.S. Congress. Focusing on the value of party reputation as an electoral resource, they develop a model of parties as institutions to solve collective dilemmas. They use this model to challenge assertions of committee dominance of the legislative process, and find strong empirical support for the continuing importance of party structures in the United States, including a resurgence of party cohesion in the 1980s. A study of foreign-policy voting similarly finds increasing party cohesion (Smith 1994).

These works suggest that, in spite of variation in party cohesion across time

[2] The Republican majority in Congress since 1994 led many to talk about a "resurgence" of party discipline, without much analysis of whether such declines and resurgences can be understood as part of a more general model rather than as an inexplicable descriptive trend.

and space, considering the role of party and the incentives partisanship creates for delegation is essential. For example, it should be important to ask whether legislators' willingness to delegate authority for international bargaining to the executive depends on divided government. Given the frequent occurrence of divided government in the United States in the last few decades and the strong expectation that party membership matters, it is necessary to consider the implications of divided government for legislative influence. We need first to ask if, as we might expect, legislators are less willing to allow the executive freedom of maneuver under conditions of divided government. A study of congressional responses to the use of military force, for example, finds that "congressional partisans tend not to trust opposition presidents to implement the law properly, and hence feel they need to scrutinize a plethora of executive-branch actions and write detailed instructions into the law" (Meernik 1995, 384). As Peterson argues, "Partisan opposition is effective opposition" (1994b, 10).

If it is in fact the case that legislators are reluctant to allow presidents of the opposing party much substantive discretion, we need to consider the implications for patterns of international cooperation. I explore the possibility that such domestic divisions substantially complicate international interaction. I also consider, in chapter 3, the effects of divided government from the executive's perspective. Just as divided government may change the willingness of legislators to give the executive certain powers, it may lead the executive to search for ways to minimize the role of the legislature in international bargaining.

Institutional perspectives on legislative organization have provided vast new interpretations of the ways that legislatures work and how they exert influence on policy.[3] For the most part, this literature has focused on domestic policy. While the specifics of problems of international interaction differ from domestic policies, many of the same kinds of dilemmas arise: how to gain information about complex problems, how most effectively to exploit divisions of labor, how to overcome collective-action problems. Models of legislative organization should thus have something to tell us about the patterns of legislative engagement in international bargaining. Two factors that theory tells us are particularly important are the similarity of preferences between the executive and the legislature and the nature of party government. The empirical studies in this book examine, among other issues, how variation in these two variables influences the nature of legislative-executive interaction on issues of international cooperation.

LEGISLATURES AND COMMITMENT

Establishing commitments is a central dilemma of politics, indeed, of social interaction in general. The commitment dilemma provides a fundamental moti-

---

[3] For an exception see Lindsay (1994a).

vation for creating and modifying institutions and an organizing device for understanding patterns of cooperation and conflict. In international politics, credibility is a scarce resource. Unless states can somehow find ways to establish credible commitments to particular courses of action, they will find it impossible to achieve many potential gains from cooperation. Indeed, the difficulties of establishing commitments in the anarchic system of international politics have given rise to the dominant theoretical approach to international politics, Realism. Assuming that states cannot credibly commit themselves to avoid attacking one another, pursuing beggar-thy-neighbor economic policies, or other mutually destructive activities, Realism creates a vision of world politics as a Hobbesian world of self-sufficiency and tacit or overt hostility. In a world where attempting to cooperate involves putting oneself at risk or adopting policies that will be costly or impossible to reverse, the ability to commit is immensely valuable.

The Realist image of the world, where commitment is impossible, is in conflict with our everyday experience of contained conflict, interdependence, and realized gains from exchange. States sometimes find ways to assure one another that they will not take advantage of temptations to achieve immediate gains at the expense of others' well-being, and they sometimes manage to achieve the benefits of long-term mutual cooperation. The systemic conditions for credibility have become the subject of many studies of international cooperation (Keohane 1984; Martin 1992a; Oye 1986a; Krasner 1983) But we also believe that domestic political structures may either complicate or enhance states' ability to establish commitments (see, for example, Simmons 1994). One of the major purposes of this book is to examine the ways in which legislative influence on foreign policy interacts with the ability to establish credible commitments. I will argue, and the empirical evidence that follows will substantiate, that institutionalized legislative influence complicates international bargaining but makes the agreements reached through these fractious bargaining processes more credible.

The Problem of Commitment in International Cooperation

The refrain of "credible commitments" runs through analyses of domestic and international politics, as well as studies of economic organization. The Prisoners' Dilemma and other variations on the theme of collective action have become common currency in our analysis of social interaction. Social scientists are now acutely aware that seemingly irrational, mutually destructive outcomes often result not from a failure to understand the situation or a lack of desire to cooperate but from an inability to commit oneself to pursue advantageous courses of action that require short-term sacrifices. Recognizing such collective dilemmas, we ask about the conditions that allow for their resolution. Resolution often comes down to the question of whether actors can devise mechanisms that allow them to establish credible commitments (Schelling 1960). Thus credibility is tightly linked to cooperation; both serve as dependent variables in the empirical chapters here.

The way that domestic institutions constrain or promote the credibility of states' international commitments remains a major theoretical and practical issue. On the one hand, we have multiple examples of legislatures interfering with executive attempts to commit to cooperate with other states, as in the U.S. Congress rejecting membership in the League of Nations. Similarly, we have examples of states attempting to adopt difficult economic reforms in which a lack of democracy appears to be a necessary condition for success, as in Chile. On the other hand, putting our faith in dictators to provide international peace and economic well-being seems a particularly frail reed. How does one find a "good dictator"? And if the dictator you have isn't the right kind, how do you go about replacing him? If we observe deep international cooperation, such as that involved in institutionalized military alliances or economic integration, democracies in fact seem more successful at providing the necessary commitments than nondemocracies.[4] The problem of credibility is too complex to answer with a simple assertion that it is necessary to minimize popular influence on policy in order to establish it.

The analysis of credible commitments quickly becomes intertwined with the analysis of institutions. Transaction-cost economics provides a framework for analyzing problems of commitment in economic exchange relationships (Williamson 1985). In general, transaction-cost approaches explain the form of economic organization—such as the range of activities undertaken within firms instead of between them—by considering how organization can minimize the costs of transactions. One of the major sources of high transaction costs lies in the possibility of hold-up or other types of reneging on bargains.

For example, consider a firm that specializes its output to produce goods that are designed to meet the specific needs of a single large buyer. Such specialization may be in the interest of both the buyer and seller, reducing production costs. However, once the commitment of specific assets takes place, the seller can find himself being held up by the buyer, who now can offer a lower price for the output since the seller has no alternative outlets for his specialized product. Fears of hold-up can prevent firms from making specific investments. Likewise, fears of reneging on bargains can prevent states from committing to control arms build-ups, create free-trade areas, or use foreign assistance productively. Transaction-cost economics suggests that actors respond to dilemmas like this by creating institutions that reduce or eliminate the opportunities for hold-up, as well as other transaction costs. In the case of specialized firms, the organizational form predicted may be a vertically integrated firm that brings under one roof the functions of both buyer and seller. In short, the choice of institutions becomes a key dependent variable for testing theories of transaction costs.

On the international level, the insights of transaction-cost economics have

---

[4] For elaboration of the concept of deep cooperation, see Downs and Rocke (1995).

been used to explain patterns of international cooperation and the functions of international institutions. Analysts have applied this approach to problems of international cooperation ranging from arms control to liberalization of international trade (Oye 1986a; Downs and Rocke 1995). An appreciation of the nature of collective-action problems and the necessity of establishing commitments in order to promote cooperation led to hegemonic-stability theory, with its prediction that the necessary commitments could only be provided by a single dominant state (Keohane 1980; Krasner 1976; Mansfield 1994). Building on and reacting to hegemonic-stability theory, institutional theorists suggested that international institutions could substitute for hegemons, performing informational and linkage functions that established the necessary conditions to allow states to make commitments (Krasner 1983; Keohane 1984; Martin 1992a).

None of these approaches has considered domestic politics systematically. In empirical studies, domestic politics arises unavoidably, and analysts are aware that actions at the domestic level interact with international commitment problems. The metaphor of two-level games suggests a tool for bringing domestic politics more rigorously into the study of cooperation and commitment (Evans, Jacobson, and Putnam 1993). But while we now have a solid picture of the systemic conditions for successful international cooperation, we remain aware that explaining a large part—perhaps the major part—of the variation in cooperation requires more careful attention to domestic politics. If the domestic situation facing a head of government, or chief negotiator, does not allow for credible commitments to negotiating partners, no set of systemic pressures short of imminent threat to the state's existence are likely to provide the necessary conditions for successful cooperation. Variation in systemic conditions helps us to understand the incentives and opportunities for international cooperation, and is one set of factors that allow for or inhibit the credible commitments necessary for cooperation. But a fuller understanding of cooperation requires systematic analysis of the domestic conditions for commitment. In the case of democracies, the institutionalized role of the legislature is a key source of variation in the ability to make credible commitments.

Figure 2.1 illustrates the commitment problem in international bargaining. Imagine bargaining between two states, Home and Foreign, on non-tariff barriers (NTBs). SQ indicates the status quo NTB level. E and L indicate the preferred outcomes of Home executive and legislature, respectively. Both prefer elimination of Foreign NTBs, while E prefers a modest reduction in Home NTBs. For simplicity, we neglect domestic politics in Foreign, indicating Foreign's preferred outcome by F.

The range of possible bargains is found by examining each actor's indifference curves running through SQ. E and L would prefer any outcome to the right of the curves SQ-E' and SQ-L', respectively, to SQ. F would prefer any outcome above the curve SQ-F'. This arrangement of preferences makes a point like A feasible as the outcome of international negotiations, since it is preferred by all three actors to SQ.

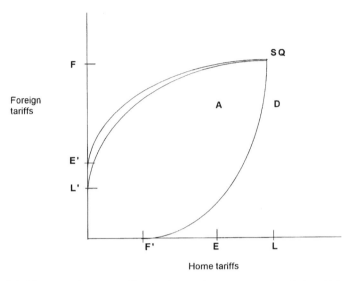

Figure 2.1. The commitment problem in international cooperation. Points F, E, and L indicate the preferred outcomes of Foreign, Home executive, and Home legislature, respectively. SQ indicates the status quo, A the international agreement, and D the outcome if Home reneges on the agreement.

Now assume that Foreign lives up to the terms of A, reducing its NTBs. Home, however, reneges on its commitment to A, and fails to reduce its NTBs. This leads to the outcome D, which leaves Foreign worse off than the status quo. If Foreign's removal of NTBs involved specific investments or is otherwise difficult to reverse, D may persist as a stable outcome, leaving Foreign aggrieved.

If Foreign anticipates the probability of such reneging behavior by Home, Foreign will be unwilling to enter into negotiations. This stylized example illustrates the value of being able to make credible commitments. Without such a capacity, Home is unable to achieve the benefits of moving from SQ to A. Since both E and L prefer A to SQ, why A cannot be achieved may appear puzzling. The solution to the puzzle arises in the failure to make credible commitments.[5] The logic of why actors who cannot commit are unable to achieve

---

[5] Studies that come to conclusions about legislatures and cooperation that differ from those in this book, such as Milner (1997), often result from different treatment of the credibility issue. Milner assumes domestic mechanisms that prevent unilateral movement from A to D. (See also Mansfield, Milner, and Rosendorff 1998.) By making these mechanisms a central variable rather than assuming them, this book comes to quite different conclusions about the effects of legislative participation.

available joint gains is the same fundamental logic as that of the Prisoners' Dilemma.

Figure 2.1 also illustrates what I mean by an exchange model between the executive and legislature. Although they have different preferences, both benefit from being able to make commitments, since many international agreements are preferable to the status quo. As in any exchange, both benefit from making a deal, while they disagree about the exact terms of a deal. In other words, a bargaining space exists between E and L, as well as between Home and Foreign. Being able to realize Pareto-improving benefits in this bargaining space requires functioning institutions of delegation and organization between the executive and legislature.

Implementation of Agreements: State Strength

International cooperation requires states to engage in two stages of interaction: bargaining and implementation.[6] During bargaining, they reach agreements about the policies they agree to adjust, usually contingent on specified policy adjustments by others. Most studies of international cooperation have in fact concentrated on the bargaining stage, asking about the conditions under which states are able to reach mutually beneficial agreements. A prominent collection of studies of two-level games, for example, is subtitled "International *Bargaining* and Domestic Politics," rather than focusing on the process of international cooperation as a whole (Evans, Jacobson, and Putnam 1993; emphasis added). But unless agreements are not only ratified but implemented, no real international cooperation, defined as mutual adjustment of policies, has taken place. In figure 2.1, an outcome of D is a case of failed cooperation, even if bargaining successfully settled on A. Attempts to explain patterns of international cooperation need to consider the conditions not only for reaching agreements but for implementing them effectively. One approach to analyzing the second stage of the cooperation problem involves attention to state "compliance" (Chayes and Chayes 1993; Victor, Raustiala, and Skolnikoff 1998). Compliance and implementation both refer to adjusting policies in ways specified in international agreements, and so could be used interchangeably. However, since the term compliance has taken on technical legal meanings and lends itself readily to legal rather than political analysis, I use the language of implementation.

Implementation is central to the models of legislatures and cooperation that I develop in this book because the process of implementation nearly always engages legislatures in democratic systems. They are directly and immediately involved in implementation if international agreements require formal legislative

---

[6] Some analysts of bargaining would identify many more stages to the process of cooperation. I use as simple a framework as possible, since my purpose is merely to argue that implementation needs to be studied as an integral part of the cooperation process.

ratification, as, for example, treaties or fast-track agreements do in the United States. Some parliamentary systems, such as Denmark's, have comparable requirements for explicit legislative approval to undertake significant international commitments. Chapter 3 considers the use of alternative forms of ratification of international agreements, to see if we can link the form of agreement used to the conditions of domestic politics in the United States.

While formal ratification is perhaps the most obvious mechanism by which legislatures influence the implementation of international agreements, it may not be the most significant or have the deepest effects. The indirect mechanisms of legislative influence discussed above play a major role in putting international cooperation into place. Even if legislatures are not asked to express their formal approval of an agreement, they have available numerous mechanisms to block, circumvent, or otherwise frustrate implementation. "Self-executing" agreements often require explicit changes in existing domestic laws to have any practical effect. One example of such agreements studied in some detail in this book is the set of directives for completion of the internal market in the EU. The directives themselves were subject to no formal domestic ratification processes. However, putting them into place in each member state is a long, contentious, sometimes tedious process of bringing domestic legislation into conformity with the directives. The process of changing domestic law provides ample opportunity for parliaments to undercut or otherwise impede faithful implementation of these important international agreements, sometimes forcing renegotiation or special treatment for individual countries, and putting the entire process of economic integration on shaky ground.

The power of the purse provides a second mechanism by which legislatures profoundly influence implementation. Most international agreements require shifting of budgetary resources—into enforcement procedures, away from producing certain kinds of arms, etc. Even in those democracies with the most extensive delegation of powers from the legislature to the executive, the legislature retains the power to control appropriations. Parliamentary control of executive expenditures is the historical, and perhaps practical, essence of parliamentary democracy. Executives find ways to gain some room for maneuver on expenditures, but it is difficult for them to circumvent legislative opposition to the extent necessary to establish a credible commitment in the face of refusal to appropriate the necessary funds for implementation.

In other specific instances, we can identify additional mechanisms and procedures that engage legislators in the process of implementation of international agreements. Appreciating the scope of legislative influence at this stage is vital, since anticipation of effective legislative opposition to implementation will feed back to affect the process of bargaining itself. Negotiators who see that their partners will have difficulty putting an agreement into place due to domestic opposition will be reluctant to commit themselves to taking the costly steps necessary for successful international cooperation. Likewise, a negotiator who knows that he will have trouble with implementation would be foolish to make substantial commitments, as long as he cares about his reputation as a reliable government representative. Implementation affects the process of international negotiation much like the threat of presidential vetoes affects the legislative process in the U.S. Congress. Anticipation of a potential future veto reaches back in time to influence the activities of rational legislators. Even when vetoes are not actually used, the president's preferences are reflected in legislation through the mechanism of anticipated reactions. Similarly, the threat of failed implementation exerts leverage on the entire process of international cooperation, providing a mechanism for expression of legislative preferences.

Anticipation of legislative reaction to international agreements has a dual effect on cooperation. First, it influences the nature of deals reached. Some have argued, drawing analogies to bargaining between labor unions and firms, that more constrained negotiators will be better placed to be tough bargainers, pulling more of the available benefits of cooperation in their direction (Putnam 1988). At times we may see such a dynamic in action, as U.S. negotiators claim that they are tightly constrained by what Congress will accept. Attempts to formalize this intuition about the distributional effects of constrained negotiation have led to mixed results. Milner and Rosendorff (1995) find results that support the notion that constraints lead to distributional advantages. But they also find that introducing uncertainty into the model substantially modifies the results. Reinhardt (1994) likewise finds that allowing legislators to behave strategically in a formal framework interferes with the supposed advantages of domestic constraint.

A second effect of domestic constraint exercised through the implementation phase is on the efficiency of international cooperation. Efficiency refers not to the distribution of benefits of cooperation between parties to international agreements but to the degree to which participants are able to realize the potential benefits of cooperation. Cooperation leads to mutual benefits: more open trade, reduced wasteful expenditures on the military, reduced threat of international conflict, etc. While the distribution of these benefits is a constant worry for negotiators, just as important an analytical issue is whether states are able to achieve cooperative benefits at all. If states cannot make credible commitments to live up to international bargains, they will not be able to exploit the gains of cooperation. Failure to cooperate in the face of potential gains is a type of inefficiency, and has been the focus of most efforts to characterize patterns of international cooperation.

If legislative involvement in implementation of agreements either facilitates or impedes establishing credible commitments, it should have a substantial impact on the efficiency of international cooperation. Many traditional studies of foreign policy, as well as the celebration of "strong states" as efficient international actors, stress the difficulties that legislative involvement creates for establishing commitments. I would argue that such claims are fundamentally misguided. It is doubtless true that attempting to cope with an active legislature further complicates the already murky process of international bargaining. Leaders of states who do not take legislative constraints into account appear to be more flexible at the bargaining table, allowing for a wider range of potential outcomes. However, as I have just argued, being able to bargain skillfully is only part of the entire process of international cooperation. Unless such bargains can be enforced back home, no amount of diplomatic skill will allow the establishment of credible commitments. In democracies, legislatures can frustrate implementation of agreements. They can do so even if—perhaps particularly if—they are closed out of the bargaining process itself. Given this fact of democratic life, regular legislative involvement in international bargaining can become a democratic asset.

Arguments about legislative influence and implementation of commitments have a close relation to theories of state strength. Analysts of comparative foreign policy and other theorists of comparative politics have turned to the concept of state strength to explain the effective pursuit of state goals, such as international cooperation or economic reform. As is usual in discussions of complex concepts, definitions of "state strength" abound. Initially, it referred to state autonomy from societal pressures (Krasner 1978a, 57–60; Nordlinger 1987; Migdal 1988). A strong state was a government apparatus that had gained autonomy, being able to choose the course of its policies without constant input and constraint from societal actors. A strong state was an autonomous state. Much of the early literature on state strength argued that autonomy was a benefit when it came to developing effective policies to deal with a complex world. For example, in a series of studies of foreign economic policies in industrialized democracies, authors found that strong states such as Japan and France were able to cope with external shocks effectively (Katzenstein 1978; Pempel 1978; Zysman 1978), while weak states like the United States found themselves stuck with inconsistent, muddled policies (Krasner 1978b). The notion of state strength as state autonomy has carried over into studies of international relations more generally (Mastanduno, Lake, and Ikenberry 1989).

More recently, analysts have applied the idea of state strength to explain the nature and success of economic reform in developing and newly industrializing economies. One line of analysis, consistent with the work just mentioned on foreign economic policy, argues that state autonomy is necessary if developing countries are to pursue difficult economic reforms. Evidence in support of this proposition is drawn from Asian states, ranging from Japan to the new economic powers of Southeast Asia, and from Latin America (Kang 1995, 573; Haggard 1990). However, these works also begin to suggest the difficulties with establishing a straightforward connection between state autonomy and successful pursuit of national goals. In fact, they often find successful states that are autonomous in only limited senses, being deeply penetrated by particular kinds of societal actors such as major financial interests.

Following such insights, another line of analysis questions the advantages of state autonomy and reconsiders the underlying notion of state strength. According to this rethinking, a strong state is not necessarily one that is able to choose its own policies without consideration of societal interests. Instead, a strong state is one that is, to put it simply, able to get things done. Mann (1986) distinguishes between "despotic" and "infrastructural" power. Despotic power is consistent with the simple authority to choose policies without constraints. But such power is nearly irrelevant to modern states. More consequential, and much more interesting, is infrastructural power: "the capacity of the state actually to penetrate civil society, and to implement logistically political decisions throughout the realm" (Mann 1986, 113).

Consistent with the discussion above of implementation, revised thinking about state strength argues that the ability to choose policies is of little consequence if policies cannot be put into place on a consistent basis. A strong state is an effective state, one that is able to mobilize popular and financial support for difficult policies. Such mobilization is perhaps not best undertaken by autonomous governments out of touch with societal actors. Instead, a deep interpenetration of government and society, expressed through institutionalized arrangements that allow efficient exchange of information, may be most conducive to effective policy. Penetrated states may indeed be constrained in the range of policies from which they can choose. But if such constraint enhances their ability to undertake fundamental reform, it can be an asset. Crone's (1988) work on Southeast Asia illustrates this point, discussing "collaborative control" as the foundation of effective states in that region. Ikenberry (1986) finds a similar result in advanced capitalist democracies. The vast literature on corporatism also falls into this framework, with its emphasis on the ways that institutionalized interpenetration of state and society allow countries to cope with modern economics and politics (Schmitter 1981, 313).

Such arguments about state strength and capacity in comparative politics are similar in tone to those in international relations about the relationship between state sovereignty and states that are successful on the international level. A sovereign state (using the term loosely) is one that can freely choose its own course of action. Yet, given conditions of interdependence, an insistence on maintaining a high level of effective sovereignty can make it very difficult for states to achieve their ultimate objectives, such as security from external threat or economic well-being. Sovereignty is perhaps best thought of as a bargaining tool under conditions of interdependence (Keohane 1993). States can choose to trade off sovereignty, for example in multilateral economic arrangements or military alliances, in exchange for other benefits. If an effective state on the international level is one that provides the maximum possible benefits for its citizens, it is not likely to be jealously protective of its sovereignty and autonomy.

Likewise, on the domestic level, an element of institutionalized cooperation with society—often expressed through legislatures—may be necessary to realize the promises of state strength.

Institutions as Commitment Devices

Discussions of the relationship between state autonomy and capacity and of patterns of international cooperation are related by a core set of concerns about the role of institutions as commitment devices. As mentioned, this core is addressed explicitly in transaction-cost economics. It provides the foundation for this book, which sees formalized legislative engagement with processes of international cooperation as a commitment device, a mechanism that allows democracies to make credible commitments on the international level. Attempts to close legislatures out of cooperative processes often backfire, for example as executives in the EU began discovering in 1992–95 when they found that they were not as free to manipulate policy toward integration without parliamentary consent as many had imagined.

The general notion that political as well as economic institutions can be understood as commitment devices has solid theoretical and empirical background. Some of the most prominent work along these lines is by Douglass North, Barry Weingast, and their collaborators. North and Weingast (1989) have studied the evolution of government institutions in England. They argue that economic growth required a foundation of stable property rights (see also North 1981). In seventeenth-century England, such a foundation was created by making the Crown accountable to Parliament, so that it became more difficult for the Crown to renege on public debt. As a consequence, England was able to borrow money at lower interest rates than would otherwise have been available, providing the foundations of a powerful modern state. Brewer (1989, 161) has expanded on this thesis, providing further evidence and historical detail.

Similar stories about transfer of authority and creation of new institutions to facilitate commitments arise in looking at groups of relations among traders. In settings where individual traders did not have long-term repeated interactions with one another, developing a reputation for being reliable was difficult. The difficulty of determining whether one was dealing with an honest or dishonest potential partner inhibited economic exchange. Some groups of traders managed to resolve such dilemmas by creating centralized institutions that allowed them to reveal information about themselves and so to establish commitments. These institutions were less important for their explicit enforcement powers than for the information they provided principals. Milgrom, North, and Weingast (1990) have applied this sort of analysis to the institution of the Law Merchant in Europe during the early middle ages. Greif, Milgrom, and Weingast (1994) have extended the model to consider merchant guilds in the late medieval period.

The stories that these authors tell about the foundations of modern political economics have much the same character as those we tell today about the rationale for international institutions or for the development of legislative institutions. In these disparate but structurally similar cases, individual actors find it necessary to develop ways to make credible commitments to one another if they wish to engage in advantageous exchange. Making such commitments in decentralized settings is difficult. Sometimes difficulties arise from lack of information about others' preferences and reputations; sometimes they arise from the short time-frame available for individual transactions. In all cases, institutions serve as commitment devices. Such a perspective does not deny that institutions also have distributional effects, determining who gets the most out of exchanges (see Knight 1992). But the commitment effects of institutions are just as important.

When we consider the place of democracies on the international stage, commitment problems should draw our attention. What is it about democracies that explains their apparent success in the twentieth century, despite concerns that internal dispersion of authority complicates international bargaining?[7] Models and empirical studies of commitment problems in other settings suggest that part of the secret of democratic success lies precisely in its supposed handicap, constant interference in policymaking by legislative actors. Not all such interference is productive. A legislature that finds itself circumvented or closed out of important decisions is likely to make a great deal of trouble. But a legislature that is consistently involved in an institutionalized, formalized manner in international bargaining can enhance the credibility of democracies' commitments. Through such engagement, legislative preferences are taken into account by negotiators. At the same time, delegation of authority to negotiate to the executive allows legislators to overcome their own internal collective-action problems and other limits on legislative capacities.

APPLYING MODELS OF LEGISLATURES TO INTERNATIONAL COOPERATION

This chapter has summarized a wide-ranging set of literatures, but finds common core insights in them. The core insights include the ideas that delegation can be a mechanism of influence; that variation in institutions is a key variable in the process of cooperation; and that credibility is central to the problem of cooperation. The reviews of the literatures have begun to suggest how these ideas might be applied to the problem of legislatures and international cooperation. The precise hypotheses to be tested will be developed and specified in a context-sensitive manner in the following chapters. This section will continue the process of developing testable implications of the models by building the basic logic of three sets of general hypotheses.

---

[7] For an alternative perspective on the reasons for democratic success, see Wittman (1989).

The major hypotheses explored in this book can be grouped into three sets. First, there is a set of hypotheses about legislative influence. A second set of hypotheses centers around the effects of legislative participation on credibility. The third, building on the first two, concerns executive-legislative interaction and international cooperation. Developing observable implications from these general sets of hypotheses requires more precise knowledge of specific substantive contexts, and so will take place in each empirical chapter. Here, I draw on the literatures summarized above to develop the overall logic and general structure of each set of hypotheses.

First, and perhaps most complex logically, we have a body of hypotheses concerning variations in legislative influence on patterns of international cooperation. As discussed above, most literature on legislatures and foreign policy suffers from one of two problems. Either it asserts that legislatures have almost no influence, or it merely describes changes in the degree of legislative influence without attempting to explain the patterns of variation we observe. Here, I draw on theories of legislative-executive interaction to explain variation in legislative influence.

Statements about variation in influence have numerous observable implications. I focus primarily on those implications that involve changes in the institutions that structure legislative participation in international cooperation. I am interested in the conditions that lead legislatures to move further toward a formal, explicit role in international cooperation; in other words, to reclaim delegated authority from executives. The null hypothesis, in general, is that legislatures have no influence on cooperation. This executive-dominance model would imply either that executives can manipulate the structures of legislative participation to evade legislative influence, or that the structures of legislative participation do not respond to the demands of international cooperation and executive behavior. In contrast, I find that these structures vary in predictable ways, but not in the ways that executive-dominance models would predict.

Under the category of legislative influence, one major expectation is the Delegation Hypothesis: *Legislatures will move to institutionalize their participation in international cooperative endeavors when there is greater conflict of interest between the executive and the legislature.* This expectation follows directly from theories of delegation, which, as discussed above, predict less legislative willingness to delegate when the executive does not share extensive common interests. Conflict of interest is operationalized in a number of ways in the following chapters, depending on the context. Divided party control of government can serve as a proxy for conflict of interest; we thus should see greater institutionalized legislative participation under conditions of divided government than under unified government. Greater conflict of interest can also arise when the issues being negotiated on the international level are particularly contentious, or when the executive has in the recent past abused delegation, taking on extensive international obligations without having obtained appropriate legislative consent. These propositions about conflict of interest between the branches and greater institutionalization of legislative participation are examined most thoroughly in the chapters on U.S. food aid, economic sanctions, and European integration. Chapter 5 shows how the Delegation Hypothesis follows from an exchange model.

The major alternative to the Delegation Hypothesis, treated as the null hypothesis here, is the Abdication Hypothesis. The Abdication Hypothesis is drawn from executive-dominance models. It states that legislatures that delegate authority to the executive thereby abdicate their ability to influence outcomes. From this perspective, there is little legislatures can do to reclaim authority from the executive if they discover that it is being abused, or if conflicts of interest between the branches grow. Thus, the Abdication Hypothesis does not predict the same patterned changes in delegation predicted by the Delegation Hypothesis.

Another expectation about legislative influence, closely related to the above, is the Influence Hypothesis: *Executives are unable to manipulate the structures of legislative participation to evade legislative influence on international cooperation.* The Influence Hypothesis follows from the above discussion of legislative organization and legislative-executive interaction. If an executive-dominance perspective were instead correct, we could summarize expectations about how executive choice of institutions varies in an Evasion Hypothesis. The Evasion Hypothesis is the major alternative to the Influence Hypothesis. I predict that there will be little empirical support for the Evasion Hypothesis. Implications regarding executive choice of institutions are tested most directly in the following chapter on the use of executive agreements and treaties in the United States.

The second major body of hypotheses regards the impact of legislative participation on the credibility of commitments. Here, the central proposition is straightforward, and labeled the Credibility Hypothesis: *Institutionalized legislative participation in international cooperation leads to greater credibility of international commitments.* This proposition is examined most closely in chapter 7, on implementation of directives within the EU. Implementation serves here as a fairly direct measure of credibility. The Credibility Hypothesis is also tested more indirectly throughout the book, in that greater credibility is expected to lead to enhanced international cooperation. Putting together this proposition with the previous one about influence, we are left with the counterintuitive expectation that, if domestic institutions are appropriately designed, credibility can actually be enhanced under conditions of executive-legislative conflict. I in fact find substantial evidence in favor of this idea in the EU, where we see that those states that have the most domestic conflict over European integration are the ones that implement EU-level agreements most faithfully. This result is surprising from a perspective that ignores institutions but consistent with my framework.

The logic of institutionalized legislative participation and credibility follows from the discussion of credibility and mechanisms of legislative influence in this chapter and the logic of legislative-executive relations as an example of exchange. Many mechanisms of legislative influence are indirect, as legislators have the capacity to undermine implementation of commitments to which they object. The specific mechanisms may include failure to change domestic law as required, failure to appropriate necessary funds, explicit overturning of executive commitments. Well-informed executives will take these ex post mechanisms of control into account, thus allowing legislative preferences to influence international bargaining and facilitating the process of implementation.

However, lack of institutionalized participation by the legislature often means that executives do not have good information about preferences or the chances that the legislature will refuse to implement international agreements. When legislative participation is not institutionalized, or when executives attempt to circumvent legislative opposition, they will reach agreements with other states that turn out to be difficult to put into effect at home. Institutionalized legislative participation—an explicit grant of authority to the executive *ex ante,* legislative oversight of negotiations, etc.—allows executives to avoid these negotiating errors, thus enhancing the credibility of commitments. If, in fact, executives were dominant, able to single-handedly implement as well as negotiate international agreements, legislative participation would be irrelevant. But as the evidence outlined above on legislative influence and the mechanisms just mentioned suggest, executives are not all-powerful. Thus, devising institutional structures whereby legislators have clear opportunities to influence bargaining is an important mechanism for establishing the credibility of international commitments.

Kenneth Schultz (1998) develops a formal model of domestic opposition and international crises that provides further logical support for the Credibility Hypothesis. Schultz finds that having an active opposition provides increased information about a state's preferences in crises, through "confirmatory signaling" that enhances the credibility of government statements. Confirmatory signaling occurs when actors whose preferences are not always precisely aligned with one another—such as an executive and a legislature in an exchange model—nevertheless make consistent statements. Even when confirmatory signaling does not occur, the credibility of government statements is enhanced by the fact that an organized opposition forces the government to be more selective about the statements it makes. While Schultz models a generalized "opposition" rather than a legislature as a second actor in the credibility game, his logic of confirmatory signaling and selective commitments echoes the logic of the Credibility Hypothesis developed here.

The third major set of expectations involves the link between legislative participation and cooperation. The logic is identical to that just outlined on credibility, and the generic form of the Cooperation Hypothesis is analogous: *Institutionalized legislative participation leads to greater levels of international cooperation.* When cooperation requires credibility, this proposition follows trivially from the previous discussion of the conditions for credibility.[8] The chapters that consider the use of executive agreements, economic sanctions, and U.S. food aid directly examine this proposition about the conditions for international cooperation.

The chapter on economic sanctions considers a related proposition about cooperation: conflict of interest between the executive and legislature can reduce the level of cooperation the executive branch can achieve, but, paradoxically, enhance the legislature's ability to achieve cooperation over the objections of the executive branch. This proposition follows from the logic of legislative efforts to influence foreign policy. Under divided government, the legislature will move to institutionalize its participation in international cooperation. In the case of economic sanctions, this leads to higher levels of international cooperation when Congress takes the lead on imposing sanctions under divided government. It also means that Congress will undermine executive-led sanctions that do not have legislative support. On the other hand, when government control is unified, the legislature will be unwilling to force its preferences on the executive branch. Foreign-policy initiatives that lack executive support, such as legislatively initiated sanctions, will thus lack credibility under unified government, and we will see low levels of international cooperation.

CONCLUSION

The theoretical framework for understanding the influence of national legislatures on international cooperation draws from a number of, at first glance, disparate perspectives. I have summarized, briefly and selectively, the relevant literatures on legislative organization, legislative-executive interaction, and institutions as commitment devices. Examination of these disparate perspectives allows us to distill some key principles for the analysis that follows. To begin with, it suggests that understanding legislative influence requires a more subtle approach than a simple count of the number of times a national legislature overturns treaties or otherwise takes dramatic public actions. Legislatures possess numerous subtle and indirect mechanisms of influence. The chapters that follow attempt to specify the nature and limits of such mechanisms, testing the Influence Hypothesis.

A related argument is that legislators transfer authority to the executive branch or other actors in order to achieve their objectives. We should not inter-

[8] For some forms of shallow cooperation—such as purely symbolic statements that require no real shift in policy, or policy changes that are easily reversed—credibility may not be a necessary condition for cooperation. I do not examine these types of cooperation in this book.

pret such delegation as a triumph of the executive branch over the legislative but remain aware of the continuing constraints that the legislature puts on policy under such conditions. Legislative-executive relations are an exchange relationship, in which the question "who dominates?" may be less important than "how can both benefit?" Considering the incentives to delegate leads us to some initial expectations about how the level of legislative activity on foreign policy will vary, summarized in the Delegation Hypothesis. In particular, we should expect greatest legislative willingness to allow the executive a free hand in foreign affairs when it trusts the executive to behave in a manner generally consistent with legislative preferences, and when control of government is not divided on a partisan basis.

Beyond providing initial expectations about the pattern of legislative activity, these literatures have a core set of propositions about institutions and credibility that will prove vital to our understanding of the role of legislatures in international cooperation. Institutionalized legislative participation in international bargaining can provide for more capacity to make credible commitments, as stated in the Credibility Hypothesis. Without this capacity, states find it nearly impossible to take advantage of the potential gains of deep forms of international cooperation. This proposition is summarized in the Cooperation Hypothesis. The credibility asset follows directly from what many feel plagues democracies most deeply: the consistent intervention of legislative prerogatives in international interactions. The chapters that follow expand on these core insights, developing more specific, testable hypotheses and providing empirical evidence. The degree of legislative influence on international cooperation varies in predictable ways, and legislative participation has direct effects on the credibility of commitments and the level of cooperation achieved. These three general propositions are developed in more detail in the following chapters.

Institutions and Influence: Executive
Agreements and Treaties

MODERN theories of legislative-executive interaction suggest that the scope for legislative influence over policy is greater than is often appreciated in studies of foreign policy. The logic behind this proposition lies in the executive's ability and incentives to anticipate legislative reactions to policy decisions, and in indirect mechanisms of influence available to legislators. The major project of this book is to extend the logic of anticipated reactions and indirect legislative influence to the realm of international cooperation and foreign policy. Establishing the potential for indirect legislative influence, as specified in the Influence Hypothesis, requires that we confront the null hypothesis: that executives are able to manipulate institutions so as to deprive legislators of the ability to exercise influence.

This chapter tests the null hypothesis directly, through examination of the use of executive agreements and treaties in the United States. Since the president can choose to make international agreements in the form of executive agreements rather than treaties, many have argued that executive agreements provide the president with a means by which to evade congressional input into international negotiations and the need for Senate ratification of agreements. The proposition that executive agreements allow the president to evade legislative influence, which I label the Evasion Hypothesis, is a specific, observable implication of the general null hypothesis that executives are able to conclude agreements to cooperate with other states without having to satisfy the demands of legislators. The Evasion Hypothesis and the Influence Hypothesis are alternatives; if evidence supports the Evasion Hypothesis, it calls the Influence Hypothesis—one of the four central hypotheses of this book—into question. This chapter tests the Evasion Hypothesis by asking whether it is capable of explaining the observed pattern of use of executive agreements. If the Evasion Hypothesis were powerful, the theoretical framework for this book would be undermined. However, I find little support for the Evasion Hypothesis. Instead, presidents' use of executive agreements appears to respond to the demands of

Chapter 3 is a revised version of "Evasive Maneuvers? Reconsidering Presidential Use of Executive Agreements," from *Strategic Politicians, Institutions, and Foreign Policy,* edited by R. M. Siverson (Ann Arbor: University of Michigan Press, 1998). ©1998 by the University of Michigan. I thank the University of Michigan Press for permission to use this selection.

credibility and complexity, lending support to the Influence Hypothesis and indirect support to the Credibility Hypothesis. Examining patterns in the use of treaties, and how they respond to shifts in domestic politics, also provides a preliminary test of the general proposition that the ability to cooperate with other states is directly related to the level of executive-legislative conflict (i.e., the Cooperation Hypothesis).

When the president chooses to complete an agreement with another country, he must choose whether to put the agreement in the form of a treaty or an executive agreement. Treaties, as provided by the Constitution, must receive the approval of two-thirds of voting senators to go into effect. Executive agreements, in comparison, are not mentioned in the Constitution. They are approved through a number of different mechanisms, from a formal legislative vote to sole executive approval. However, they have the same legal effect as treaties (Millett 1990).[1] While Congress has attempted to specify criteria for determining the form of international agreements, the president continues to make these decisions unilaterally. Explaining variation in the form of agreements thus allows us to gain insight into the executive's strategic calculations about the use of domestic institutions.

In this chapter I question the evasion perspective. Two lines of argument should lead us to suspect that executive agreements do not provide the president with an effective way to avoid Congress. First, Congress is not as easy to evade as would be necessary for the Evasion Hypothesis to have much force. Even without the formalities of treaty ratification, the president operates within the boundaries of congressional consent, and although these boundaries most likely vary under different ratification procedures, they do not disappear. Second, and related, considerations of making credible commitments to other states should lead us to question the value of executive agreements that are intended simply to avoid Congress. If other states understand that domestic evasion is the motivation behind executive agreements, they should question the credibility of the commitment made by the executive under such a procedure and therefore be reluctant to accept informal agreements.

If the evasion argument were correct, we would expect to see predictable patterns in the use of executive agreements and treaties. However, the data presented here suggest that such patterns provide only minimal explanatory leverage. They lend support to the notion that executive agreements are not effective evasive devices. While the president may try to use them in this manner, congressional constraints and the need to make credible commitments to other countries put limits on his ability to do so. Alternative explanations for the

---

[1] Agreements that have been reached on sole-executive authority, not pursuant to legislation or otherwise involving the legislature, may not in fact have the same legal standing as treaties. See Congressional Research Service (1993, xvii).

choice of institutional form lie in considerations of credibility as well as the need to deal with increasing complexity in the international environment. Additional evidence of congressional influence and its interaction with credibility comes from examining congressional reactions to executive agreements over time, particularly congressional attempts to force the president to provide information about such agreements.

Beyond a test of the Evasion Hypothesis, patterns in the completion of international agreements allow an initial test of the domestic conditions that facilitate international cooperation, as predicted by the Cooperation Hypothesis. We can use the number of agreements completed as a rough measure of cooperation, and ask whether it declines in the face of executive-legislative conflict, as predicted. The chapter begins by elaborating the Evasion Hypothesis, then outlines alternative hypotheses about institutional choice. It then moves on to tests of the Evasion Hypothesis and the conditions for cooperation. It concludes with discussion of congressional attempts to gain control over the use of executive agreements, showing how these efforts have provided the framework for legislative influence.

THE NULL HYPOTHESIS: EVASION

The theoretical framework for this book highlights indirect mechanisms of legislative influence and examines the connection between this influence and the ability to make the necessary credible commitments to cooperate with other states. However, in the area of foreign policy many have questioned the notion that the legislature has substantial, consistent influence. The Influence Hypothesis, while widely accepted in studies of domestic policy, is highly controversial in the context of foreign policy. In particular, critics point to the ability of the executive to manipulate institutions so as to prevent legislators from gaining access to imporant decision-making processes. One prominent example of such supposed manipulation lies in the ability of executives to reach agreement with one another via informal agreements rather than agreements, such as treaties, that require formal legislative ratification. Thus, the key null hypothesis for this project is that executives can evade legislative influence by strategic choice of institutions, such as the form of agreements.

In traditional U.S. foreign-policy analysis, the relationship between Congress and the executive branch has been conceptualized as a "struggle for power" (Crabb and Holt 1992). Most analysts find that the executive branch is privileged in this struggle. The powers of the executive branch, its task of negotiating with other countries, and congressional weakness all contribute to an executive branch that is able to get its way on foreign-policy issues. While most analysts see a resurgence of congressional activism since the early 1970s, they conclude that the executive retains a dominant position (Peterson 1994c). Such analysis, however, stands in contrast to that of comparative foreign-policy analysts. When put in comparative perspective, the United States is singled out for having a strong legislature and an activist Congress (Katzenstein 1978). As this confusion in the political-science literature suggests, our understanding of executive-legislative relations in U.S. foreign policy remains plagued by a number of unexplained anomalies. Explanation of these anomalies demands an analytical framework that will allow us to identify and make sense of the patterns of legislative influence on foreign policy.

The previous chapter summarized modern work on legislative organization and legislative-executive interaction that provides such a framework. A central insight of the modern literature on legislatures is the necessity of distinguishing between action and influence. On foreign-policy issues, in particular, the locus of *activity* lies in the executive branch. But it would be a fundamental logical error to infer from this observation that legislatures lack the interest or means to influence international cooperation. We should take seriously, as a hypothesis worthy of rigorous scrutiny, the proposition that legislatures can use indirect means of influence to express their preferences on foreign policy as well as on domestic policy. When the executive acts without explicit legislative approval, it is natural to assume that legislative preferences will have little impact on his actions. But if we consider the potential for indirect mechanisms of influence, for example those that legislators might have available to them at the implementation stage, and if we assume that executives are far sighted and able to anticipate such ex post facto legislative influence, we have identified a channel by which even sole executive decisions can reflect legislators' policy preferences.

One oft-cited piece of evidence to support a claim of lack of congressional influence is the use of executive agreements as a method for making binding commitments to other countries. Such agreements are not mentioned in the Constitution. Because they do not involve the Senate in its constitutionally prescribed "advise and consent" role, they are seen as a method by which the president makes commitments independent of the wishes of Congress. Thus, increasing use of executive agreements, according to the Evasion Hypothesis, is evidence of decreasing legislative influence.

As figure 3.1 shows, the use of executive agreements has increased from very low levels in 1930 to 300 to 400 per year by the 1990s. At the same time, the number of treaties has remained about constant, at approximately fourteen per year.[2] Prior to 1930, the president used executive agreements only infrequently. The Congressional Research Service (1993, 14; hereafter cited as CRS), citing

---

[2] Figures are from CRS (1993, 14). The CRS obtained these data from the Office of the Assistant Legal Adviser for Treaty Affairs in the Department of State. Figures do not include classified agreements, and the criteria for reporting an international understanding as an executive agreement occasionally change. For example, the decrease in the number of executive agreements in 1991 and 1992 resulted from a change in reporting rules. In 1990, the State Department decided to discon-

a study by Borchard (1947), calculates that between 1789 and 1929 the United States signed a total of 667 treaties and 1,028 executive agreements. Today, the United States typically signs this many executive agreements in less than three years. Their use particularly accelerated in the late 1940s, as the United States assumed a more active role in international affairs. The numbers continued to grow until the mid-1970s, and appear to have settled to a fairly constant rate since then.

The trend toward increasing use of executive agreements has worried most interested observers, whether legal scholars, senators, or political analysts. The legal community engaged in a spirited debate in the 1970s about the constitutionality of executive agreements (Millett 1990; Paige 1977). The conclusion of the legal debate, and of Supreme Court cases, was that the president did indeed have the power to bind the United States through the use of executive agreements. Like treaties, they became the "supreme law of the land," once the president agreed to them. Only if an international commitment were to come into conflict with specific provisions of the Constitution would problems arise. In the Senate, as discussed further below, many expressed concern that the use of executive agreements diminished their ability to influence the content of international agreements.

The consensus view among political scientists is expressed well by Nathan and Oliver: "Presidents . . . have developed and employed the executive agreement to circumvent Senate involvement in international agreements almost altogether." The trend toward using these agreements is considered part of the development of the imperial presidency during the Cold War. Executive agreements were also "a potent device in the hands of activist presidents who sought means to further their conception of an energetic presidency" (1994, 99). Because members of Congress are not by law involved in consultations during the negotiation of executive agreements, and often do not have to vote on them, it seems plausible to interpret them as one of the tools presidents use when they wish to avoid congressional scrutiny. Executive agreements are thus perhaps antidemocratic, a way for the president to avoid keeping international commitments within the range acceptable to Congress. This executive-dominance perspective from students of U.S. foreign policy is consistent with arguments that see international cooperation as a kind of "executive cartel," designed to strengthen the executive at the expense of the legislature (Moravcsik 1994; Vaubel 1986; Kaiser 1971).

Why question this commonsense view? Because it neglects constraints on the president's ability to evade Congress. Recent studies of domestic political issues have taught us that such inferences frequently mischaracterize the actual nature of legislative influence. In the case of executive agreements in particu-

tinue reporting agricultural-assistance agreements under PL 480 as executive agreements (CRS 1993, xxxvii).

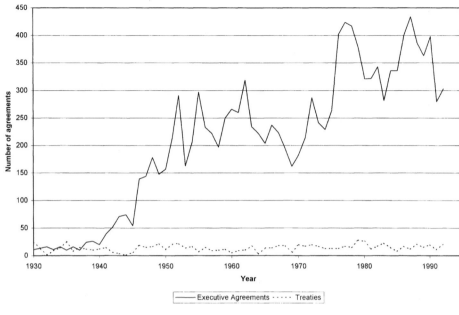

Figure 3.1. Number of agreements, 1930–1992.

lar, I would suggest two sets of reasons that we should look more skeptically at the claims made by the executive-dominance school. One set of reasons lies in mechanisms of influence that remain in the hands of members of Congress even in the case of executive agreements. To argue that the president can make far-reaching commitments without taking note of these mechanisms requires a demonstration that they have no effect. If Congress retains mechanisms of influence, this fact has far-reaching implications. In particular, it implies that a president using the executive-agreement procedure to avoid a Congress that will refuse to implement an international agreement or will overturn it through legislation will bring the credibility of any U.S. commitment into question. Such questions about credibility are a second reason that we should examine the Evasion Hypothesis more deeply. If other states question the credibility of commitments, and suspect that executive agreements are being used as evasive devices, they will be reluctant to sign agreements that call for deep cooperation.

Congress has in its hands a number of mechanisms by which it can exert influence on international agreements, even if they do not take the form of treaties. Executive agreements come in a number of varieties, including congressional-executive agreements, agreements pursuant to treaties, and sole-executive agreements. Congressional-executive agreements, which include most executive agreements, are "either explicitly or implicitly authorized in advance by Congress or submitted to Congress for approval" (CRS 1993, xvii). In some areas, such as the relatively technical issue of postal conventions or occasionally the more politicized issues of foreign trade or military assistance, Congress explicitly has authorized the conclusion of international agreements. The Reciprocal Trade Agreements Act of 1934, in which the president was authorized to negotiate reciprocal reductions in trade barriers within limits set in the legislation, is a good example. At other times, such as the fast-track procedures used to approve most recent trade agreements, including NAFTA, the president is required to submit negotiated agreements for congressional approval.

Agreements pursuant to treaties include those that have been either expressly authorized in a treaty or are clearly implied by a treaty's provisions. For example, the president has concluded a large number of executive agreements under the terms of the NATO treaty, without explicitly coming back to Congress for approval. The final category, sole executive agreements, are those that do not have any explicit or underlying implicit authorization from Congress. Legally, the president invokes constitutional authority such as that as Commander-in-Chief to justify the conclusion of sole executive agreements. While the legal status of sole executive agreements remains fuzzy, it appears that they cannot supersede a prior act of Congress (CRS 1993, xvii).

When agreements explicitly or implicitly are authorized in advance by Congress, it is difficult to sustain the argument that Congress has no influence on their content. Delegation of authority does give the president room to maneuver, for example by creating issue linkages not anticipated by Congress but that Congress finds difficult to reject. But only under narrowly defined circumstances does delegation negate the potential for congressional influence on agreements. Even when dealing with complex issues, structures of oversight, delegation, and legislative organization allow legislators to learn enough about the issues and proposed policies at stake to evaluate and make decisions about international commitments (Lupia and McCubbins 1995). Thus, congressional preferences continue to set constraints on executive action, although the nature of these constraints varies depending on institutional form, legislative interest, and the difficulty of learning about the issues being negotiated.

Similarly, when the president concludes agreements pursuant to treaties, the Senate's preferences have been taken into account during the initial ratification process. If the president's actions pursuant to the treaty go beyond the bounds of what the Senate anticipated, the power to abrogate the treaty or otherwise punish the president remains, and should serve to put constraints on executive actions. It is necessary for the Senate to learn about international interactions to exercise these powers effectively. But once again delegation of authority to interested specialists within Congress, as well as organized oversight of executive actions, allows the Senate to meet the learning conditions, which are not as stringent as we might first imagine. It is not necessary for Congress to be aware of every individual executive action in order for legislative preferences to place consistent constraints on the activities of a far sighted executive, especially one who cares about his reputation as a source of information or a representative of national interests. The nature of the international system demands that states be able to act strategically, and delegation of authority to the executive is often necessary to allow strategic maneuvering. It is not a signal of legislative impotence or indifference.

Johnson (1984), in a comprehensive study of international agreements, distinguishes between statutory agreements (what I have called congressional-executive agreements or agreements pursuant to treaties) and sole-executive agreements. He concludes that the conventional wisdom that executive agreements have replaced treaties is incorrect, since almost 87% of all U.S. international agreements are statutory rather than sole-executive agreements (Johnson 1984, 10–12). He finds that sole-executive agreements account for only about the same number of agreements as treaties (7% and 6%, respectively). Johnson concludes that the notion that Congress has been closed out of the process of international negotiation is therefore misplaced. Another estimate puts the number of executive agreements that involve some legislative action at 97% (Stevens 1977, 907; see also Pyle and Pious 1984, 274). The level of legislative action or explicit delegation to the executive that is present in most executive agreements belies the notion that they give the president unconstrained authority to make unilateral commitments for the United States.

Sole-executive agreements clearly present the greatest opportunity for the president to evade congressional will. However, various legislative powers beyond formal approval mechanisms provide the opportunity for influence on most types of international agreements, including sole-executive agreements. The keys to indirect influence are powers of implementation and appropriation. Many international agreements require changes in domestic law, so that implementation engages normal legislative processes. Not only does this implementation stage provide congressional influence, it brings in the House as well as the Senate (CRS 1993, xxxii–xxxiii). Chapters 6 and 7 examine the possibility of exerting influence on the content of negotiations through anticipation of the implementation stage in the case of agreements within the European Union. A similar pattern surely should apply in the United States, with its more powerful legislature. In addition, any international agreement that requires appropriation of funds will be scrutinized and can be overturned, de facto, by the House. The need to appropriate funds has been used to exert leverage over executive agreements, for example, when the president has tied foreign assistance to various political commitments from recipient states (see chapter 5). Since all foreign-aid appropriations pass through the House, and often are scrutinized closely, the potential exists at this stage for a de facto legislative veto. Anticipating such problems, the president should take congressional preferences into account. In addition, many international negotiations involve congressional representatives in a formal or informal consultative role, often in response to anticipation of a potential legislative veto (O'Halloran 1994).[3]

These mechanisms of congressional leverage suggest that, at the domestic level, there are reasons to expect the president to be sensitive to congressional concerns. While it is surely incorrect to assert that Congress "controls" international negotiations, the numerous methods by which the two houses of Congress effectively can veto or otherwise complicate implementation of an international agreement should suggest that it is not easy to circumvent congressional wishes entirely. Further reasons to question the Evasion Hypothesis arise when we model the problem of strategic interaction with other states. Strategic interaction is a central factor when we consider international relations, but it has been neglected by those who consider executive-legislative relations on domestic policy issues. Models of domestic-policy delegation assume that, after delegation, the executive sets policy. However, in international issues, delegation leads to negotiations (tacit or explicit) with other states rather than to unilateral setting of policy. It is reasonable to expect that this change in the structure of the situation will lead to differences in patterns and effects of delegation.

In particular, the United States' negotiating partners must consider whether the commitments made by the United States are credible. Concerns that commitments will be overturned by Congress are reasonable, and not infrequently expressed by other states. Knowledge that the president is using executive agreements to circumvent congressional opposition surely would add to concerns about credibility. Since Congress often has the power effectively to abrogate executive agreements, through the appropriations process or by otherwise refusing to implement an agreement, other countries will not take the president's word at face value in such situations. Unless other mechanisms make the commitment credible, states should be reluctant to commit themselves to take costly steps through executive agreements if they are primarily evasive devices. Other states may have incentives to demand more explicit and formal ratification processes, such as fast-track procedures. The most far-reaching commitments are precisely those where concerns about evasion are most likely to arise, so that the executive agreement would become less effective as an executive technique as U.S. credibility becomes more questionable.

The Evasion Hypothesis, consistent with the executive-dominance approach

[3] Since the *INS v. Chadha* decision, which struck down a form of legislative veto, legal scholars have questioned whether any forms of legislative vetoes are constitutional, and whether the Supreme Court's decision has made much of a difference in the ability of Congress to exercise influence. It appears that Congress retains many ways to change executive decisions in spite of *Chadha*. Korn (1994–95) makes a good argument that the importance of this decision has been overblown. Vázquez (1995) examines additional legislative mechanisms with particular attention to international agreements.

to foreign policy, suggests that executive agreements provide the president with an effective means to circumvent congressional opposition. Those who prefer to see congressional influence on international commitments therefore find the increasing use of executive agreements threatening. However, the logic of the executive-dominance approach is not sound. Congress retains indirect mechanisms of influence even in the case of executive agreements. These mechanisms should not only constrain the president, they should make other states skeptical of U.S. commitments that are made through executive agreements designed only to circumvent Congress. Indirect congressional influence should therefore lead to a different pattern in the use of executive agreements than that predicted by the Evasion Hypothesis.

THE LOGIC OF LEGISLATIVE INFLUENCE ON EXECUTIVE AGREEMENTS

As long as Congress retains some capacity to overturn or undercut international commitments with which it disagrees, negotiating partners suspecting congressional disagreement with a commitment will question its sincerity. They may demand a more formal approval process, such as a treaty, to establish credibility. One example of such a demand came in the process of establishing military bases in Spain. Beginning in the 1960s, the United States committed to bases there through secret executive agreements. When these agreements came to light in 1970, they caused an uproar in the Senate. Congress nevertheless agreed to renew funding. By 1975, after a series of complaints, the renewal agreement for the bases was submitted as a treaty. What is interesting here is that demands for moving toward a treaty did not only come from the Senate. Spain also pushed for the more formal treaty procedure (Atwood 1981, 218).

The logic of interbranch relations suggests that we need to go beyond the evasion perspective if we are to understand the use of executive agreements. In this section, I suggest two alternative frameworks for explaining variation in the use of ratification procedures: complexity and credibility. Both of these arguments are more consistent with the logic of congressional influence than is the evasion perspective, and both consider the impact of the international strategic environment in addition to the domestic political strategies of the president. Treating the use of ratification procedures as the dependent variable, the Evasion Hypothesis and the hypotheses developed in chapter 2 give rise to alternative observable implications.

The rationale originally given for the use of executive agreements was the complexity of U.S. relations with the rest of the world. Complexity often provides the fundamental incentive for delegation in principal-agent settings, and there is no reason to rule it out as an explanation here. While most authors acknowledge that complexity is an important motivation for executive agreements, the implications of this insight for understanding patterns in their use have not been explored.

The literature on agency problems and solution of informational dilemmas may provide some explanatory leverage. For example, as discussed in chapter 2, this literature suggests that delegation is most effective when the agent has preferences similar to those of the principal. This insight implies that we should see extensive use of executive agreements on those issues on which a consensus on basic policy has been reached. For example, after the debate about Spanish bases was settled with the 1975 treaty, and as Spain became a more attractive alliance partner in the post-Franco era, Congress explicitly delegated to the president authority to conclude executive agreements relating to military bases in Spain pursuant to the treaty. More controversial issues, on the other hand, should continue to be dealt with by more formal ratification procedures. As the Delegation Hypothesis suggests, Congress will be less willing to delegate authority when more conflict of interest exists.

Preliminary evidence in support of the complexity explanation comes from a simple examination of the number of executive agreements used over time. Prior to the twentieth century, U.S. engagement with the rest of the world was minimal and the number of international agreements negotiated reflected that fact. In contrast, after World War II the frequency and complexity of U.S. international relations increased suddenly and dramatically. If the United States had handled this rapid increase in interactions with other countries solely through treaties, the sheer difficulty of getting them all through the cumbersome ratification process would have brought the Senate machinery to a halt and put a straitjacket on the U.S. ability to play the active role in the world it has ever since. Not surprisingly, the upsurge in international engagement was reflected in an increased use of executive agreements. While it is possible for such a movement to limit legislative influence on foreign policy, models of delegation show that delegation for reasons of complexity can preserve legislative influence (Krehbiel 1991). Delegation is not equivalent to abdication.

A complementary perspective to the focus on complexity considers how the use of executive agreements is related to the general problem of making credible commitments in foreign policy. The major drawback of an executive agreement is that the commitment inherent in it is, *ceteris paribus,* not as credible as one that has been ratified in a treaty. The reasons lie in two analytically distinct, although practically intertwined, considerations: signaling and commitment.

Signaling considerations refer to the information that actors send one another about their preferences and intentions. A state concluding an international agreement with the United States requires information that will allow it to assess the probability that the agreement has received widespread consent and that the U.S. government intends to abide by it. More open, formal ratification mechanisms, particularly those that involve a vote in the legislature, send more information about the preferences and intentions of those who will be responsible for implementing the agreement. This logic closely parallels that of Schultz (1998), which models a government and an opposition that may provide confirmatory signaling, thus enhancing the credibility of government commitments. A president that chooses to use the executive-agreement mechanism for a potentially controversial agreement may be sending precisely the wrong signal, telling other states that there is not much support for the agreement in the legislature or public at large. An executive agreement kept secret would exacerbate these fears. Such a signal would raise legitimate doubts about the credibility of the U.S. commitment expressed in the agreement.

In contrast to signaling, considerations of commitment need not rely on the assumption of uncertainty about preferences. Commitment mechanisms allow actors to bind themselves to a particular course of action, even one that all parties involved know will be difficult to sustain when the time comes. Ulysses binding himself to the mast, or Schelling's teenage driver throwing his steering wheel out of the window during a game of chicken, exemplify commitment mechanisms that do not rely on a signaling logic. In both, there is little doubt about preferences. The problem instead is time inconsistency, where actors know that they will not be able to live up to desirable courses of action in the future unless they take some action to bind themselves today.

Choosing to undergo the rigors of a treaty-ratification process can serve as a commitment mechanism as well as a signaling device. Gaining ratification of a treaty is a course that is not lightly reversed in the future, even by a new executive. Systems like that in the United States, with multiple veto points, are well known for inducing a status-quo bias (Tsebelis 1995b). Once put in place, policies are difficult to change. This is certainly the case with treaties. Once Senators have gone on record by ratifying a treaty, they will be more reluctant to allow a president to abrogate it than if they had not gone through the formal ratification process. Part of the logic of commitment lies simply in the complexity of the legislative process. Another dimension lies in audience costs, the notion that an actor that has publicly approved an agreement will suffer costs to its reputation for backing down from that commitment unless circumstances have changed substantially (Fearon 1994).

Whether treaties serve as signaling devices, commitment mechanisms, or both, there is strong reason to expect that they are more credible indicators of future U.S. behavior than are simple executive agreements. While gaining treaty ratification is certainly more difficult than merely signing an agreement, the costs of ratification will result in more credible commitments. While credibility may not be an overriding issue in all international interactions (such as one-shot assistance deals or actions that are entirely noncontroversial), it is extremely important in most long-term interactions and provides a justification for forgoing the easier, executive-agreement path in such circumstances. The credibility of commitments, as well as the complexity of international relations, provide explanations for variation in the use of ratification procedures that are consistent with current understandings of legislative influence. The following section provides a series of statistical tests of two alternative perspectives: the

Evasion Hypothesis and the hypothesis that outcomes reflect congressional influence (the Influence Hypothesis) and concerns about credibility (the Credibility Hypothesis).

TESTING THE EVASION HYPOTHESIS

Since indirect legislative influence is, by definition, difficult to observe directly, we must look for other methods to sort out the logic behind the use of executive agreements. Simply noting congressional oversight activity, or pointing to cases in which the president has taken actions not explicitly authorized by Congress, cannot settle this debate. Instead, we need to turn to aggregate evidence on patterns in the use of executive agreements and treaties.

If the Evasion Hypothesis is correct, it has clear implications for the frequency with which executive agreements are used. If their intent is to circumvent Congress, we should see them used most frequently when the president is confronted with a Congress with preferences different from his or her own. When the Senate tends to agree with the president's foreign policies, there will be a reduced need to use the escape route provided by executive agreements. Instead, we should see a shift to the use of treaties when the Senate is in agreement with the president's foreign policies.

To test the Evasion Hypothesis, I begin by considering the percentage of executive agreements as a function of party control of the Senate and presidency. When the Senate is controlled by the same party as the presidency, we can assume that it generally has preferences closer to those of the president than when it is controlled by the opposition party. Even if there is some divergence in foreign-policy preferences within the party, the constraints of party membership provide the president with a source of support within Congress under unified government (Cox and McCubbins 1993). Margolis (1986) finds evidence that the use of executive agreements increases under divided government, and argues that this result is convincing support for the Evasion Hypothesis. However, his tests are only bivariate, do not control for time trends, and do not consider problems of statistical significance. The following models correct for these flaws. They use data from CRS (1993, 14) on agreements concluded between 1930 and 1992.

Margolis (1986, 45–47) argues that the best indicator for the Evasion Hypothesis is the percent of all international agreements that are negotiated as executive agreements in each year. Table 3.1 shows a model of the percent of all agreements as executive agreements that tests for the effects of divided government and different points in the electoral cycle.

The key independent variable for the Evasion Hypothesis is SENNUMB, the number of Senators from the president's party. If the Evasion Hypothesis is correct, we should see decreasing use of executive agreements when SENNUMB increases, since there will be a reduced need to circumvent the Senate under

TABLE 3.1
Percent of International Agreements as Executive Agreements, 1930–1992

Variable	Estimated Coefficient	Standard Error	T- statistic
SENNUMB*	−0.003	0.0018	−1.693
FIRSTYR	0.0162	0.0288	0.564
ELECT*	0.0385	0.0227	1.698
AR1*	−0.461	0.134	−3.438
AR2	−0.16	0.132	−1.214
Constant	0.0077	0.0082	0.941
Number of observations:	63		
Standard error:	0.103		
Log likelihood:	55.61		

these conditions. Therefore, SENNUMB should have a negative coefficient. The value of SENNUMB ranges from 34 to 75, with a mean of 53.9.

I also include a dummy, FIRSTYR. This variable takes on the value 1 when the president is in his first year of office. A new president, learning how to deal with a new Congress, might be expected to rely more heavily on the use of executive agreements than one that, through experience, has learned the ropes in Washington. We would therefore expect a positive coefficient on FIRSTYR. The third independent variable, ELECT, is a dummy for election years. Those who see executive agreements as an evasive device have also argued that presidents will use a higher percentage of executive agreements in election years (King and Ragsdale 1988, 115). The rationale is that since executive agreements provide autonomy, they are particularly useful tools for presidents engaged in an election campaign. Therefore, the Evasion Hypothesis suggests that ELECT should have a positive coefficient.

The data on treaties and, especially, executive agreements show strong time-series effects. To control for these, the following models have been estimated with two parameters for autoregression. These parameters, AR1 and AR2, take account of the persistent effects of random errors through time. Also to control for time-series effects, the dependent variable is the first difference of the percent of all agreements as executive agreements (or, in later models, the first difference of the number of agreements), i.e., the change in executive agreements from one year to the next. Modeling the change rather than the total agreements provides a control for the strong secular trend of increasing use of executive agreements over time. The estimation technique used, unless otherwise noted, is Ordinary Least Squares (OLS).

The results in table 3.1 initially appear encouraging for the Evasion Hypothesis. I use a one-tailed T-test as a measure of statistical significance, since we have strong priors about the direction of effects, and to avoid making the test for the Evasion Hypothesis too stringent. As predicted, an increase in the number of Senators from the president's party leads to a significant decrease in the percent of executive agreements concluded. In addition, we see a significant increase in the percent of executive agreements negotiated in election years. These results suggest that the president turns to the use of executive agreements in order to avoid partisan opposition in the Senate, and to provide room for unconstrained foreign-policy accomplishments during election years. Both results are consistent with the Evasion Hypothesis.

Previous work on executive agreements has used party control of government, as I have thus far. As we will see later in this book, party does matter a great deal in determining the nature of legislative-executive relations. But it may not be an adequate indicator of levels of congressional support for the president. For example, if the Democratic and/or Republican parties are split on the major foreign-policy issues at stake in international negotiations, a count of the number of Senators from the president's party may be too crude a measure of support to give a fair test to the Evasion Hypothesis. At a minimum, we should consider other measures and see how they perform relative to the party control variable.

One alternative measure of support comes from analysis of patterns of congressional voting. A common measure of congressional support is the number of congressional votes supporting the president divided by the total number of votes on which the president took a position. *Congressional Quarterly* collects these data (Stanley and Niemi 1994, 276–77), and in table 3.2 I include them in the model as the variable SUPPORT. Because support data are only available beginning 1953, the following models are limited to the period 1953–1992. SUPPORT scores range from a low of 0.51 to a high of 0.93, with a mean value of 0.74.

The model in table 3.2 shows that SUPPORT predicts presidential choices better than a measure of party membership did. We find a significant negative coefficient on SUPPORT, consistent with the Evasion Hypothesis. When congressional support for the president increases, he less frequently turns to executive agreements. The effect of SENNUMB disappears in this estimation, suggesting that SUPPORT is picking up the relevant variation in congressional support. In the following models, to avoid problems of multicollinearity, I include only SUPPORT, dropping SENNUMB.

This alternative specification of congressional support also shows an interesting change in the effects of the election cycle. Now, the effect of election years has disappeared. Instead, we find that the president tends to negotiate a larger percentage of executive agreements during his first year. This is an effect not predicted by the Evasion Hypothesis. It suggests that regular fluctuations in support for the president during the electoral cycle produced a spurious positive result on the variable ELECT in the former model. The increase in use of executive agreements during election years seems to have been caused by fluc-

TABLE 3.2
Percent of International Agreements as Executive Agreements, 1953–1992

Variable	Estimated Coefficient	Standard Error	T-Statistic
SENNUMB	0.0005	0.0004	1.174
FIRSTYR*	0.0241	0.0076	3.172
ELECT	0.0002	0.0055	0.0363
SUPPORT*	−0.0974	0.0434	−2.242
AR1*	−0.8883	0.1642	−5.409
AR2*	−0.3865	0.1608	−2.403
Constant	−0.0002	0.0015	−0.1154
Number of observations:	40		
Standard error:	0.020		
Log likelihood:	100.3		

tuations in congressional support during these years. Once we control for support, we do not find the president turning to executive agreements as an electoral device. So this piece of evidence supporting the Evasion Hypothesis disappears when the model is more properly specified, using a better measure of congressional support for the president.

While congressional support for the president has a statistically significant effect on the percent of executive agreements used, we also need to ask about the substantive significance of this result. A contrast between the years 1959 and 1965 provides an illuminating perspective. In 1959, Eisenhower received the lowest support score in this data set, 52.9%. In 1965, Johnson received one of the highest support scores, 93.1%. We should therefore expect to see a dramatic difference in the percent of executive agreements used in these two years, according to the Evasion Hypothesis.

In fact, however, the predicted percentages for these two years are not very far apart. The model predicts that in 1959 Eisenhower would have negotiated 96.1% of total agreements as executive agreements, while in contrast Johnson would have negotiated 94.4% as executive agreements.[4] Because Eisenhower's congressional support was low, he turned more frequently to executive agreements. This difference, of less than two percentage points, is disappointing evidence for the evasion perspective. A dramatic shift in levels of congressional support gives rise to only a minor shift in the use of executive agreements. These results imply that while presidents predictably attempt to use executive agreements to evade congressional opposition, their ability to do so effectively is tightly constrained. Such constraints are consistent with the complexity and credibility explanations developed above.

[4] In practice, in 1959 the measure of executive agreements was 95.4%, while in 1965 it was 93.6%. While somewhat off scale, the difference between these two years is the same size as predicted by the model.

The results in table 3.2 necessitate a reevaluation of the Evasion Hypothesis. The predicted effect of election-year behavior does not appear once we control for levels of congressional support. And while congressional support does have a regular effect, leading to a shift toward the use of a higher percentage of executive agreements, the size of this effect is small. It seems appropriate to further disaggregate these results to determine whether some other framework for analysis provides more leverage.

The percent of executive agreements negotiated may not, in fact, be the best indicator of executive behavior. Changes in the aggregate percentage can result from a number of underlying trends, obscuring the real influences at work. The Evasion Hypothesis offers a clear prediction about the causes of change in this percentage. It predicts that presidents attempting to evade congressional restraints would both increase their use of executive agreements *and* decrease their use of treaties. According to the Evasion Hypothesis, presidents can substitute executive agreements for treaties when they anticipate opposition in the Senate, thus evading congressional influence. Thus, the Evasion Hypothesis predicts that divided government should lead to both an increase in the number of executive agreements completed and a reduction in the number of treaties. Both effects contribute to a change in the percentage of executive agreements. Testing these predictions about the *number* of treaties and executive agreements provides a more sensitive test of alternative theories than does the cruder approach of modeling only the percentage of executive agreements.

Tables 3.3 and 3.4 present estimations of the effects of congressional support and the electoral cycle on the numbers of executive agreements and treaties, respectively. The number of executive agreements signed per year ranges from a low of 10 to a high of 434, with a mean of 209. The number of treaties ranges from 1 to 28, with a mean of 14.1. Table 3.3, examining the number of executive agreements, shows no statistically significant effects whatsoever. While we find a negative coefficient on SUPPORT, the standard error of this coefficient

TABLE 3.3
Number of Executive Agreements, 1953–1992

Variable	Estimated Coefficient	Standard Error	T-Statistic
SUPPORT	−61.94	98.95	−0.0361
FIRSTYR	−13.49	14.79	−0.912
ELECT	10.05	12.52	0.803
AR1	−0.0062	0.172	−0.0361
AR2	−0.164	0.186	−0.882
Constant	2.385	7.149	0.333
Number of observations:	40		
Standard error:	51.46		
Log likelihood:	−206.1		

TABLE 3.4
Number of Treaties, 1953–1992

Variable	Estimated Coefficient	Standard Error	T-Statistic
SUPPORT*	18.76	8.426	2.227
FIRSTYR*	−7.093	1.804	−3.931
ELECT	1.181	1.426	0.829
AR1*	−0.8322	0.1629	−5.11
AR2	−0.303	0.1636	−1.85
Constant	0.1557	0.3998	0.3895
Number of observations:	40		
Standard error:	5.14		
Log likelihood:	−116.5		

is very large, so that the effect of congressional support cannot reliably be distinguished from zero. Similarly, we find the predicted positive coefficient on ELECT, but it is not statistically significant. These results are a challenge to the Evasion Hypothesis. It does not appear that an increase in the percent of executive agreements negotiated when congressional support is low results from an increased number of executive agreements, as predicted.

Turning to the evaluation of treaties in table 3.4, we find a solution to the puzzle of how to account for changes in the percent of executive agreements. This table shows that we find a significant increase in the number of treaties negotiated when levels of congressional support are high. We also see a decrease in the number of treaties negotiated during a president's first year in office. To gain a sense of the magnitude of the congressional-support effect, compare the years 1959 and 1965, as above. In 1959, Eisenhower's low level of congressional support leads to a predicted 7.7 treaties being negotiated. In contrast, the model predicts that Johnson would negotiate 14.9 treaties in 1965, almost double the number predicted for Eisenhower.[5] This is a sizable effect, suggesting that the president finds it quite difficult to conclude treaties when he lacks overall congressional support. The increased percent of executive agreements used when congressional support is low results not from a regular increase in the use of executive agreements but from a reduced ability to conclude treaties. This decrease does not reliably show up as a shift to using more executive agreements, contrary to the prediction of the Evasion Hypothesis. Similarly, the higher percentage of executive agreements concluded during a president's first year in office results from a failure to conclude treaties, not from a substitution of executive agreements for treaties.

Because the number of treaties negotiated each year is fairly small, OLS may

[5] The actual numbers of treaties concluded were 12 in 1959 and 14 in 1965.

TABLE 3.5
Treaties, 1953–1992, Poisson Regression

Variable	Estimated Coefficient	Robust Standard Error	T-Statistic
SUPPORT*	1.162	0.4548	2.555
FIRSTYR*	−0.4048	0.1539	−2.63
ELECT	0.0483	0.1149	0.4204
YEAR*	0.0206	0.0056	3.679
Constant	−38.8	11.22	3.458
Number of observations:	40		
Log likelihood:	1009.6		

not provide a good statistical model for this dependent variable. To check for this possibility, table 3.5 estimates a Poisson model of the number of treaties. A generalized-event-count model showed no evidence of overdispersion in the number of treaties, so the Poisson model is appropriate. The variable YEAR is included to control for some time-series effects, which is more difficult in Poisson than OLS models. The results of the Poisson estimation are consistent with those found in the OLS model: an increased use of treaties when congressional support is high, and fewer treaties concluded during presidents' first year in office.

What do these statistical results suggest about alternative frameworks for understanding institutional choice? While the initial results appeared consistent with the Evasion Hypothesis, deeper probing makes a credibility story appear more persuasive. While we see an increased percent of agreements being negotiated as executive agreements when congressional support is low, the size of this effect is small. We find no evidence of increased use of executive agreements during election years once we properly control for congressional support. The significant effect is not increased use of executive agreements but diminished ability to conclude treaties when congressional support is low. This effect is contradictory to the imperial-presidency argument. The president's ability to conclude treaties depends heavily on his or her level of support in Congress, and the president is not able to substitute executive agreements for treaties, at least not robustly.

If the president cannot substitute executive agreements for treaties at will, he or she cannot use executive agreements as effective evasive devices. Thus, the evidence here supports the proposition that Congress maintains numerous mechanisms of influence over international agreements, supporting the Influence Hypothesis more strongly than the Evasion Hypothesis. In addition, if we treat the number of agreements concluded as a rough measure of cooperation, we can view these models as preliminary tests of the hypothesis that executive-legislative conflict makes international cooperation problematic. When congressional support for the president is low, he or she finds it more difficult to conclude treaties and cannot simply substitute executive agreements for the forgone agreements.

In the statistical models, I have assumed that the congressional-support score is an adequate proxy for whether Congress is willing to go along with the president on the issues under negotiation with other governments. From the evidence given here, it is not possible to say whether lower support-scores matter because they reflect more fundamental disagreement on policies between the branches, or whether they mean that the president has fewer bargaining chips to with which to buy support on difficult foreign-policy questions. While distinguishing between these two dynamics is certainly worthy of further investigation, for the purposes of understanding patterns in international cooperation they give rise to the same kinds of difficulties. A president who lacks congressional support will find it difficult to conclude agreements that can satisfy the demands of both other countries and the legislators who will be involved in implementing agreements. However, if the president were largely unconstrained on foreign policy, he or she could avoid legislative constraints by substituting an informal procedure, and thus would only need to satisfy the demands of the other state. The fact that such substitution does not occur with any regularity suggests that attempts to avoid legislative constraints are not credible. Substituting an informal procedure does not free the president from considering legislative preferences.

Further evidence in support of the influence and credibility argument comes from considering other mechanisms that might establish credibility in international negotiations. Ratification is only one factor that lends credibility to a commitment. If commitment has been established through another mechanism, or if it is not an issue for some other reason, then we may see less pressure to negotiate a formal treaty.

Consideration of the credibility problem suggests that the use of executive agreements and treaties should vary across the type of issue. Where other mechanisms exist to establish commitment, we should see relatively frequent use of executive agreements. The demand for formal ratification to establish credibility will fall if alternative commitment devices are in place. Political observers have often noted that military commitments, in particular, are made credible through mechanisms other than ratification. Overseas bases are established; joint planning and military maneuvers take place; extensive military assistance programs are put in place. All of these should tie the hands of the United States more surely than any ratification procedure would. Therefore, we should expect to see more extensive use of executive agreements on military matters than on those where alternative commitment mechanisms are harder to identify.

Margolis (1986) collects data on the type of agreements negotiated from 1943 to 1977, providing a preliminary assessment of the use of different types of agreements on different issues. He divides international agreements into

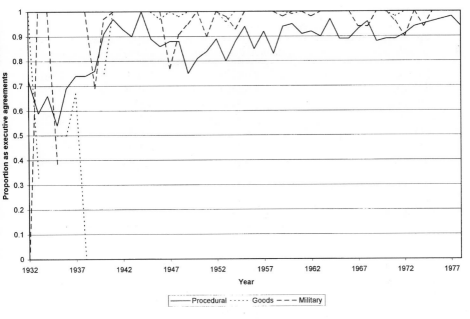

Figure 3.2. Proportion as executive agreements by type.

three types: goods (economic agreements), military, and procedural. Figure 3.2 shows the percentage of each type of agreement that takes the form of an executive agreement. We should, if the credibility perspective is correct, expect to see a relatively high percentage of executive agreements on military issues. Procedural issues, on the other hand, may be those where commitment mechanisms are difficult to identify, so we should see a low percentage of executive agreements here. Figure 3.2 supports this expectation, with procedural agreements consistently having a lower percentage of executive agreements than those on military issues or on goods. In this period, 90% of procedural agreements were executive agreements, compared with 97% of military and virtually 100% of economic agreements.

One type of military agreement, however, does not have built-in commitment mechanisms: those on arms control. Arms-control agreements are difficult to monitor effectively. In addition, undetected cheating on an arms-control agreement could have devastating consequences, so that credibility is an important issue (Downs and Rocke 1990). Given these considerations, we should expect that arms-control agreements should more often take the form of treaties than do other military agreements. And this is precisely what the CRS (1993, xxx, 203) has found.

Further probing of the data turns up additional evidence that backing down

Table 3.6
Treaties 1955–1992, Separate Support Scores

Variable	Estimated Coefficient	Standard Error	T-Statistic
HOUSE*	0.1727	0.0731	2.361
SENATE	−0.0401	0.0903	−0.4446
FIRSTYR*	−6.348	1.81	−3.508
ELECT	0.5613	1.495	0.3754
AR1*	−0.8658	0.1724	−5.023
AR2	−0.3163	0.1757	−1.8
Constant	0.195	0.3967	0.4915
Number of observations:	38		
Standard error:	5.17		
Log likelihood:	−113.2		

from the use of treaties is not just a matter of avoiding the Senate but of credibility problems created by more general lack of congressional support. As argued above, Congress maintains many indirect forms of influence over international agreements, many of which rely on the implementation of those agreements. The implementation process continues after formal ratification and thereby often allows the House to influence international cooperation, although perhaps not as immediately as the Senate. Based on this reasoning, table 3.6 substitutes separate measures of House and Senate support for the overall support score used above, in a model of the number of treaties concluded. Because separate measures of support are not available until 1955, this model relies on only 38 observations.

This model shows a surprising fact: the president's ability to conclude treaties is significantly related to his support in the House, but not to his support in the Senate. This result is again inconsistent with the Evasion Hypothesis, which expects that it is low levels of support in the Senate that lead the president to move to using executive agreements. Instead, we find something more consistent with a model based on credibility concerns. When the president's support in the House is low, he has a hard time concluding treaties. This pattern suggests that more general concerns about implementation of negotiated agreements, not just problems getting them ratified in the Senate, account for the number of treaties agreed.[6]

The statistical patterns found here show stronger evidence for considerations

[6] Other statistical models substituting separate House and Senate support scores for the overall support score show consistent results. The percentage of executive agreements concluded depends on House support, but not on Senate support; and the number of executive agreements concluded is not significantly related to any of the independent variables considered here.

of influence and credibility than for the Evasion Hypothesis. When we look at the percentage of all agreements negotiated as executive agreements, we initially seem to find support for the Evasion Hypothesis. It appears that as congressional support for the president goes up, he less frequently turns to the executive-agreement mechanism. However, the size of this effect is small, with even large movements in congressional support leading to only a couple of percentage-point shifts in the use of executive agreements. On further examination, we discover that the shift in percentages appears to be the result of a decreased ability to conclude treaties rather than increased use of executive agreements. This result is consistent with a perspective focusing on legislative influence and credibility, not with the evasion perspective. Further support for the influence and credibility perspective comes in the time trend in the use of executive agreements; increased use of executive agreements in the first year of a president's term; more executive agreements being used for military agreements other than arms control; and the influence of support in the House, not just the Senate. We can conclude that while the president is tempted to use executive agreements as an evasive device, his ability to do so is tightly constrained by considerations of credibility necessitated by the international strategic environment.

CONSTRAINING THE EXECUTIVE: CONGRESSIONAL MECHANISMS

Empirically, the hypothesis that executive agreements provide the president with an efficient means of evading congressional opposition does not find much support. While there are reasons to suspect that the president attempts to use executive agreements in this manner, the extent to which he is able to do so is limited. Earlier, I suggested two related sets of constraints. The first lies in the mechanisms that Congress maintains to exercise influence on agreements other than treaties. The second lies in the fact that negotiating partners can appreciate these constraints and so will be reluctant to make commitments to executive agreements that are intended to circumvent Congress. In this section, I examine congressional oversight of executive actions. Such oversight is a necessary condition for indirect mechanisms of congressional influence to have any effect. This section provides evidence relating to the causal mechanisms underlying the aggregate patterns found above.

Congressional concern about the use of executive agreements has led to two concentrated efforts to reform the procedures for approving international agreements. The first, in the 1950s, led to near passage of a constitutional amendment that would have severely restricted the president's ability to negotiate executive agreements. The second, in the 1970s, was more modest in its ambitions but ultimately more successful in establishing a clear and formalized role for Congress.

The two major attempts to reform procedures could hardly have come from more different ideological backgrounds. The first, led by Senator John W. Bricker (R-Ohio), was grounded in conservative political principles, especially the isolationist variety of conservatism. It was motivated by fears that U.S. commitments to multilateral institutions would override traditional visions of states' rights. The 1970s reforms were part of a more general revolt against the imperial presidency. They were led by liberals, especially those who opposed U.S. involvement in Vietnam. The Brickerites were protesting the actions of a fellow Republican president, Eisenhower, and the debate tended to split each party between its isolationist and internationalist wings. The 1970s debate split somewhat more along party lines, although its major emphasis was on the powers of the legislative versus the executive branch of government. It involved both houses of Congress, while the 1950s debate took place solely in the Senate.

The Bricker revolt aimed to put strict limitations on presidential authority to reach international agreements. It also sought to minimize the effects of such agreements on domestic law, especially the prerogatives of the individual states.[7] The main focus of concern was that U.S. participation in the UN would increase presidential control of policy at the expense of the states. The debate became framed as one of human rights versus states' rights, as fears were expressed that the UN's Genocide Convention and other human-rights agreements would severely curtail the autonomy of states. In response to such concerns, in 1951 Bricker began efforts to limit the president's ability to commit the United States to multilateral organizations. His proposed amendment would have specified issues on which the United States was not allowed to enter into international agreements, particularly issues involving individual rights. It also prevented delegation of any legislative, executive, or judicial powers to any international organization or foreign country. It sought to prevent the president from substituting executive agreements for treaties, and would have required all executive agreements to be publicized and in effect for only a limited period.

By 1953, the Senate Committee on the Judiciary began holding hearings on Bricker's proposals. The Eisenhower administration first tried to sink the amendment while avoiding open confrontation, but eventually pulled out all stops in an attempt to fend off Bricker's challenges to its authority. According to Tananbaum (1988), this effort represented one of Eisenhower's most effective uses of the "hidden-hand presidency." After the Judiciary Committee reported an amendment that would have put severe constraints on the executive favorably to the floor, the president put his support behind an alternative amendment introduced by Senator William F. Knowland, the Republican majority leader. The Knowland amendment was significantly weaker than the Bricker, merely making explicit already existing conditions, for example that treaties that conflict with the Constitution would have no force.

---

[7] The following discussion of the Bricker amendment is drawn largely from Johnson (1984) and Tananbaum (1988).

By the time floor debate began on the Bricker amendment in 1954, it appeared that Bricker had gained enough support to get his amendment through Congress. Eisenhower moved to open confrontation now, for example putting an open letter in the *Congressional Record* stating that he was "unalterably" opposed to the Bricker amendment. After much maneuvering, introduction of amendments, and administration lobbying, the Bricker amendment was defeated by a vote of forty-two to fifty on 25 February 1954. However, this was not the end of the story. The Bricker forces regrouped and threw their weight behind a slightly weaker amendment introduced by Senator Walter George (D-Georgia). The George amendment focused less on states' rights, but required that Congress explicitly approve all executive agreements. Since this was a proposed constitutional amendment, it would have required sixty-one votes (two-thirds of those Senators present at the time) for passage. In the end, the administration managed to find the single necessary defector and the amendment was defeated, sixty to thirty-one. While similar amendments were on occasion introduced in later years, none went very far.

By the 1970s, concern about the use of executive agreements resurfaced, as part of a general concern about the aggrandizement of executive power. However, this time reform attempts concentrated on gaining information from the executive, rather than changing voting procedures. They were more successful. The pattern of success and failure of reform attempts tells us much about congressional incentives and influence, and the logic behind the use of executive agreements. As I have argued, Congress has a number of mechanisms by which to influence agreements besides formal ratification power. However, none of these mechanisms will be very effective if the administration can keep agreements secret from Congress. Much information about agreements comes through leaks and other nonofficial channels, as predicted by a fire-alarm understanding of congressional oversight. However, to supplement these sources of information, in 1972 Congress passed the Case Act, requiring the State Department to notify Congress of all executive agreements within sixty days of their entry into force.[8]

This second round of attempts to revise the usage of executive agreements began in 1969, when Senator Stuart Symington (D-Missouri) began an investigation of U.S. international agreements in the Foreign Relations Committee. The Symington investigation was stimulated by U.S. involvement in Vietnam and general military commitments in Southeast Asia (Stevens 1977). The hearings of the Symington subcommittee (formally known as the Subcommittee on U.S. Security Agreements and Commitments Abroad) uncovered information about previously unknown executive military commitments. These findings led Congress to pass the National Commitments Resolution, which reaffirmed that commitments to other nations should require affirmative action by both the ex-

---

[8] For a discussion of the background and effects of the Case Act, see CRS (1993, 169–202).

ecutive and legislative branches (Nincic 1992, 87–88). However, this resolution was not binding, and did not appear to have much impact on executive behavior.

Senator Clifford Case (R-New Jersey) introduced legislation in 1970 to require notification within sixty days of any international agreement not submitted to the Senate as a treaty. This bill became law in 1972. Classified agreements as well as unclassified are transmitted, although through a different procedure designed to assure their secrecy. It took a number of years for the provisions of the Case Act to be implemented effectively, but consistent oversight by Senator Case and a series of amendments led to what appears to be a more consistent flow of information about executive agreements to Congress. One initial problem of implementation came more from lack of cooperation among executive agencies than from outright executive noncompliance. The State Department apparently complied immediately. But many international agreements are negotiated by agencies other than State, and State did not have information about these agreements to transmit to Congress. A system was set up within a few years to require agencies to send their information to the State Department. State appeared to cooperate quite enthusiastically in this endeavor, as it enhanced its role as the central actor coordinating U.S. activities overseas.[9] While there have been a series of investigations that have turned up some failures to notify Congress about agreements, these investigations appear to have had the intended effect of increasing compliance with the Case Act (CRS 1993, 185).

What impact has the Case Act had? The Evasion Hypothesis would lead us to expect that it would have a negative impact on the use of executive agreements. If such agreements are intended to circumvent Congress, being forced to make them public should curtail their use. However, we see no evidence of this in the numbers of executive agreements concluded, as shown in figure 3.1. In fact, beginning in 1976, at about the time the Case Act gained effectiveness, we see what appears to be a jump in the number of executive agreements used. We probably should not make too much of this increase, since it may have resulted in part from improved counting procedures, with more international commitments being considered executive agreements as a result of Case Act procedures. However, there is no sign that the president is now less willing to use executive agreements than prior to 1972. This suggests that the logic of such agreements throughout the entire period rests on much more than attempts to circumvent congressional oversight.

What does this brief legislative history suggest about the logic of executive agreements and the powers of Congress? The branches do struggle to enhance their influence, and it is clear that at times the executive branch has attempted

---

[9] In chapter 4, looking at sanctions against South Africa, we see a similar dynamic of the State Department joining forces with Congress as a result of conflict within the executive branch.

to evade congressional oversight by using executive agreements. However, it also suggests that Congress has mechanisms to discover such uses and has now institutionalized a procedure to facilitate the flow of information about international commitments. This information provides Congress with the means to make more indirect mechanisms of influence, such as denying appropriations or taking legislative action to overturn commitments, effective. Anticipating such actions, the president is likely to be more sensitive to congressional concerns in negotiating agreements with other countries (Stevens 1977, 929). In fact, we do see increasing provisions for consultation with members of Congress during important international negotiations (CRS 1993, 201). In spite of congressional action and oversight, the use of executive agreements continues at high levels. Thus the motivations for using executive agreements likely lie in credibility and complexity concerns rather than in an ability to evade legislative constraints.

CONCLUSION

The central hypotheses of this book are that legislatures have consistent influence on international cooperation, and that such influence enhances the ability of states to make credible commitments and so to engage in difficult cooperative endeavors. These hypotheses would be impossible to support if executives were able to manipulate domestic institutions, such as the form of international agreements, so as to evade legislative influence. However, modern understandings of legislative influence suggest that the Evasion Hypothesis may be mistaken. The legislature maintains numerous mechanisms to influence international agreements, particularly during their implementation, and so is not as easily circumvented as the image of an imperial presidency implies. Therefore, executive agreements used as evasive devices can cast serious doubt on the credibility of international commitments.

The evidence presented in this chapter shows, on balance, that the Evasion Hypothesis cannot explain patterns in the use of executive agreements. Shifts in the use of executive agreements and treaties are accounted for by a reduced ability to conclude treaties when congressional support is low, consistent with the Cooperation Hypothesis. The Evasion Hypothesis expects any reduced ability to conclude treaties to lead to increased use of executive agreements, but we do not find this pattern in the data. Instead, low congressional support leads to low credibility, and therefore fewer treaties. In addition, we find that first-year presidents find it more difficult to conclude agreements, and that executive agreements are more frequently used when alternative commitment mechanisms exist, as in the case of military agreements. Support in the House is as important for the ability to conclude agreements as is support in the Senate. All of these findings are consistent with the general hypothesis that legislatures influence international cooperation in numerous and subtle ways, and that such influence is directly tied to the ability of states to make credible commitments to one another.

The Evasion Hypothesis is one specific implication of executive-dominance models, an implication that applies specifically to the issue of institutional choice and that has been articulated in numerous studies on the use of executive agreements and treaties in the United States. But when we push beyond the most superficial evidence, we find that the Evasion Hypothesis explains very little variation in institutional choice. Instead, we find patterns that are consistent with the proposition that executives anticipate credibility dilemmas and choose institutions based at least in part on such anticipation. However, this chapter has not presented any evidence directly showing that institutions give rise to different levels of credibility. This issue becomes a major focus of later chapters, especially those on sanctions and the European Union.

CHAPTER 4

Economic Sanctions: Domestic Conflict of Interest and International Cooperation

CORE HYPOTHESES tested in this book involve the degree to which national legislatures influence processes of international cooperation and the ways in which institutionalized legislative participation in cooperative processes enhances the level of cooperation achieved. Systematic study of economic sanctions imposed by the United States provides direct tests of both the Delegation and Cooperation Hypotheses. Since sanctions have been imposed under conditions of both divided and unified government, and since they originate in either Congress or the executive branch, these cases provide the necessary variation on the explanatory variables to test propositions about both influence and international cooperation. So beyond addressing an issue of immediate political concern—how domestic politics determines the use of economic sanctions—these cases allow us to operationalize and examine central theoretical concerns of this study.

Since World War II, the United States has often turned to economic sanctions as a tool with which to influence other countries. During the Cold War, American presidents used sanctions and other forms of economic denial and warfare to confront the Soviet Union. By the 1970s, the situations in which the United States chose to use sanctions had expanded considerably, to include protests against human-rights violations throughout the world, attempts to force others to settle expropriation disputes, and attempts to punish states for aggressive foreign policies. With the end of the Cold War, sanctions have become a more valuable, if still controversial, policy tool. From sanctions tied to military threats in Iraq, Haiti, and the former Yugoslavia, to the apparent success of sanctions in encouraging South Africa to discard its system of apartheid, the United States frequently finds itself in situations where putting pressure on an adversary's economy satisfies the many demands and constraints on U.S. policy.

Through the post–World War II period, Congress has become more willing to use sanctions to pursue its own foreign-policy goals, sometimes in defiance of the foreign policy of the executive branch. Because both branches of government can and do initiate the use of economic sanctions, they provide a set of cases by which we can evaluate the different strategies of the two branches and their ability to achieve international cooperation. This chapter considers the level of international cooperation achieved, exploring how cooperation varies depending on the source of sanctions and conflict of interest between the branches. It also examines the nature of independent legislative activity. The first section contrasts the behavior of the two branches, considering the different strategic incentives facing each and how these incentives lead to different patterns of international cooperation. The central question of this section is how congressional willingness to limit or override executive discretion varies, an implication of the Delegation Hypothesis. The second section builds on this understanding to examine the effects of political parties on international cooperation, an implication of the Cooperation Hypothesis. In particular, this section examines how divided government affects the ability of either branch to generate international support for its sanctions policies. The third section turns from examination of aggregate data to look more carefully at one particular case: the extension or denial of Most-Favored-Nation (MFN) status to China.

The evidence in this chapter suggests, in the first instance, that the executive is on average better placed to gain international cooperation than is the legislature. However, this finding becomes more nuanced once we consider the impact of party. The ability of the legislature to achieve cooperation in the face of executive opposition is highly contingent on party control of the government. Under some conditions, specified in this chapter, Congress approaches or equals the president in the level of cooperation it achieves. Examination of the China-MFN case substantiates these aggregate statistical findings by demonstrating how the interbranch politics of economic sanctions are highly dependent on party control. Overall, this chapter establishes that Congress exercises substantial control over the use of economic sanctions, particularly under conditions of divided government, and, more surprisingly, that congressional sanctions can achieve substantial levels of international cooperation under these same conditions. The problem of establishing credible commitments to sanctions provides the causal mechanism linking partisan politics to the level of international cooperation achieved.

THE BRANCHES AND INTERNATIONAL COOPERATION

In order to understand the political logic of economic sanctions, and to develop observable implications of our core hypotheses about influence and cooperation, we need to understand in some detail the incentives facing the branches when they consider the use of economic sanctions. This section explains the incentives. It first considers the international-level problem, explaining why all actors generally prefer to use multilateral over unilateral sanctions. In other words, all actors face incentives to gain international cooperation if they can. The international-level dilemmas involved in multilateral sanctions also mean that the actor organizing them needs to worry about establishing credible commitments. Second, this section turns to the domestic problem, that between the branches. Here I argue that partisan incentives have a direct impact on the ability of either branch to establish the necessary credible commitments to sanctions. This section then presents some preliminary results. On the domestic level, we find evidence on congressional activism that supports the partisan logic developed here. On the international level, we see preliminary evidence on the relationship between the branch imposing economic sanctions and the level of cooperation achieved. This evidence is examined more thoroughly in the following section.

The International Problem: Organizing Multilateral Sanctions

As American efforts in the 1990–91 Persian Gulf crisis, the Yugoslav succession crisis, and the 1994 attempt to encourage democracy in Haiti demonstrate, states prefer multilateral economic sanctions to unilateral ones. Even for a country as large as the United States, with its high volume of international trade and financial transactions, unilateral sanctions have severe deficiencies. If the government imposing sanctions (the "sender," which is the United States in the cases considered here) cares about the economic impact of sanctions on the target state, it will prefer international cooperation. Refusal of other states to cooperate in a sanctions effort or active attempts to undermine sanctions, as in the Soviet Union's long-term support for Cuba in the face of a U.S. embargo, are commonly cited reasons for the failure of sanctions (von Amerongen 1980; Paarlberg 1978). Unilateral sanctions can have little more than transitory effects unless the country imposing them is in the unusual position of a monopolist or monopsonist with no potential entrants in the goods being sanctioned or close substitutes.

Even if the sender intends sanctions primarily as a signal rather than anticipating a substantial economic impact on the target, multilateral sanctions have advantages over unilateral ones. Sanctions imposed by only one country reveal conflicts of interest among potential sanctioners, sending precisely the wrong message to the sanction's target. This is particularly true when states impose sanctions in support of supposedly widely held principles, such as encouraging democracy, protesting international aggression, or attempting to stop actions like ethnic cleansing. In addition to these signaling concerns, domestic considerations lead to a preference for multilateral sanctions. Domestic groups forced to bear the costs of sanctions, such as farmers in the United States, are more resistant when their competitors in other countries can pick up sales lost due to government policy (Paarlberg 1980). Once a country decides to impose economic sanctions, it prefers to gain international support.

However, studies of economic sanctions show that such cooperation is usually difficult and costly to achieve (Martin 1992a, 46–53). Typically, one state has a strong interest in using sanctions, while many others are content to free-ride on its efforts. Considerations of international security often give rise to this asymmetrical pattern of interests. For example, during the Cold War the United States often found itself with a dominant strategy to impose sanctions regardless of the efforts of its allies, due to its unique role as a superpower and leader of the NATO alliance (Waltz 1979, 170–76). In 1982, Britain found itself in a similar situation in its conflict with Argentina over the Falkland Islands (Malvinas). Although other European countries were not indifferent to the outcome of the Falklands conflict, they did not believe that the potential benefits of sanctions outweighed their costs (Daoudi and Dajani 1983; Martin 1992b, 160). In other situations, regional considerations lead to asymmetrical interests, as in U.S. policy toward Haiti.

Due to this asymmetrical pattern of interests, in most cases of sanctions one country will find itself a "privileged group" of one, with incentives to impose sanctions regardless of the level of cooperation it achieves. However, this leader would prefer to gain the support of other countries. To overcome this dilemma, the leading sender engages in tactical issue-linkage, the use of threats and promises, in an attempt to gain higher levels of international cooperation (Schelling 1960, 31–32; Martin 1993a). We can see such a dynamic of suasion in the Gulf crisis, for example, with the United States offering inducements like debt relief and military assistance, and threatening such actions as reductions in foreign aid, to convince other states to join in the sanctions effort (Freedman and Karsh 1993, 143–44). "International consensus" provides only part of the explanation for cooperation in the Gulf episode and in most others; persuasion and arm-twisting play at least as important a role.

Thus, tactical issue-linkage is a central element of attempts to organize sanctions coalitions. However, tactical issue-linkages are notoriously unstable and difficult to maintain in international politics (Oye 1979; Keohane 1984, 91–92). On the domestic level, similar exchanges are commonplace, for example as legislators construct elaborate logrolls that are stabilized by domestic institutions (Weingast and Moran 1983). Strategies of side-payments and logrolling are more difficult to carry out on the international level, where institutions are relatively weak and interactions often sporadic rather than regularized. Thus, states wishing to use linkage strategies face a problem of credible commitment as others question their ability or willingness to carry through with threats or promises, or are tempted to accept side-payments and then renege on agreements. Credibility concerns therefore permeate all aspects of multilateral sanctions.

In order to assure international cooperation on economic sanctions, therefore, the leading sender needs to demonstrate a strong commitment to the issue at stake. If other governments question the credibility of threats of countersanctions if they don't cooperate, or wonder whether the leading sender is seriously committed to maintaining sanctions, they will be unlikely to engage in costly actions. Given the high profits available from trading with the target country (note, for example, the Dominican Republic's violation of sanctions against Haiti in 1994), incentives to free-ride and call the leading sender's bluff are high. On the other hand, countersanctions actually carried out can be highly damaging. For example, in the 1982 Siberian natural-gas-pipeline-sanctions episode, the United States threatened to cut off European firms from their access to American technology if they continued to provide pipeline equipment to the Soviet Union (Jentleson 1986, 172–214). These countersanctions would have been very painful for the blacklisted firms. However, the ability of the Reagan administration to carry out countersanctions was highly questionable, and the Europeans refused to cooperate.[1]

Studies of the use of economic statecraft by other states have also shown that government capacity to carry out policy explains significant variation in outcomes (Spaulding 1991; Baldwin 1985). All these considerations mean that credibility is a key variable if we wish to understand international cooperation on economic sanctions. The ability of the sender to establish a credible commitment, both to the original sanctions themselves and to any threats or promises used to generate international cooperation, will in large measure explain the level of international cooperation we see. Turning to the American use of sanctions, we need to ask how interaction between the branches of government enhances or undermines the credibility of U.S. commitments. Are critics of the American system accurate in their arguments that the dispersal of powers handicaps the United States in its interactions with other countries? The answer to this question provides a test of the Cooperation Hypothesis.

The Domestic Problem: Incentives to Impose Sanctions

The usual fragmentation of political power in the United States is reflected, perhaps even exaggerated, in provisions for imposing economic sanctions. In fact, the "confusion" about who has the right to impose sanctions has led to recurrent calls for reform (National Academy of Sciences 1991, 86–87). Legal provisions for using sanctions are lax; the United States is somewhat unusual in this respect (Carter 1988). Due to the complexities of the legal system, either the administration or Congress can initiate sanctions against other countries, for almost any reason. When the president imposes sanctions, Congress could, in theory, decide to override these measures by exercising its power of the purse, forcing an end to sanctions. While some members discussed such action during the 1982 pipeline crisis (*Congressional Record,* 22 July 1982, E3429), Congress has never actually taken such a step. Congress also has the ability to impose sanctions through a variety of measures. MCs can impose trade and other

---

[1] In this case, the United States did eventually back down (*Weekly Compilation of Presidential Documents,* 13 November 1982, 1475–76).

sanctions through specific legislation. In addition, general legislation links U.S. foreign assistance to political developments, such as human rights, in other countries. Congress implements general legislation of this sort through foreign-aid bills, which sometimes result in the imposition of sanctions. The president can veto general foreign-aid legislation, and sometimes does. However, Congress has also overridden such vetoes (Congressional Research Service 1979). Since the late 1960s, Congress has imposed sanctions quite frequently. Thus, Congress has ample provisions by which to play an active role on sanctions. But the extent to which it does so, and a test of hypotheses about legislative influence, requires consideration of domestic political incentives facing MCs.

Although sanctions can originate in either the legislative or executive branch, the structural advantages of the presidency mean that the executive is often the source of sanctions in crisis situations. The president can invoke emergency provisions of legislation like the Trading with the Enemy Act or the International Emergency Economic Powers Act to react quickly to other states' actions, such as an invasion or the imposition of martial law. Congress, on the other hand, finds it more difficult to move quickly and often follows the administration's lead in crisis situations. In addition, the executive's immediate access to information through its embassies and other bureaucracies and its closer contact with other governments gives it an advantage in imposing sanctions quickly in response to particular international events.

Congress responds to somewhat different incentives in its decisions to impose sanctions, based on its differential access to information, ties to constituents, and relatively nonhierarchical organization. The historical evidence suggests that Congress usually reacts to ongoing problems in other countries, rather than to crises. For example, Congress has often imposed sanctions in an attempt to pressure other states to improve their human-rights records. These human-rights problems tend to be a chronic, persistent issue, rather than an acute situation such as the Iraqi invasion of Kuwait. While the president rather than Congress often responds to crises, he or she also occasionally addresses more chronic problems with sanctions.

Because of their institutional capacity for rapid action, if presidents are in favor of using sanctions they typically will put them in place before Congress is able to act. Therefore, congressional sanctions usually imply resistance or, at best, indifference on the part of the executive branch. If both branches favor sanctions, the president will impose them; only if the president questions the wisdom of sanctions or doesn't feel they are worth the effort does Congress act on its own. This logic is important to the following analysis: when Congress imposes sanctions, the executive branch is unlikely to be an enthusiastic supporter of this move, and often will actively oppose it. The rest of the chapter therefore assumes that sanctions that originate in the legislative rather than executive branch reflect a relatively high level of conflict of interest between branches. Based on this assumption, we can test hypotheses about the impact of conflict of interest and legislative activity on the ability to cooperate with other countries.

Domestic Outcomes

The first implication of the above analysis is that we should observe Congress imposing sanctions under different conditions from those under which we observe sanctions originating in the executive branch. Specifically, congressional sanctions should respond primarily to chronic problems in the target, while the executive responds to crisis situations, such as international aggression. To test such propositions, I use data collected by Hufbauer, Schott, and Elliott in *Economic Sanctions Reconsidered* (1990; hereafter cited as HSE). HSE collects data on and presents summaries of most cases of sanctions in the twentieth century, through 1989. The United States was the primary source of sanctions in 82 cases, which constitute the data-set used in this chapter.[2]

Based on the case summaries in HSE, and additional primary research where necessary, each case has been coded as to whether the executive or Congress initiated sanctions. The coding shows, as we would expect, that the president has been responsible for initiating most sanctions: 56 out of 82, or 68%. HSE code each case for the policy goal at stake. They use four categories: modest policy goals; destabilization of the target government; disrupting or preventing military adventures; and other major policy goals. "Modest policy goals" include improvements in human-rights conditions, settlement of expropriation disputes, and similar issues. According to the analysis above, the president should disproportionately be responsible for sanctions in pursuit of major policy goals. When major international events appear to demand a response from the United States, the president is placed so that he or she can respond quickly. Congress, in contrast, is slow to react, typically preempted by the president in crisis situations. This logic leaves Congress to impose sanctions primarily in those situations where the president has chosen not to respond to some chronic situation overseas and so has no particular interest in sanctions.

To determine whether these patterns of activity by the two branches appear in the data, I have collapsed HSE's latter three categories into one, labeled "major policy goals." We should expect that Congress is disproportionately responsible for sanctions in support of modest policy goals, and the president for major policy goals. The cases in this data-set are evenly split between modest and major policy goals, with 41 cases of each. Figure 4.1 shows the distribu-

---

[2] The data-set omits two cases studied in HSE. These are sanctions against South Africa and sanctions against Zimbabwe. The rationale for excluding such cases is that they are outliers, having extraordinarily high levels of international cooperation, so that they exert a disproportionate influence on the statistical results. For further discussion of the reasons for omitting these cases, see Martin (1992a, 51–52). The South African case is unusual in a number of important respects, and discussed later in this chapter.

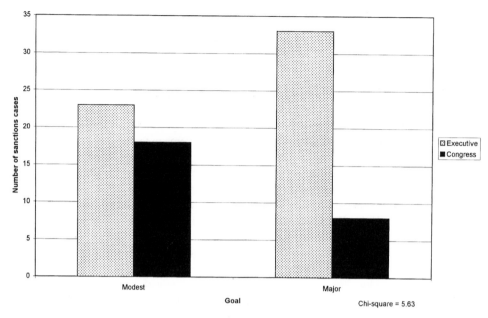

Figure 4.1. Branch originating sanctions by goal. Chi-square = 5.63.

tion of sanctions by policy goal and the branch responsible for initiating them. The data conform to the pattern expected. While well over half of all executive sanctions were imposed in pursuit of major policy goals, less than one-third of congressional sanctions were. To put this result another way, when the United States imposes sanctions in pursuit of major policy goals, the executive originates sanctions more than 80% of the time. Congress, in contrast, is responsible for nearly half of all sanctions in pursuit of modest policy goals. The chi-square statistic reveals that the difference is significant. On average, when Congress imposes sanctions they are in pursuit of less ambitious goals than those imposed by the president. It appears, based on this preliminary result, that the office of the executive is better placed to respond to major crises than is Congress, leaving Congress to respond to domestic demands to "do something" that the executive chooses to ignore.

As discussed above, states imposing sanctions prefer that they be multilateral. International cooperation is valuable when using this policy tool (like most others), but difficult to achieve because there are high incentives to defect or free-ride. States need to establish credible commitments to sanctions and associated threats or promises intended to generate international support. However, the two branches of government may have differing abilities to establish credibility. The aggregate analysis in this chapter sorts among alternative hypotheses about legislative and executive credibility.

As a null hypothesis, an executive-dominance model would predict that Congress could not establish credible commitments unilaterally over presidential objections (Crabb and Holt 1992; Peterson 1994c). Remember that when Congress imposes sanctions, it is typically under conditions in which the executive is either opposed to using sanctions or, at best, indifferent. Conventional analyses that argue that the president is dominant on foreign-policy issues would expect Congress to find it extremely difficult to undertake independent policy initiatives under such circumstances. When Congress does impose sanctions, according to this logic, it would be for purely symbolic purposes. As such, Congress would not have the tools available with which to make credible commitments, and so would gain little international cooperation. A corollary of this argument would assert that legislators have no reason to value international cooperation very highly. Either because legislators are unable to impose their will on the executive, or because they have no wish to do so on foreign-policy issues, the conventional executive-dominance approach would expect that Congress would achieve little or no international cooperation. Thus the null hypothesis, as in the previous chapter, is drawn from an executive-dominance approach.

An executive-dominance model predicts that Congress will find it more difficult to make credible commitments to sanctions than will the president. If credible commitments are necessary to generate support for sanctions, as argued above, we should therefore expect that Congress will be less successful in gaining international cooperation. Variation in the level of cooperation achieved thus provides an indirect test of propositions about credibility. Figure 4.2 presents evidence on the level of international cooperation achieved by the Congress and the executive branch in the 82 cases of U.S.-led sanctions. I use a four-category measure of cooperation developed by HSE. According to their scale, a value of one indicates no international cooperation (i.e., unilateral sanctions); two indicates minor, primarily symbolic cooperation; three indicates modest cooperation that is limited in time and scope; and four represents significant, widespread international cooperation (HSE 1990, 44).

The first result that appears in this figure is that achieving high levels of international cooperation is quite rare. However, the executive clearly has a greater success rate than does Congress on this dimension. Nearly half of all cases fall in the "no cooperation" category. However, only 33% of presidential sanctions are in this group, while 70% of congressional sanctions are. The president has achieved "modest" or "significant" cooperation in 34% of cases, while Congress has attained this level in only 8%. The chi-square statistic shows that the chance of this pattern being observed if there were no relationship between branch and international cooperation is less than 5%. Thus, we can conclude that Congress does not achieve as much cooperation from other states, on average, as does the president.

Thus far, the evidence does little to refute the conventional wisdom of exec-

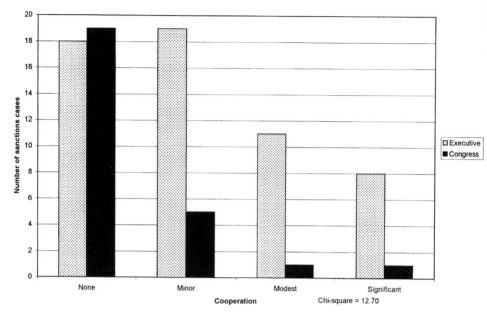

Figure 4.2. Branch by international cooperation.

utive dominance in foreign affairs. The president imposes more sanctions than does Congress, and far more in support of major policy goals. In addition, the president is more successful in gaining the support of other countries for his sanctions efforts. So we may be tempted to conclude that legislative attempts to take the lead on economic sanctions are misguided, and that the legislature is unable to gain the cooperation of other states for its policies. This conclusion would support the null hypothesis and undermine the alternative hypotheses about legislative influence outlined in chapter 2. However, we found in the previous chapter that initial aggregate support for executive dominance crumbled when we moved to more sensitive and appropriate tests. I follow the same strategy in this chapter, further breaking down the data on international cooperation to test alternative hypotheses about legislative influence and credibility. In particular, I introduce divided government as an explanatory variable. The results suggest that the failures of legislative initiative are contingent, not absolute, and that under some circumstances the legislature is capable of organizing itself to gain significant levels of international cooperation.

DIVIDED PARTY CONTROL AND INTERNATIONAL COOPERATION

This section develops and tests more nuanced hypotheses about international cooperation. In particular, it examines an interaction effect between divided government and the branch responsible for imposing sanctions. Controlling for the effects of divided government provides a direct test of general hypotheses about conflict and cooperation. These general hypotheses give rise to specific, observable implications about the effect of divided government on the level of international cooperation achieved. The logic is that conflict between the branches, measured here by divided government, gives rise to the institution-alization of legislative activity, which in turns enhances the credibility of com-mitments and the level of international cooperation achieved.

Partisan Control of Government

Problems of dispersed authority in the U.S. government are exacerbated, many authors argue, when control of the presidency, the Senate, and the House is not maintained by a single party (Pfiffner 1991; McCubbins 1991; Sundquist 1992). Over the last twenty years, divided government has become common in the United States. The causes of divided government are the subject of much con-cern and debate, but will be treated as exogenous here (see Jacobson 1990; Fio-rina 1992). Instead, our concern is with the consequences of divided govern-ment for international cooperation on economic sanctions.

While there is a lively debate on the consequences of divided government, little of this debate involves rigorous theoretical development or empirical test-ing of propositions. The literature is dominated by a presumption that divided government forces the American people to pay a high price in terms of effi-ciency, as it creates gridlock and allows multiple veto points in the system, pre-venting substantial policy initiatives. Analysts point to examples of perceived government failure, such as the high budget deficits of the 1980s, and attribute these to divided government, but often without adequately controlling for al-ternative explanations. Only a couple of efforts have been made systematically to examine the evidence relating to divided government (Mayhew 1991; Fio-rina 1992). These empirical studies, which look at figures such as the amount of major legislation passed and the percentage of treaties ratified, throw into question the prevailing view that divided government is a major handicap for the United States. While some authors argue that we do not yet have a good un-derstanding of how to include political parties in our models of American gov-ernment (Krehbiel 1993), others have developed an image of parties as coordi-nating devices that allow politicians to overcome many of the difficulties posed by the separation of powers and multiple veto points in the U.S. government (Cox and McCubbins 1993). Yet, existing studies are far from the final word on the subject, and make clear the need for more theoretical and empirical analy-sis of the consequences of divided government.

Divided government creates and reflects serious conflicts of interest between the branches. To the degree that the parties hold different policy preferences, divided government means that veto players who most likely do not agree on their preferred policy hold power. Beyond this preference effect, divided government creates partisan incentives to obstruct the activities of the other branch, as discussed above. Given these drawbacks, we might expect that divided government would undermine any capacity to establish credible commitments and therefore jeopardize attempts at international cooperation. However, the logic of institutionalized legislative influence suggests a way in which conflicts can be overcome, and may in fact turn out to be constructive. Under divided government, Congress has an incentive to institutionalize its participation in foreign policy, according to the Delegation Hypothesis. Without the worry that it might undercut a president of its own party, Congress can pursue an relatively independent foreign-policy agenda and set up the necessary monitoring and other mechanisms to establish credible commitments to this foreign policy. If Congress does institutionalize its pursuit of economic sanctions, focusing seriously on the problem of international cooperation and how to achieve it, it may have much more success in gaining cooperation than a view that neglected institutional incentives would suggest. Thus, institutionalized legislative activity can go a long way toward overcoming the handicaps of divided government.

Divided government in the United States can take two forms: a president of one party confronted by unified congressional control by the other party; or split congressional control, with the House controlled by one party and the Senate by the other. Consider first the latter case, split congressional control. Leaving aside for the moment the question of interaction with the executive branch, how would we expect a split Congress to behave on issues involving economic sanctions? One hypothesis, building on Cox and McCubbins (1993), would begin from the assumption that parties are a coordinating device. Within the legislature, parties allow their members to overcome the collective-action problems posed by the large, unwieldy, nonhierarchical organizations of the House and Senate. In this framework, party leadership becomes an important factor in explaining policy outcomes. While acknowledging that party discipline in the United States today falls below that in most other democracies (particularly parliamentary systems), and below the level found in some earlier eras of U.S. politics, the collective-action model assumes that parties nevertheless exercise some influence on legislators' voting patterns. They do this not by coercive measures, forcing individual MCs to vote against their constituency interests, but by providing the necessary functions to allow MCs to adopt more long-term perspectives on their interests and to coordinate with one another, thus overcoming collective-action problems and making all MCs better off.

If the collective-action model is accurate, we would expect split congressional control to have a significant impact on the pattern of economic sanctions imposed by Congress. Specifically, it predicts that Congress will find it quite difficult to impose sanctions when the two chambers are controlled by different parties. Congressional sanctions require coordination between the two branches. Without unified party control, such coordination—particularly under

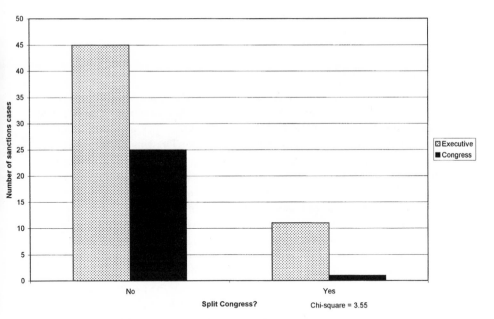

Figure 4.3. Branch by split congressional control.

conditions where the president is not enthusiastic about the use of sanctions—
will be extremely difficult to achieve.

Figure 4.3 examines how imposition of sanctions depends on split control of
Congress. Split control has not occurred very often, so that we have only a few
opportunities to observe behavior under these circumstances, making tests of
statistical significance problematic. As figure 4.3 shows, when Congress has
been split it has imposed sanctions only once in the cases included in this data
set.[3] This occurred in 1986, when Congress passed legislation cutting Exim-
bank loans to Angola until Cuban troops were withdrawn (HSE 1990, 2:593).
Even in this case, although Democrat Dennis DeConcini proposed an amendment forcing the president to impose a trade embargo, Congress was unable to
agree to make sanctions very stringent, sticking with only financial sanctions.
U.S. policy on Angola is an issue on which the legislative and executive
branches have struggled for decades, so that congressional action on this matter is not terribly surprising. Imposition of sanctions under conditions of split

[3] As discussed above, sanctions against South Africa have been excluded from this data-set.
Were they included, we would find another case of sanctions imposed under split control, as Congress imposed new sanctions on South Africa in 1986. Although this case throws off the statistical
results and so is reasonably excluded from most of the analyses here, it is examined later in this
chapter.

congressional control is rare. On this evidence, it appears that party does matter, at least within Congress.

Divided Control and International Cooperation

Now we turn to the more complex question of how divided control between the branches might influence patterns of international cooperation. As argued above, one of the key determinants of international cooperation is the ability of the leading sender to make credible commitments. Drawing on the above reasoning about the impact of divided government, our first hypothesis might be that commitments would be more difficult to make under divided government. In this circumstance, presidents would face a Congress without the benefit of party-coordination mechanisms when they decided to pursue sanctions policies. We might plausibly expect that under such circumstances, other states would reasonably question the ability of the president to carry through with costly threats or promises that adversely affected some congressional constituencies. On the other hand, an executive-dominance approach would not expect that we would see any significant difference in the executive's ability to make commitments under conditions of unified or divided government. Starting from the presumption that the executive is able to get his or her way on foreign-policy issues, other states would have little reason to question the executive's credibility regardless of party control of Congress.

One line of reasoning that seems particularly useful for helping to sort out the logic of credible commitments under divided government is to focus on the incentives for Congress to "micromanage," or tightly oversee and monitor, the president's activities. One implication that follows directly from thinking about partisan incentives is that congressional willingness to exercise tight control over the president should be greatest when the president is of a different party than the majority in Congress (Kernell 1991, 96–97). If Congress is controlled by Democrats and the executive by Republicans, for example, the legislature will have greater reason to distrust the executive, anticipating that the executive will attempt to circumvent or otherwise fail to implement fully congressional sanctions and countersanctions. Thus, Congress is likely to exercise stringent monitoring and oversight procedures under divided government, rather than relying on systems that leave greater room for shirking. We see such a dynamic in congressional activity on human rights, as Democrats in Congress came to find that they could not trust Presidents Nixon or Ford to carry out legislation on this issue as they intended. The Democratic leadership thus consistently increased both the precision of legislation and the resources devoted to oversight (Schoultz 1980; U.S. House 1976), as predicted by the Delegation Hypothesis: legislatures move to institutionalize their participation in policymaking in the face of conflict with the executive.

Under divided government, individual MCs have greater incentives to monitor the president closely, anticipating electoral benefits from revealed presidential shirking. When the legislative and executive branches are controlled by different parties, individual MCs can score political points by revealing evidence of presidential shirking and evasion of legislative intent. Thus, the tradeoff between monitoring costs and control should favor tighter control under conditions of divided government. When interacting with the executive branch on foreign policy, Congress constantly confronts a trade-off between allowing presidential discretion to pursue foreign policy and devoting scarce resources to oversight, and the optimal level of control varies with party control of the two branches.

When Congress and the executive are controlled by the same party, however, legislators' calculations change. Now, to the extent that party reputation is a public good from which all party representatives benefit, revelation of presidential shirking is not an unconditional benefit. MCs may, for good reason, be reluctant to expend resources to show that a president of their own party is refusing adequately to carry out legislated sanctions. Such revelations could have negative electoral consequences for the party as a whole. In addition, they could make public conflicts within the party over the utility of sanctions, undermining the electorate's confidence in the governing party's performance. Thus, Congress will be unlikely to exert as much control over the president under conditions of single-party control as under divided government.

Considerations about incentives to monitor presidential activity lead to the counterintuitive expectation that *congressional* sanctions will be more credible, and so gain greater international cooperation, when the presidency and Congress are controlled by different parties. Under unified government, MCs are constrained in their willingness to bind and monitor the president too tightly; they are more inclined to delegate significant authority to the president under these conditions. This pattern of constraints gives the president leeway to circumvent congressional intent, leading to congressional sanctions that lack credibility and so will gain little international cooperation. Under divided government, congressional incentives change substantially, so that members of the majority party now have high incentives to monitor the president closely and otherwise "micromanage" foreign policy. In fact, studies of divided government have argued that precisely this pattern of behavior is one of the major drawbacks of divided government (Kernell 1991).

However, in the context of economic sanctions divided government is likely to lend further credibility to congressional efforts. Therefore, in something of a paradox, we should expect to see Congress gaining greater international cooperation for its sanctions efforts under conditions of divided government. This hypothesis is an observable implication of the general proposition that conflict between the branches leads to institutionalization of legislative participation, which in turn enhances credibility and the chances of gaining international cooperation. This prediction also allows us to differentiate between the executive-

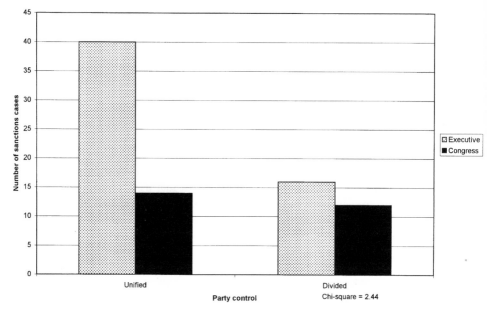

Figure 4.4. Branch by divided party control.

dominance model and partisan-politics explanations. An executive-dominance model would expect Congress to have problems imposing sanctions regardless of party control; it would give us no reason to expect more success under conditions of divided government.

The first implication of the partisan model is that we should see greater congressional willingness to delegate authority to the president when government is unified, as implied by the Delegation Hypothesis. For example, we should see more reluctance in Congress to take the initiative in imposing economic sanctions, instead allowing the president to take the lead on foreign policy. We can hypothesize that we will see proportionately fewer congressional sanctions under unified than under divided government. Figure 4.4 presents data on this issue.

The evidence in figure 4.4 is suggestive, but not conclusive. We do observe a difference in the ratio between executive and congressional sanctions under conditions of unified and divided government. Under unified government, Congress initiates only 14 out of 54 cases of sanctions, or 25.9%. When government control is divided, Congress initiates 12 out of 28 cases, or 42.9%. More congressional activism under divided government is consistent with the Delegation Hypothesis. Under divided government, Congress is happy to follow its own foreign-policy course, and so more likely to impose sanctions. However, these data are only suggestive, not conclusive. The observed pattern is not sta-

TABLE 4.1
Ordered Probit: Dependent Variable = International Cooperation

Independent Variable	Estimated Coefficient	Standard Error	T-Statistic
Constant	−1.36	0.565	−2.40
CONGRESS*	−1.44	0.436	−3.31
CONGRESSXDIV*	1.42	0.638	2.22
DIVIDE	−0.428	0.341	−1.26
TARGET	−0.204	0.194	−1.05
GOAL	0.134	0.284	0.472
COSTD*	1.42	0.362	3.94
Thresh 1	1.08	0.150	7.20
Thresh 2	1.84	0.199	9.23
Number of observations:	82		
Percent correctly predicted:	48.8%		

tistically significant. The chi-square statistic of 2.44 does not allow us to rule out the possibility that the observed pattern was the result of random variation, even though the difference in percentages appears substantively significant. In order to gain further explanatory leverage, I next turn to slightly more sophisticated statistical analyses and a more direct test of patterns of international cooperation.

Tables 4.1 and 4.2 present a statistical test of the hypotheses about the relationship between divided government and international cooperation. I use the four-category measure of cooperation discussed above as the dependent variable. For an ordered categorical variable like this, ordered probit is an appropriate method of analysis. Probit analysis, unlike the figures presented thus far in this chapter, allows me to control for alternative explanations of international cooperation, thus isolating the independent effects of branch and divided government. I include three control variables here. The first is TARGET, which is a measure of the economic and political condition of the target country developed by HSE. We might expect that sanctions against stable, wealthy states are more likely to be futile and costly, and therefore less likely to generate much international support, than those against poor, unstable targets. HSE develop a three-point scale that very roughly measures the condition of the target. A value of 1 indicates a poor and unstable target, while a value of 2 indicates one that is quite rich and stable.[4] The mean value of TARGET in this data-set is 2.04.

---

[4] Because TARGET is measured on a three-point ordinal scale, the technically correct procedure would be to substitute two dummy variables for it in this model. However, statistical analyses have shown that this substitution makes no observable difference in the results, so the original variable is included here for simplicity of interpretation and to save degrees of freedom.

Above, we considered how the goals of sanctions might be related to the branch of government that imposed them. We might also expect that these goals will be related to the degree of international cooperation achieved. When policy goals are ambitious, sanctions with little international support are unlikely to succeed. Cooperation is valuable in this case. But when policy goals are more modest, unilateral U.S. sanctions might have a greater chance of working. We might therefore expect that the United States would put more effort into generating international cooperation when it is pursuing sanctions with ambitious goals. To test for this possibility, I include the dummy variable GOAL in the model. It takes on the value 1 when the United States is seeking major policy changes in the target. The cases are evenly split between modest and major policy goals.

As discussed above, one of the major factors influencing the level of cooperation attained is the commitment the United States makes to the sanctions effort. When this commitment is not credible, cooperation is unlikely. However, factors other than the branch initiating sanctions will contribute to credibility. In particular, earlier studies have found that the sender's effort is more credible when it shows a willingness to bear high costs (Martin 1992a). To control for this effect, I include the variable COSTD in the model. COSTD is a dichotomous variable, coded 1 for low-cost sanctions (such as cutting foreign aid) and 2 for high-cost sanctions (such as extensive trade sanctions). I have recoded it from HSE's original four-point coding of costs. Thirty-four cases have a value of 1, and forty-eight a value of 2.

The variables relevant to the divided-government hypothesis that is our primary interest here are CONGRESS, CONGXDIV, and DIVIDE. CONGRESS is a dummy variable that takes on the value one if Congress is responsible for imposing sanctions. DIVIDE is another dummy, which codes for those sanctions imposed during periods when the presidency is controlled by a different party than the majority in Congress. Fifty-four of the cases of sanctions in this data set occurred under unified government, and 28 under divided government. CONGXDIV is an interaction term for these two variables, so it is equal to 1 only when Congress imposes sanctions under conditions of divided government. The key effect of divided government will show up in the interaction term, CONGXDIV. If Congress exercises tighter control over sanctions under divided government, and so is able to achieve greater credibility then, we should see a positive coefficient on CONGXDIV. The result would support the counterintuitive expectation that Congress is best able to establish credible commitments, and so gain the cooperation of other states, under conditions of divided government. This proposition follows from considering the Delegation and Cooperation Hypotheses in the context of economic sanctions.

Given the rough measurements used in this model, the results are surprisingly strong. CONGRESS has a negative coefficient, while the interaction term has a positive one, as expected. Both of these results are statistically significant.

TABLE 4.2
Fitted Values

CONGRESS	PRES	Fitted score	Fitted COOP
0	0	1.22	3
1	0	−0.227	1
0	1	0.789	2
1	1	0.764	2

They suggest that Congress has less difficulty establishing its credibility when the president is of a different party. Congress shows a significantly better record of achieving international cooperation under divided government than under unified government. In fact, under divided government, Congress and the president show about the same ability to gain international cooperation. The only other variable showing a statistically significant effect is COSTD, which was also included as a result of thinking about credibility concerns. This result shows that the United States as a whole achieves greater international cooperation when it bears relatively high costs; refusal to bear these costs results in a loss of credibility. We can see this dynamic in the 1982 pipeline episode. In this case, the Europeans were angered by U.S. refusal to bear the costs of a grain embargo. The administration's reluctance to bear these costs helped persuade European governments that U.S. threats of countersanctions were a bluff (Stern 1982, 78; Martin 1992a, 234–39).

To aid in interpretation of these results, table 4.2 presents some fitted values for cooperation, given the results of this analysis. In this table, I have set TARGET = 2, GOAL = 1, and COSTD = 2. Under these conditions (a moderate-income target, ambitious policy goals, and fairly high-cost sanctions), if both branches are controlled by the same party and the president imposes sanctions, we expect "modest cooperation" (COOP = 3) as the outcome.[5] Congress, however, can expect to achieve no cooperation under the same circumstances. The results change significantly when government control is divided. Now, the president and Congress can expect to achieve essentially the same level of cooperation, a minor level (COOP = 2). Congress receives significantly more cooperation when government is divided, while the president achieves somewhat less.

The Outlier: South Africa

Sanctions against South Africa have been excluded from the data-set used here. They were excluded because this case is a statistical outlier, where the level of

---

[5] Under no conditions does the model predict "significant cooperation."

international cooperation was exceptionally high so that it exerts disproportionate influence on any statistical results. In many ways, sanctions against South Africa are a unique case. The level of public support for sanctions to push the South African government to abandon apartheid, not only in the United States but throughout most of the world, far exceeded public support for sanctions in other sanctions cases. Public support, and pressure on the government to respond to such support, resulted from the intensive efforts of many domestic and transnational groups over many years (Klotz 1995). However, strong preferences for a particular outcome, such as an end to apartheid, or a policy, such as sanctions against the South African government, do not imply that politicians stop behaving strategically. The analysis of political strategies should remain a central part of our understanding of even popular issues.

Including the South African case in the data-set would have made some difference to the results presented thus far. In particular, we find here another example of Congress imposing sanctions when the Senate and House are run by different parties, in the Comprehensive Anti-Apartheid Act (CAA) of 1986. In 1986 the House was in Democratic hands, but the Senate in Republican. Not only did Congress manage to overcome partisan incentives in this instance, it did so to the extent that it overrode (Republican) President Reagan's veto of the CAA. Such unusual action demands a more careful look, since it so prominently deviates from the general pattern.

U.S. efforts to put pressure on South Africa to change its racial policies go back to 1963, when the Kennedy administration imposed a voluntary arms embargo and some restrictions on loans from the Export-Import Bank. This step, as well as actions on the part of the UN and other international actors, followed shootings in March 1960 of demonstrators in Sharpeville, South Africa, that killed sixty-nine people. Further violence in 1976, beginning with protests by students in Soweto, led to more American and international sanctions. In 1978–79 the Carter administration strengthened the 1963 measures, extending the ban on loans and banning the sale of all goods to the police and military in South Africa (Lipton 1988, 4–18).

In the 1980s, renewed violence in South Africa and a new constitution that excluded all black South Africans from representation led to a new round of international pressure. The United States took steps, but only as a result of congressional pressure (Becker 1987, 147). The Reagan Administration opposed further sanctions, arguing instead for a policy of "constructive engagement" (Menges 1988). The administration argued that only by engaging potentially progressive forces in South Africa could the rest of the world have any leverage. Sanctions, according to this argument, would only harm the black population and cause resentment, blocking political change. However, pressure from the legislature to take action grew in 1985, and in an attempt to fend off legislation Reagan imposed some sanctions, using an executive order. The steps taken in this order included extension of the bans on sales to the police and military, a ban on the import of Krugerrands, and an end to most exports of nuclear technology, as well as diplomatic and voluntary measures.

However, the situation in South Africa continued to deteriorate and the administration's measures were not enough to satisfy anti-apartheid groups in the United States, who continued to put pressure on legislators to take more forceful steps. As a result, Congress passed the CAA in September 1986. The CAA prohibited new investment in South Africa, loans to the South African government, export of computers and oil, direct air traffic, and the import of many products (Congressional Information Service 1986). Reagan vetoed the legislation but enough Republican senators defected from the administration's line to support an override. 1986 thus contrasts strongly with 1985, when Majority Leader Robert Dole (R-Kansas) and Foreign Relations Committee chair Richard Lugar (R-Indiana) conspired, in response to administration pressure, to prevent a vote on anti-apartheid legislation.

It is the actions of the Republican defectors in 1986, those who were willing to ignore intense lobbying from the president, that are the most puzzling, and out of character for the usual course of partisan politics on economic sanctions. Democratic support for sanctions was nearly unanimous, in 1985 as well as 1986, and enough support existed in the House to override a veto. The potential swing votes among Republicans in the Senate are the key to explaining the 1986 outcome. As usual, when one constructs an explanation for a single puzzling event in retrospect, it begins to look overdetermined. A number of factors came together in 1986 to encourage a statement of bipartisan opposition to the administration's policies. The situation in South Africa had deteriorated substantially in the year prior to the passage of the CAA, beginning with the declaration of a state of emergency in July 1985. Rates of violent death and reports of death in detention rose rapidly. Other states and international institutions, including the European Community and the Commonwealth, were moving toward imposing sanctions in spite of resistance from powerful states like Britain (*Congressional Quarterly,* 27 September 1986, 2270–71; Hermele and Odén 1988, 42–43; Treverton 1988). Public outcry against the situation in South Africa continued to be loud and supported by organized lobbying groups such as Trans Africa. The administration's claims that constructive engagement could moderate the policies of the South African government were discredited by all these developments.

However, perhaps most significant for purposes of persuading the Republican defectors to sacrifice party loyalty for the sake of a popular vote (and for their consciences) was the effect that the events of 1985–86 had on positions within the administration itself (Baker 1989). Throughout this book, we tend to treat the executive branch as a unified, or at least hierarchical, actor. And for most purposes this simplification is adequate. But when an issue like apartheid gains such a high level of public attention and outcry, and the existing policies of the president look increasingly ineffective and immoral, we might expect splits to occur within the executive branch. As we have since learned of the Reagan administration, the control of agencies by the president was quite weak, exacerbating the tendency created by deep policy disagreements for agencies to go in their own directions.

In the case of sanctions against South Africa, the agency that most significantly deviated from the administration line was the State Department. While in 1985 the administration had managed to present a united front, in 1986 the president's policy was undermined by open conflict with State, which was supported to some extent by the National Security Council. Whereas the president and CIA portrayed the African National Congress (ANC) as a group of Communists devoted to violent overthrow of the South African government, with whom the South African government should not be forced to negotiate, Secretary of State George Schultz met the head of the ANC in his office in 1986. Schultz testified before the Senate Foreign Relations Committee in July 1986 that he still opposed sanctions, but broke with the president on the other dimensions of his constructive-engagement policy (U.S. Senate 1986). Congress read Schultz's testimony as a signal that the State Department no longer supported the president on this issue (Menges 1988, 74). When State broke with the administration's previous policy, Lugar no longer felt bound to prevent a vote on sanctions. With the defection of this key committee chair, the battle in the Senate was lost, and the legislative process led to passage of the CAA.

The CAA thus looks like an exception that proves the rule, so to speak. It is exceptional in that the ties of party loyalty did not prevent a split Congress from acting to impose major sanctions against the direct, public wishes of the president. But a look at the dynamics of the case suggest reasons that party loyalty broke down. In particular, deep disagreement and defection of agencies from the president's policy within the executive branch encouraged similar behavior on the part of Republicans in the Senate. Given intense public pressure to take part in the international sanctions effort, and evidence that party unity had broken down within the administration, few incentives remained for the Republicans to toe the party line. The CAA case suggests that activists hoping to rely on legislative action to impose sanctions when control of Congress is split between the parties will have an extraordinarily difficult task. Only if the level of public pressure is fierce enough to create divisions within the executive branch can we expect to see enough defections to make a difference in the legislative process. On reflection, the CAA case substantiates the claim that partisan considerations profoundly influence legislative behavior on economic sanctions.

Overall, the statistical results support the contention that party control of government has interesting impacts on the ability to gain cooperation, but they are somewhat more subtle than one might first expect. With two exceptions, Congress has never imposed sanctions when one party controls the House and the other the Senate. In general, Congress has a harder time demonstrating credible commitments to sanctions than the executive, reflected in lower levels of international cooperation. However, this result is dependent on whether the same party controls both branches of government. Under unified government, Congress finds it nearly impossible to achieve international cooperation. But when control is divided, Congress performs as well as the executive. These results strongly suggest that party-control matters, and cast doubt on a simpler executive-dominance explanation of patterns of cooperation. The aggregate results are quite promising, and suggest a nuanced understanding of the interaction between legislative involvement, divided government, strategic interaction, and international cooperation. The Delegation Hypothesis leads us to expect that Congress will exert tighter control over the sanctions it imposes under divided government. The Cooperation Hypothesis leads us to expect that such control will lead to higher levels of cooperation on congressionally led sanctions. This is indeed the pattern we observe. To lend further insight into these complex relations, I turn next to a more detailed case study that will allow us to follow the dynamics of sanctions politics. I focus on the question of granting MFN treatment to China, following the course of this contentious issue through two administrations.

MFN TREATMENT FOR CHINA

The linkage between human rights and economic relations with the United States is a long-standing and controversial issue in American politics. The human-rights practices of Latin American countries have led to ongoing debates about the use of sanctions. In these cases, sanctions most often have taken the form of limiting foreign assistance, but have occasionally escalated to limits on trade (Martin and Sikkink 1993). One case of human-rights sanctions that spans a number of administrations is MFN treatment for China. This case therefore provides a direct test of the Delegation Hypothesis.

Background

In dealings with Communist countries, including China, foreign assistance is a moot point since they do not receive substantial foreign aid from the United States. Instead, advocates of economic statecraft have had to turn to trade sanctions. Trade sanctions are often more controversial and difficult to impose than restrictions on aid, since trade sanctions directly harm business interests in the United States. But, if credibly put into place, they can have substantial economic impact on their target. For these reasons, we find recurrent heated debates about tying trade with the United States to the human-rights practices of Communist countries.

The fundamental piece of legislation involved in this debate is the Jackson-Vanik amendment to the 1974 Trade Act (Stern 1979). This amendment, presented by Senator Henry Jackson, ties Most-Favored-Nation treatment to the emigration practices of Communist countries. From 1951 to 1975, all "non-market" countries had been denied MFN status. MFN status means that a country is entitled to the same low levels of tariffs that the United States extends to its major trading partners (excluding special discriminatory arrangements, such as NAFTA). Without MFN treatment, tariffs revert to the last level specified in the U.S. code, which is often an order of magnitude higher than the MFN level. Thus, denial of MFN treatment constitutes a major trade barrier to countries wishing to export to the United States.

The 1974 Trade Act provided a mechanism for allowing Communist countries to attain MFN status. But the use of this mechanism was tightly constrained by the Jackson-Vanik amendment, which came out of traditional Cold War considerations and has been seen as a signal of the end of détente (Gasiorowski and Polachek 1982). The amendment provides that the benefits of MFN or any other trade agreement can be extended to Communist countries if the president certifies that a country allows free emigration. If the president cannot make such a certification, he can still grant MFN through the use of a one-year waiver, on the grounds that emigration policies are being improved. Granting of such waivers has become a hot political issue, particularly in the case of China after the Tiananmen Square massacre of 4 June 1989.

The waiver mechanism itself has undergone some changes, which are worth considering because they have deeply influenced the ability of Congress to exert its will when it disagrees with the president. Originally, either house could overturn a presidential waiver of Jackson-Vanik (i.e., a finding that MFN treatment should be extended for one year in spite of a lack of free emigration). The single-house legislative veto was implicated as unconstitutional by a 1983 Supreme Court decision, *Chadha v. Immigration and Naturalization Service,* which found all such vetoes unacceptable as they deprived the president of the right to use his constitutionally specified veto power (Pfiffner 1991; Korn 1993). Since the *Chadha* decision, efforts to reject a presidential waiver require a joint resolution of both houses of Congress. Such a joint resolution is subject to presidential veto, which would require a two-thirds vote of both houses for an override. Thus, since 1983, congressional ability to impose sanctions through the Jackson-Vanik amendment has been seriously eroded. Now as few as thirty-four Senators (a blocking minority willing to uphold a presidential veto) are able to prevent the denial of MFN treatment.

China has benefited from MFN treatment since 1980, through annual waivers. Each year, the deadline for renewing MFN treatment has been 3 June. Through 1988, the waivers generated little controversy, as the growing international economic activity of China and explosive growth of American investment there created a constituency strongly in favor of unimpeded economic relations.

However, MFN treatment for China became controversial after the Tiananmen Square crackdown on pro-democracy demonstrators in June 1988, in which hundreds gathered in the square and elsewhere in Beijing were killed by army troops. Immediately after the crackdown, the United States did impose some sanctions on China. These initial sanctions included a suspension of high-level visits and withholding support for World Bank loans and military sales (Sullivan 1992, 10). They were widely perceived as primarily symbolic, not at all stringent or punitive, and designed to protect U.S. economic interests. Immediately after the crackdown Bush decided to renew Chinese MFN treatment, and his decision provoked no quick response from Congress. After the initial demands for punishment of China and demonstrations of American disapproval faded away, continuing detention of leaders of the pro-democracy movement by the Chinese government led to calls to use economic leverage to protest and attempt to change Chinese behavior. The annual waiver of the Jackson-Vanik amendment became a focal point for this debate. On the pro-sanctions side, supporters argued that it was immoral not to punish China for its behavior, that U.S. economic leverage could be effective, and that it was inconsistent to hold the reforming Soviet Union's (later Russia's) feet to the fire by denying MFN while letting the repressive Chinese government off the hook. On the anti-sanctions side, business and pro-free-trade interests argued that sanctions would harm the most progressive and international sector of Chinese society, that growing economic engagement was the best way to encourage Chinese democracy, and that the economic harm to the United States from starting a trade war with China was not worth the potential benefits of sanctions.

Under the Bush administration, executive decisions about sanctions against China appear to have been made in a highly centralized manner. President George Bush, an ex-ambassador to China who considered himself something of an expert on how to promote democratic reforms through a deep understanding of Chinese society, made the primary decisions himself. His experience and inclinations led him to agree with the anti-sanctions side of the debate, arguing that cutting off economic ties would only lead to more repressive behavior, in addition to hurting U.S. economic interests. Thus, as 3 June 1989 approached—coincidentally, only one day from the first anniversary of the Tiananmen Square massacre—Bush declared that he would renew China's MFN status. This decision led to congressional efforts to craft a legislative override of the Jackson-Vanik waiver, efforts that lasted until 1994. Study of these efforts allows us to further test the Delegation Hypothesis, since legislative efforts began under divided government and continued in the first Clinton administration, under unified government. If the party-control approach developed above is correct, we should see a difference in congressional incentives and behavior across the two administrations. Specifically, we should see greater monitoring activity and other kinds of micromanagement under the Bush administration, and greater willingness to delegate policymaking to the executive during the Clinton administration.

Legislative Behavior: Bush Administration

In 1989, MCs began introducing legislation that would revoke China's MFN status. Some measures introduced would revoke MFN unconditionally; others would make renewal of MFN conditional on specific actions by the Chinese government, such as releasing dissidents from prison, and on a general improvement in human-rights conditions in China. Senator Daniel Patrick Moynihan (D-New York), for example, introduced conditional legislation in 1989. Initially, anti-MFN bills made little progress through the legislative process. In 1989, Congress only managed to pass a bill introduced by Representative Nancy Pelosi (D-California), who was to become a major figure in the MFN struggle. Her 1989 bill, which passed the House on a 403–0 vote and the Senate on voice vote, merely allowed Chinese students in the United States to extend their visas. Bush vetoed this bill. Apparently he hoped to prevent congressional interference in policy toward China, not intending to signal disagreement with the substance of the bill, since simultaneously with his veto he signed an executive order extending Chinese students' visas. The president's veto was upheld in the Senate on a 62–37 vote (*New York Times,* 31 January 1990), signaling the future fate of legislation directed at China.

In 1990, Congress took further steps toward revoking MFN. After Bush renewed MFN in June, both houses took up legislation to overturn the president's waiver. By June 1990, a dozen pieces of such legislation had been introduced (*Congressional Quarterly [CQ]*, 23 June 1990, 1944). Initially, efforts to revoke MFN seemed to have widespread bipartisan support. For example, Stephen Solarz (D-New York), chair of the House Foreign Affairs Subcommittee on Asian and Pacific Affairs, stated after hearings that there was a risk of immediate termination of MFN. "I assure you, Congress will move forward," he claimed (*CQ,* 26 May 1990, 1639). Moynihan also claimed that "[we] will propose legislation," and we will enact legislation to prevent this measure [the extension of MFN]" (*CQ,* 26 May 1990, 1686). Senate Majority Leader George Mitchell (D-Maine) joined in as a vocal supporter of the anti-MFN forces. The administration continued to oppose vigorously any MFN linkage.

The first bills to make it past the stage of a floor vote came in October 1990. On October 18, the House passed two different bills, one that denied MFN treatment immediately and one that put tight restrictions on the resumption of MFN treatment (*CQ,* 20 October 1990, 3490). Both passed by comfortable margins and with bipartisan support. However, the Senate never acted on these bills, nor did it pass any bills of its own, in spite of Mitchell's efforts to introduce legislation, so that the House bills expired with the end of the congressional session. Bush once again renewed MFN status for China in May 1991.

By spring 1991, observers believed that support for MFN revocation was growing. Their belief was not only due to continuing discomfort with China's human-rights practices but also to dissatisfaction with other Chinese policies, including its military sales and trade surplus with the United States. A lobbyist for apparel importers who favored MFN extension worried that "MFN is really in jeopardy this year. . . . China's not very popular, and since we're in the middle of a recession, free trade is not very popular either" (*CQ*, 27 April 1991, 1044). The same lobbyist thought that "the administration does not have the stomach for a veto fight" (*CQ*, 1 June 1991, 1434). Mitchell introduced a bill in the Senate revoking MFN, and Pelosi did so in the House. Both of the bills were widely cosponsored. At this point, the debate began to take on partisan dimensions, although a number of Republicans were willing to support anti-MFN measures. The leadership for introducing legislation came from the Democratic side of the aisle. The more adamant Bush became about refusing to put any conditions on MFN, the more support grew among Democrats for taking this issue into their own hands (*CQ*, 8 June 1991, 1512; *CQ*, 29 June 1991, 1737–41).

The House approved a bill attaching conditions for renewal of MFN on 10 July 1991 by a vote of 313–112. This bill imposed even stronger conditions than those in the original bill introduced by Pelosi, following action by the Ways and Means Committee (*CQ*, 13 July 1991, 1880). The House bill would make MFN treatment conditional on release of prisoners arrested in 1989, an end to coerced abortions and sterilizations, an end to the export of certain military technologies, and an end to the export to the United States of goods made with prison labor. The Senate passed its own bill, with even tougher conditions, on 23 July by a 55–44 vote (*CQ*, 27 July 1991, 2053–56). While an apparent victory, anti-MFN forces saw this narrow margin of victory as a defeat, since it signaled that the Senate would not override a guaranteed presidential veto.

Perhaps sensing certain defeat, Congress did not rush ahead to reconcile the House and Senate bills and so get legislation to the president's desk. A conference report finally appeared in November, and the House approved it by a vote of 409–21 (*CQ*, 30 November 1991, 3517). The Senate finally approved it, in the face of a promised presidential veto, on 25 February 1992, by a vote of 59–39 (*CQ*, 29 February, 1992, 460). Since the Senate vote fell short of the two-thirds margin needed for an override, prospects for revocation of MFN were dim. The president subsequently vetoed the bill, and the House approved an override, but the Senate sustained the veto by a vote of 60–38 on 18 March (*CQ*, 21 March 1992, 716). In the Senate, partisan effects on voting were clear. Even Senators who publicly disagreed with Bush's strategy voted to uphold his veto, in order to avoid handing him an "embarrassing defeat" (*CQ*, 6 June 1992, 1594). Bush duly announced in June a renewal of MFN status, and congressional Democrats duly introduced new legislation to overturn his decision.

In 1992, Democrats hoped to generate wider support for anti-MFN legislation by targeting it more narrowly. In particular, they aimed sanctions only at state-owned industries. They hoped that this targeting would devalue arguments that sanctions would only hurt progressive forces in China by exempting private enterprises (*CQ*, 4 July 1992, 1933). Legislation revoking MFN passed the

House in July, and the Senate in September. The House accepted the Senate's version of the bill, but it was predictably vetoed by Bush. The Senate once again upheld the veto, in spite of the narrowing of the legislation's provisions, by a vote of 59–40 on 1 October (*CQ,* 3 October 1992, 3027). The decision to uphold the president's veto once again appeared to hinge on partisan decisions by Senate Republicans. During 1989–92, efforts to tie China's MFN treatment to its human-rights policies closely followed the predictions of the party-control model. With a Republican president, Democrats led the charge in attempting to deny MFN treatment, showing themselves unwilling to believe the president's pledges to pursue human-rights improvements through other channels. However, their efforts to manage Chinese MFN policy in the face of presidential opposition ran afoul of a Republican contingent in the Senate willing to support the president in spite of misgivings about his policies, and of *Chadha,* which had given Bush veto power he would not have had prior to 1983.

Legislative History: Clinton Administration

According to the Delegation Hypothesis, we should see marked shifts in congressional behavior once Democratic President Bill Clinton took office in 1993. Congressional Democrats, who previously were happy to introduce legislation overturning presidential decisions and vote to override vetoes, should now be more willing to allow the president to take the policy initiative. They should be more willing to delegate authority to him, exercising less stringent control over policy and being less willing to vote against him. The Republican minority in Congress, on the other hand, should now be more active in pushing for legislation, particularly since many of them had been publicly skeptical of arguments in favor of MFN extension.

In fact, the legislative history of 1993 and 1994 fits this model nicely. While Mitchell and Pelosi still introduced legislation, it did not generate enough Democratic support to make it to Clinton's desk. On the other hand, Republicans became more active in introducing their own versions of bills tying MFN treatment to Chinese behavior. China and MFN treatment had become an issue during the 1992 campaign, with Clinton criticizing Bush's refusal to impose sanctions. He pledged to take a tougher line with China, pushing harder for human-rights improvements and conditions on MFN treatment.

However, Clinton did not follow up on campaign rhetoric by revoking MFN on taking office. Instead, he continued it for one year, while stating that renewal in 1994 would be contingent on clear improvements in specified areas. He sent Secretary of State Warren Christopher and Assistant Secretary of State for East Asia and Pacific Affairs Winston Lord to testify in congressional hearings that the administration wanted the one-year renewal in order to have a lever with which to push for changes in Chinese policy. Although such arguments were almost identical to those made by the Bush administration, they provoked quite a different response on Capitol Hill. Republicans such as Senator Jesse Helms (R-North Carolina) now vocally supported MFN conditionality (*CQ,* 3 April 1993, 855). While Mitchell and Pelosi still introduced legislation to make MFN conditional, Mitchell stated that he hoped there would be no need to pass the bill, in effect calling for presidential leadership (*CQ,* 24 April 1993, 1011). Mitchell and Pelosi did little to push their legislation through Congress in 1993. In fact, the only legislation to be reported out of committee was introduced by Republicans. President Clinton hailed this congressional approval of room for maneuver, claiming that "we no longer have an executive branch policy and a congressional policy. We have an American policy" (*CQ,* 29 May 1993, 1349).

However, 1993 proved no better for American efforts to pressure China than had the previous three years. The Chinese government steadfastly refused to make its internal practices contingent on American approval, daring the United States to deny MFN treatment. It went so far as to imprison a number of dissidents just before a visit by Christopher, refusing even to give him a face-saving agreement to fend off congressional criticism. In effect, the Chinese government was calling the American's bluff. And a bluff the Clinton policy turned out to be.

As the 1994 deadline for MFN renewal approached, very different sounds came out of Congress than had been heard previously. Now, many congressional leaders began arguing that the MFN lever was ineffectual, and that the United States had to find new methods to pressure China. They specifically called for breaking the link between MFN and human rights. Even Mitchell was reported to be willing to give Clinton "an opportunity to resolve the policy quandary without Congress intensifying the political pressure. . . . Congressional Democrats are prepared to give Clinton plenty of leeway on China—a sentiment that was not nearly as forthcoming when Republican George Bush was president" (*CQ,* 30 April 1994, 1054).

In 1994, as these discussions suggested, the annual linkage of MFN and human rights was finally dropped. Instead, the administration pledged to use other, more credible methods to pressure China to respect human rights. These methods would include quiet diplomacy and "lower intensity" economic measures (*CQ,* 28 May 1994, 1372). Pelosi, in particular, argued against such a change in policy, reasoning that the continued threat of MFN denial was essential in the effort to exert leverage on Chinese policy. Democratic leaders did introduce legislation calling for tougher trade sanctions in June 1994 (*CQ,* 18 June 1994, 1587). But such arguments now found little support. The House Ways and Means Committee, which under the Bush administration had reported sanctions bills with a favorable recommendation to the floor, now voted by a margin of 31–6 against a sanctions bill introduced by Gerald Solomon (R-New York) (*CQ,* 2 July 1994, 1774), and also against Pelosi's bill on a voice vote (*CQ,* 30 July 1994, 2119). The bills were nevertheless scheduled for a floor vote, under the special treatment specified by the Jackson-Vanik amendment.

But on 9 August, the House upheld Clinton's decision to delink MFN and human rights, rejecting the Solomon bill by a vote of 75–356 and the Pelosi bill by 158–270. Instead, the House voted to approve a bill introduced by Lee Hamilton (D-Indiana) that put into practice the measures Clinton had outlined in May (*CQ,* 13 August 1994, 2317). The Senate took no action on sanctions measures.

The pattern of behavior in 1994 contrasts strongly with that of Congress during the Bush administration. In spite of continuing support from congressional leaders and continuing dissatisfaction with various aspects of Chinese behavior, Congress was unwilling to challenge the president's decisions by passing legislation as it had during the Bush administration. Republicans became somewhat more active in calling for sanctions, but support among the Democratic majority fell below the level at which even a bare majority could be put together to call for sanctions. It is difficult to tie the change in legislative behavior to changed behavior by the executive branch. In fact, one of the most striking aspects of the China-MFN case is the similar behavior by Bush and Clinton, in spite of Clinton's rhetoric condemning the Bush administration's policies toward China. While Clinton at first appeared to take a tougher line, threatening a cutoff of MFN status in 1994, his threat turned out to be a bluff, exposed by the Chinese government's blatant refusal to make any concessions to American demands. In the face of Chinese brinkmanship, the Clinton administration decided to put aside the MFN card and to rely instead on the same methods that had been used in the previous administration. In contrast to congressional reactions through 1992, Clinton's action did not instigate legislation. Congress showed itself willing to follow Clinton's lead on this issue, in effect delegating him significant authority to determine policy toward China. This case thus strongly supports the Delegation Hypothesis, providing evidence that aggregate differences in outcomes under divided and unified party control are explained by different incentives for legislators to delegate to the executive branch.

CONCLUSION

U.S. use of economic sanctions shows definite patterns of legislative activism and the impact of such activism on the ability of the United States to cooperate with other countries, returning us to the central questions of this book. Initial analysis of patterns of use of sanctions and cooperation shows that Congress does not often undertake sanctions unless the president refuses to do so, and that congressional sanctions are on average less effective in generating international cooperation than those originating in the executive branch. However, as in chapter 3's examination of the use of executive agreements and treaties, once we push beyond these initial patterns we find a more nuanced understanding of legislative incentives and capabilities. The simplest tests give results that are consistent with executive-dominance views, but also with models that allow for legislative and partisan influence. We must turn to more complex statistical studies, supplemented by case studies to establish causal relations, in order to sort among alternative models.

In the case of economic sanctions, we find that partisan effects go a long way toward explaining both legislative activity and the success of attempts to generate international cooperation. Under unified government, Congress is generally happy to allow the executive branch to take the lead, and when it does take the initiative into its own hands is not particularly effective. This pattern is consistent with the Delegation Hypothesis. When we introduce divided government into the models, controlling for potentially confounding factors, we find that Congress is more likely to impose sanctions when government is divided. This result is perhaps not terribly surprising, but it leads to the more intriguing and revealing result that congressional success in gaining cooperation from other states increases significantly under divided government. Congressional success when legislators confront an opposition president suggests that Congress does indeed possess the necessary tools to establish credible commitments, but is inhibited in its use of these tools when such action would bring it into conflict with a president of the same party. Since legislators of the same party as the president are more likely (though far from guaranteed, as the South Africa case shows) to have preferences similar to his on foreign policy, greater executive than legislative effectiveness under unified government likely reflects successful delegation rather than executive dominance. The pattern of international cooperation on economic sanctions thus reflects the interaction of the Delegation Hypothesis and the Cooperation Hypothesis.

In sum, systematic analysis of the domestic politics of economic sanctions has provided a powerful tool for testing the central hypotheses of this book about legislative influence and patterns of international cooperation. The major argument of this chapter has been that conflict between the branches motivates Congress to institutionalize its foreign policy activities, thus allowing it to establish more credible commitments to economic sanctions and therefore achieve higher levels of international cooperation. We find evidence that Congress limits its executive discretion under divided government; that it is able to exercise substantial influence on foreign policy, seen through its ability to generate international cooperation with its sanctions policies; and that the executive's ability to gain cooperation declines in the face of conflict between the branches. Although this chapter provided no direct measures of credibility, the logic of credibility is central to determining the incentives facing the branches and developing observable implications of the relationship among divided government, the branch imposing sanctions, and the level of international cooperation achieved. Overall, considering sanctions has provided insight into all of the central concerns of this book. The next chapter follows up on these insights, turning to the history of U.S. food-aid policy to provide another test of the Cooperation Hypothesis.

CHAPTER 5

U.S. Food-Aid Policy: The Politics
of Delegation and Linkage

As a major component of U.S. foreign assistance since the mid-1950s, the food-aid program has been subject to remarkably well-contained debates, escaping the frequent public clashes and negative public opinion that follow other forms of economic and development assistance (Wallensteen 1976, 289). In large part, the relatively strong public support for food assistance comes from its overtly humanitarian character. Food aid goes directly to alleviate hunger and starvation overseas, at least as typically portrayed. However, as this chapter will demonstrate, the motivations and consequences of food aid are more complex than this simple humanitarian motive suggests. In fact, precisely because of its humanitarian character and the support it provides U.S. agriculture, food aid is a popular program. Its popularity means that the political struggle over its use has taken on unique and intriguing dimensions.

This chapter does not examine food aid solely because it provides an illuminating and little-known window on U.S. foreign policy. The history of U.S. food assistance provides the necessary empirical detail and variation for us to examine and link the two central questions of this book: the causes and consequences of variation in executive discretion on issues of international cooperation. Like the previous chapter, the primary focus here is the Delegation and Cooperation Hypotheses. This chapter builds on the findings of earlier chapters to see if they carry through to another issue-area, and to further elaborate the mechanisms of delegation. While some analyses of foreign aid see it as a prime example of how congressional "interference" undermines U.S. policy, I argue here that it makes a positive contribution to the task of establishing credible linkages to other states' policies.

Theories of legislative delegation, as discussed in chapter 2, suggest that legislative willingness to allow the executive a high level of discretion depends on the perception of common interests or other mechanisms that persuade the legislature that the executive will not abuse such discretion. In contrast to most traditional studies of foreign policy, theories of delegation suggest that a high level of executive discretion is not always an advantage in international politics because it creates questions about the credibility of the commitments made by the executive. The scope for executive arbitrariness and the ability of the legislature to undercut commitments at the implementation stage create credibility problems, as summarized in the Credibility Hypothesis.

Such issues of arbitrariness and credibility prove to be central to understanding food-aid policy. As explained below, the high level of support for the food-aid program in Congress has led it to grant the executive an exceptionally high level of discretion, especially when contrasted to other forms of foreign assistance. The executive has taken advantage of this high level of discretion to use food aid strategically, in a sustained way in the cases of aid to India and to South Vietnam discussed in this chapter. Strategic executive action results in a pattern of food-aid provision that varies substantially from year to year, undermining any objectives that require donors to make a long-term commitment to aid provision. When executive manipulation of food aid has the support of Congress, as in the case of pushing India to adopt self-help programs in agriculture, the strategic use of aid can be effective. But when the president uses food aid in ways not supported by the legislature, his behavior leads to legislative action to prevent such uses in the future and to further institutionalization of and limitations on the use of food aid. The pattern of executive-legislative interaction on food aid thus is consistent with the expectations of the Delegation, Credibility, and Cooperation Hypotheses.

Since the history of U.S. food-aid policy is not common knowledge, this chapter begins with a historical overview of the development of the program. One of the key features we see in the history is change in the level of delegation to the executive over time. The second section analyzes the causes and consequences of these changes in the range of executive discretion. We find that the popularity of food aid is the most important factor explaining the level of delegation, and that high levels of delegation give rise to strategic manipulation of aid. As argued in chapter 2, an exchange model of executive-legislative relations is most powerful for explaining the pattern of delegation. The third and fourth sections examine the dynamics of changing patterns of delegation in some important food-aid programs, those to South Vietnam, India, and Egypt. This chapter provides further evidence on the central hypotheses of this book: that legislatures are more willing to delegate to the executive when they share common interests, and that institutionalized legislative participation in processes of international cooperation leads to greater credibility of commitments and so greater cooperation.

HISTORICAL BACKGROUND

The United States developed an institutionalized program of food aid in the early 1950s. During World War II and reconstruction, the United States had provided significant food assistance to Western Europe and Japan. But these programs were seen as temporary, not considered part of the overall foreign-assistance program. Another large but still ad hoc provision of food aid occurred in 1951, when India approached the United States for emergency food-assistance to cope with the effects of massive crop failures (Prasad 1980, 1–43).

At the same time, the agricultural price-support systems initially put in place during the 1930s were beginning to lead to the creation of large "surpluses," food that could not be sold on the open market as it would drive prices below officially established levels. Postwar demand for food imports had masked the size of these surpluses for a while. Prices began to fall in the late 1940s as the demand for exports diminished, then rose with disruptions caused by the Korean War. But by 1953, prices were once again falling as European and Japanese production rose. This presented the Eisenhower administration with a major problem: how to dispose of the agricultural surpluses it was accumulating without undermining its own complex price-support systems.

Finding ways to dispose of surpluses overseas was an attractive policy option, particularly if such action could create regular customers for U.S. exports in the future. With the prodding of Secretary of Agriculture Ezra Taft Benson, President Eisenhower created an interdepartmental committee to study alternative methods of surplus disposal (Peterson 1979, 34). Although Congress was not generally inclined to be generous with foreign aid, strong Republican support on the Hill and a common interest in the surplus-disposal question led Eisenhower to believe that the time was ripe to institutionalize a new program (Peterson 1979, 33). The interdepartmental committee worked quickly and developed a draft surplus-disposal bill by December 1953, leading Eisenhower to call for the creation of such a program in his 1954 budget message. However, disputes about the exact nature of the program led to delays in developing a bill that could be presented to Congress.

One problem in drafting legislation also gave rise to some of the unusual characteristics of executive-legislative interaction on the issue of food aid. While there was enthusiastic support for a large program in the Agriculture Department as well as in Congress, the State Department was much less enthusiastic. State's concern was that a massive American program would depress demand for imports from third countries and so complicate U.S. relations with allies and friends that were agricultural exporters. However, once the House Agriculture Committee began holding its own hearings on the issue of surplus disposal, the specter of losing the initiative to Congress led the executive-branch committee to compromise and develop a bill (Peterson 1979, 41). As it turned out, there was a supportive constituency for surplus disposal in Congress, which in the end prodded the administration into action (Toma 1967, 40). After substantial consultation with interested members of Congress, a bill moved quickly through the legislative process and was signed by July 1954.

The Agricultural Trade Development and Assistance Act of 1954, usually known as Public Law (PL) 480, thus had its origins in an urgent domestic problem with foreign-policy implications. The bill was intended as a measure to dispose of surpluses, which accounts for its popularity in Congress. Only incidentally was it a "foreign-assistance" bill. Until the 1970s, the program was handled entirely within the agriculture committees of the House and Senate, not by the committees on foreign relations. The legislative language specified the objectives of the bill as including surplus-disposal and foreign-policy goals; humanitarian implications were also mentioned, but by no means a fundamental motivation for the creation of this program. Senator Hubert Humphrey, in particular, was intent on designing the program so that it could be used for foreign-policy goals. He recognized, for example, that such usage would require coordination and multiyear planning, rather than an ad hoc approach (Toma 1967, 42).[1]

In contrast to other foreign-aid programs, particularly other forms of economic assistance, PL 480 left the executive with a great deal of discretion. The president was limited by the amount appropriated for surplus disposal in each year and by the commodities determined to be in surplus by the Agriculture Department, but faced almost no restrictions on how these funds were to be used. Congress often appropriated more money than requested by the administration. Legislation specified no criteria for which states could receive food aid, other than the limitation that it go to "friendly nations," which was understood to mean that it could not be supplied to Communist countries. This restriction was not likely to be found constraining by the president, and could at any rate be waived if he determined such a waiver to be in the "national interest." According to a comprehensive study by Trudy Huskamp Peterson (1979), the implementation phase was key to the use of food aid, as it has proven to be in other cases considered in this book. In the food-aid case, "it was here, in the implementation phase, that the administration's real policy freedom lay. The programming priorities, the allocation of resources, the selection of tools, all were left to the discretion of the Republican administrators" (Peterson 1979, 50).

Beyond substantive discretion, the president had an unusually high degree of procedural and institutional discretion. Congress did not specify which agencies were to be involved in administering the food-aid program, leaving this decision entirely up to the president. Conflicts between agencies reappeared as they competed for control over PL 480. Initially, the administration created no formal structure and numerous agencies played some role in dispersing food aid. Quickly finding such a system debilitating, the president created an Interagency Committee on Agricultural Surplus Disposal (Peterson 1979, 45).

Congress did create an agency to handle the technical implementation of PL 480, the Commodity Credit Corporation (CCC), under the auspices of the Department of Agriculture (USDA). The CCC was responsible for financing the sale and export of commodities. However, in creating the CCC, Congress was careful to give it a great deal of independence from legislative oversight, in

---

[1] Pastor (1980, 281) claims that the executive branch tends to favor long-term commitments, while Congress insists on single-year authorizations. However, the cases studied in this chapter do not support his generalization. Often, Congress has favored multiyear programs in order to reduce the level of political manipulation available to the president in short-term programs.

order to provide it the flexibility to respond to "market forces" (Krupadanam 1985, 60). The structure of the CCC freed food aid from the usual mechanism of annual funding reviews and the scrutiny that accompanies them. Congress gave the CCC borrowing authority, so that if the administration wished to conclude an agreement that would exceed appropriations it could simply borrow the necessary funds (Wallerstein 1980, 24–25). Thus even funding provided only a loose, long-term constraint on the president, while in the short term his ability to make spending decisions was nearly unconstrained by the usual legislative processes.

PL 480 consisted of three separate programs, or titles. Title III provided for emergency distribution of food through voluntary agencies or barter. It has always been a small program, and not controversial. Title II is slightly larger and provides for grants of food aid. However, it has also remained small and has escaped controversy, for the most part.

Title I is by far the largest part of PL 480, has been the focus of debates about food aid, and will be the focus of this chapter. It provides for the sale of U.S. agricultural products overseas on special terms. Initially, Title I allowed for the sale of these products by recipient governments for local currency. The local currency generated by such open-market operations was put into a special account for the use of the U.S. government or the local government for purposes specified in legislation. The acceptable purposes were very broadly defined and included general security interests, thus putting few constraints on the use of local currencies. The U.S. government generally used up to 20 percent of the local currencies to support the costs of diplomatic, military, and other operations in the country. The rest could be used by the local government as it desired. The Title I program thus allowed recipient governments to avoid using scarce hard currency (i.e., U.S. dollars) to pay for food imports and provided them with a source of funds to use for domestic purposes. For example, the South Vietnamese government in the early 1970s used the local currency generated from Title I sales to cover a share of its military expenses. In the mid-1970s local currency sales were replaced by long-term dollar credits, as huge accounts of local currencies had accumulated in some cases. Dollar-credit sales still provided the foreign-exchange benefit, but were not quite as subject to misuse by recipient governments as local-currency sales. Amendments to PL 480 in 1985 reinstituted some local-currency sales (USDA 1988, 1–2).

The high level of discretion allowed the executive branch led inevitably, given the differences of opinion about the value of food aid, to battles between agencies. Initially Congress appropriated $700 million for Title I and $300 million for Title II, for a three-year period. The distribution of appropriations across years and across countries was not specified. The administration decided, after internal debates, to send most of this assistance to NATO allies, other European states, and Japan. Putting the program into practice took some time. By the time the first semiannual report appeared, only four Title I agreements had been signed: with Japan, Turkey, Pakistan, and Yugoslavia. No deliveries had yet been made (Peterson 1979, 59). Potential recipients were reluctant to accept some of the commodities the American government was pushing on them, such as tobacco, and disagreed about how much control the United States would have over the use of local currencies generated by PL 480 agreements. Members of Congress expressed concern that the administration was not moving fast enough to complete agreements, indicating their support for food aid. In the early years, the major source of congressional dissatisfaction with PL 480 was that the Eisenhower administration could not move commodities fast enough (Toma 1967, 56; Ruttan 1993, 8, 11).

The political uses of PL 480 aid quickly appeared. In particular, the executive used its discretion in this program to provide "common defense" support to states that it viewed as threatened by the Soviet Union. For example, after Congress denied military assistance to Iran in 1955, the administration concluded a Title I program that provided the Iranian government with funds to meet its military budget (Peterson 1979, 63). It established similar programs in Greece, Formosa [Taiwan], Korea, Burma, India, and Egypt. The executive branch learned quickly that it could use the discretion expressly delegated to it in PL 480 to meet objectives that Congress made difficult to meet through other means. Table 5.1 provides data on the top ten recipients of Title I sales from 1955 through 1988. (Figures have not been corrected for inflation.)

One issue on which Congress decided to assert itself, and thereby marginally reduce executive discretion, was the loan of local currencies generated by Title I to private firms. Initially, the CCC proposed that some portion of these currencies be loaned to American shipping firms in order to make more shipping available. The Commerce Department opposed such a measure, for fear that it would create scarcities of shipping for commercial sales. These debates meant that less than 15 percent of the currency approved for such loans was actually lent in 1956, none of it to American companies. Complaints by American shipping companies moved Congress to action, creating in the 1957 extension of PL 480 the "Cooley Loan" program (named after the House Agriculture Committee chair Harold Cooley) (Peterson 1979, 65–66). The 1957 legislation specified that 25 percent of local currencies generated by Title I sales go to loans to private firms, either American or foreign. This action was a rare case of legislative intrusion into the operation of PL 480 in its early years, and clearly motivated by distinct domestic pressure. In addition, most executive-branch actors supported such a move.

Congress did review the PL 480 program frequently in its early years, but support for it continued to be high and few significant changes, or manipulation of the level of delegation, occurred. The continuing high level of delegation was a conscious legislative choice, rather than a matter of neglect or a low level of interest in the program. Support for the surplus-disposal program remained high and appropriations increased, for example to $3 billion in 1956.

TABLE 5.1
Title 1 Sales, Top Ten Recipients ($ thousands)

	India	Egypt	Pakistan	Indonesia	South Vietnam	South Korea	Bangladesh	Yugoslavia	Brazil	Morocco	Total Title 1 Sales, All Recipients
1955	0	0	34,300	0	0	14,800		78,000	0	0	466,100
1956	0	36,100	28,900	143,900	0	53,700		110,300	73,400	0	958,100
1957	546,000	0	115,100	0	0	21,700		143,200	204,800	0	1,468,500
1958	73,900	0	99,800	0	6,100	69,900		104,600	0	0	995,400
1959	372,600	65,500	124,500	62,400	0	51,100		135,000	0	0	1,129,200
1960	978,800	101,800	172,100	19,000	8,300	0		26,500	0	0	1,702,500
1961	1,717,400	119,600	64,500	29,900	14,400	71,300		40,100	173,700	0	2,727,600
1962	53,000	226,700	826,800	174,900	40,100	101,800		132,600	93,200	22,000	2,206,900
1963	79,200	548,500	0	78,900	35,800	115,800		142,000	68,200	8,000	1,713,500
1964	600,700	22,400	0	0	97,200	192,300		26,300	127,300	5,200	1,411,900
1965	305,100	0	0	0	48,300	0		0	0	11,400	455,600
1966	826,300	60,900	130,900	0	219,200	74,900		0	0	14,000	1,451,400
1967	628,700	0	198,600	23,000	152,700	58,000		0	39,300	40,200	1,355,000
1968	176,900	0	32,700	142,400	40,800	125,800		0	37,100	20,800	776,200
1969	326,600	0	35,800	138,900	140,200	106,000		0	24,500	6,200	1,002,100
1970	196,993	0	66,966	114,499	110,914	102,453		0	20,171	2,221	772,538
1971	146,600	0	63,600	126,600	117,200	0	0	0	0	17,500	1,102,400
1972	33,400	0	67,200	114,900	108,400	0	0	0	0	24,800	1,101,000

Year											
1973	0	0	70,600	103,800	176,900	0	0	0	0	1,200	977,500
1974	0	0	30,242	5,355	233,919	5,726	18,901	0	0	6,927	573,448
1975	103,148	76,106	78,646	3,482	22,625	73,869	204,094	0	0	0	762,316
1976	27,595	147,829	91,497	43,909	0	62,764	156,556	0	0	0	649,792
1977	41,789	198,925	51,359	125,411	0	72,096	49,488	0	0	9,593	759,766
1978	27,793	175,486	59,252	149,491	0	63,306	84,981	0	0	12,168	731,988
1979	0	218,725	38,580	89,636	0	42,094	57,581	0	0	7,266	747,944
1980	0	285,387	49,996	97,061	0	32,532	58,360	0	0	8,705	853,267
1981	0	286,731	48,747	54,497	0	27,576	47,589	0	0	22,462	769,572
1982	0	274,410	49,989	17,421	0	0	63,867	0	0	34,660	722,301
1984	0	246,051	49,995	0	0	0	59,773	0	0	0	762,687
1985	0	218,417	40,657	40,652	0	0	91,651	0	0	41,118	723,589
1986	0	201,345	5,194	3,048	0	0	48,635	0	0	26,531	589,280
1987	0	174,260	37,220	29,203	0	0	75,155	0	0	46,682	695,576
1988	0	179,507	80,000	15,000	0	0	44,960	0	0	35,999	693,290
Total	7,262,518	3,864,679	2,843,740	1,947,075	1,573,058	1,539,516	1,061,491	938,600	861,671	425,632	

Sources: 1955–1969 and 1974–1988, USDA Semiannual and Annual Reports to Congress; 1970–73, Wallerstein (1980), 132.

At this point the administration was more skeptical about the success of PL 480 than was Congress. Concerns arose in State, since the program created potential foreign-policy complications with third countries; Commerce, since PL 480 could compete with commercial exports; and Agriculture, since plans to use PL 480 to encourage agricultural development overseas could lead to the creation of competitors for U.S. exports. "Unlike the questioning administration, Congress easily passed the PL 480 extension in the summer of 1957, largely along lines agreeable to the administration" (Peterson 1979, 83). In this year, the administration had proposed a one-year extension with an appropriation of $1.5 billion for Title I. In a move unimaginable on other foreign-assistance programs, the Congress appropriated for a longer period than the administration requested: $2.25 billion for eighteen months.

Faced with the fact that legislative support was creating a permanent food-aid program, the administration began to consider more seriously how to reform the program so that it would better serve administration ends. The State Department, in a report written by John H. Davis, called for moving to multiyear agreements rather than renewing them on a year-by-year basis. The report reasoned that PL 480 programs might create dependence on food aid, which created a dangerous situation for recipient countries if no multiyear agreements were in place. State supported integrating food aid with development assistance and suggested renaming the program "Food for Peace." Agriculture, with its concern for the interests of American agricultural exporters, resisted the development emphasis and multiyear programming, but such a proposal was nevertheless presented to Congress in 1959 (Peterson 1979, 87–89). Treasury, concerned with budgetary implications, also expressed a preference for year-by-year programming.

The idea of multiyear planning received some support in Congress, for example from Senator Humphrey. Within Congress, two different viewpoints emerged. Agricultural interests favored programs that would dispose of surpluses most efficiently. Since crop prices and supplies varied widely from year to year, these interests preferred to keep programming on a one-year basis. Humphrey and others with stronger foreign-policy interests pushed for recognition of food aid as a major foreign-policy program and for multiyear extensions. The battle between these two factions was resolved in the usual legislative way, by the exercise of procedural power. Agricultural interests had control of the legislation since it originated in the agriculture committees. They killed Humphrey's bill proposing five-year extensions by instead taking up the administration bill, which called for two-year extensions. However, the administration did not get everything it wanted. The program remained focused on surplus disposal, with provisions to use proceeds for economic development killed in committee. The name Food for Peace was officially approved in the 1959 legislation.

The next substantial changes in PL 480 came in the mid-1960s. The legislature moved to emphasize agricultural development, referred to as "self-help measures" in the jargon of the time (Singer, Wood, and Jennings 1987, 23; U.S. Senate 1973a, 158; Nau 1978, 223). Another congressional concern was the accumulation of local currencies. This concern led Congress to legislate a move toward long-term dollar-credit sales, although the change was phased in over a number of years (U.S. House 1964a, 1964b; U.S. Senate 1964, 1965). Congress also tightened up the provisions for sales to Communist countries and those trading with Cuba (Toma 1967, 90–98).

As discussed in more detail below, President Johnson believed PL 480 was a valuable diplomatic tool and used it strategically in interactions with Egypt and India. Because other forms of aid involved many more congressional restrictions, they could not perform the same function if food aid were cut. Therefore, the Johnson administration lobbied to maintain high funding levels for PL 480 (Paarlberg 1985, 116–17). In particular, the administration pushed to remove the requirement that commodities be declared "in surplus" before they could be programmed. This lobbying was successful, with Congress merely requiring USDA to find that commodities were "available" before they could be used for PL 480. While most observers see the legislative revisions of 1966 as substantial (see, e.g., Weinbaum 1982, 118), they involved little decrease in the level of delegation to the executive branch. The emphasis on self-help was one already being pushed by the executive branch, and the provisions to encourage self-help programs were not specific enough to provide many restraints on executive actions. Freedom to choose recipients remained in the hands of the executive.

Legislative changes to PL 480 in the mid-1970s had a larger impact on executive flexibility. In 1973 and 1974, Congress cut off other forms of aid to South Vietnam. In response, as discussed later in this chapter, the administration increased PL 480 sales to the South Vietnamese government. As the overall level of funding for PL 480 fell, sales to South Vietnam and Cambodia became a large share of the total PL 480 budget. The primary changes came in the 1974 Foreign Assistance Act, which now covered food aid (still known as PL 480). One change made local currencies generated by Title I sales no longer eligible to be used by the local government for defense expenditures. The move that generated most executive resistance, however, was a requirement that at least 75 percent of all food aid be distributed to countries with per-capita incomes under $500 (Paarlberg 1985, 119). While this provision still allowed the executive branch a significant level of discretion—after all, many countries had per-capita incomes below $500, and 25 percent of expenditures were freely available for political purposes—it did signal the end of the massive fluctuations in food-aid distribution that had characterized the earlier years of PL 480. Congress also wrote in a provision prohibiting food aid to governments that consistently violated human rights, although the country-specific legislation tying aid to human rights that appeared in development aid did not extend to food aid (see Martin 1992a, 99–130).

Since the changes of the mid-1970s, the debate over PL 480 has been much less intense and legislative changes to the program have been modest. In 1977, a "Food for Development" program was established, specifying that 15 percent of long-term credit sales be distributed to countries that agreed to use the benefits to encourage agricultural development (Revel and Riboud 1986, 163). In 1984, the Reagan administration announced measures that would increase exports. These measures, while responding to a Task Force on Hunger report, were also motivated by increasing surpluses. The agricultural-development program became known as Food for Progress and was intended to relieve financial pressures in countries with large debt problems, as well as to increase production capacities. The program also created emergency stockpiles of food in Africa and an emergency food-aid fund of 1.5 million tons of grain (Revel and Riboud 1986, 163). In addition, the sale of agricultural products for local currencies was reintroduced in this "Food for Development" initiative (Ruttan 1993, 29). A general review of foreign-assistance programs at the end of the Reagan administration led to legislative reform of food aid in 1990. The major impact of these reforms was to concentrate authority for implementation in the hands of AID and USDA, reducing the role of the State Department and NSC (Ruttan 1993, 32–38). The food-aid program continues to respond to the agricultural situation in the United States. For example, with hog prices at a thirty-year low, domestic pressures to include pork in the "Food for Peace program" appeared in 1998 (*New York Times*, 13 December 1998, 29).

EXPLAINING DELEGATION AND ITS CONSEQUENCES

The history of the food-aid program allows us to test a number of the hypotheses developed in chapter 2. The legislative history just summarized provides a direct test of the Delegation Hypothesis, which states that the level of delegation to the executive will increase as common interests between the branches increase. In the context of food aid, predictions about delegation become slightly more complex because there are at least two distinct policy dimensions involved: surplus disposal and foreign policy. This section will develop an exchange model of interbranch relations that explains the pattern of delegation observed. Food aid also allows us to test the Credibility and Cooperation Hypotheses: that the credibility of commitments and level of cooperation, defined as mutual policy adjustment, increase when the legislature is involved in policymaking in an institutionalized, regularized way. These propositions will be tested most directly in the two case studies in the following section.

International cooperation is an exchange relationship. States cooperate when they make mutual adjustments in their policies. Mutual policy adjustments rely on reciprocity, one state exchanging its own policy modifications for those of others. Based on this definition, it is clear that uses of foreign assistance other than the purely altruistic or humanitarian are instances of international cooperation.[2] As one analyst has noted, "Just as there is no free lunch, there is nothing like aid without strings" (Krupadanam 1985, 107). Sometimes the terms of exchange are quite obvious and explicit, as when the United States agreed to increase various forms of assistance to Egypt and Israel as part of the package of deals concluded at Camp David in the late 1970s. Another common form of explicit exchange, but one not considered in this chapter, is "tied aid," where recipients agree to use some portion of aid to purchase goods from the donor. Sometimes the terms of exchange are not made explicit, even in private discussions, with aid instead forming part of a longer-term pattern of diffuse reciprocity between friendly states (Keohane 1986). The policy adjustments that aid recipients make are sometimes political, as in the Camp David example, and sometimes economic, as when recipients agree to modify domestic or foreign economic policies as a condition for receiving aid. Studying patterns of delegation in foreign-aid programs thus gives insight into the more general problem of patterns of delegation in international cooperation.

Explaining Delegation

This chapter considers both the causes and the consequences of delegation to the executive branch on U.S. food-aid policy. The historical overview has introduced the basic puzzles about the level of delegation. Why does the executive have substantially greater discretion on the implementation of food aid than on other foreign-assistance programs? Within this generally high level of delegation, how can we account for changes such as the reduction of executive discretion in the mid-1970s? I argue here that high levels of executive discretion are not the result of legislative ignorance, lack of interest, or inability to control what the executive does in foreign affairs. Instead, consistent with modern theories of executive-legislative relations, the decision to allow the executive high levels of discretion was an intentional one, motivated by high support for agricultural-surplus disposal in Congress.

Variation in delegation fit closely the patterns found in other chapters. Legislative distrust of the executive branch, for example that generated by blatant misuse of aid appropriations, prompts tighter oversight. Divided government in this case tends to covary with the level of distrust, and so is not possible to distinguish the two effects reliably. However, studies such as Peterson's (1979, 50)

---

[2] For an argument that altruism is a major motivation for aid policies, see Lumsdaine (1993). However, Lumsdaine acknowledges that aid programs initially motivated by humanitarian concerns can take on political dimensions, making their characterization as an instance of international cooperation accurate.

argue that presidents are more successful in gaining high discretion on food aid if they confront a Congress controlled by their own party.

To summarize the pattern of delegation from the historical overview given above, in 1954 the level of discretion allowed the executive was extraordinary. While executive discretion continues to be high relative to other foreign-aid programs, it has varied substantially over time. Congress seriously reconsidered the level of delegation in 1964 and 1966, and again in 1973–74. However, these reviews had different outcomes. In the 1960s, changes in delegation were quite modest. The changes of the 1970s were much more significant. In this section, I discuss the way in which the basic pattern of delegation is explained by congressional attitudes toward the program. Within these broad parameters, legislative trust of the executive seems to explain the difference between the 1960s and the 1970s.

The basic idea, one that may look counterintuitive at first glance, is that Congress is likely to delegate high levels of authority to the executive branch on those programs to which it is most favorably disposed, even if the executive branch is more skeptical of the value of those programs. Why wouldn't Congress choose to micromanage the most popular programs? The answer lies in the dynamics of executive-legislative relations, and the logic becomes clearer if we conceive of these relations as a set of exchange relationships. Consider the debate over some new program, such as food aid in the 1950s. The more the proposed program is highly valued by both branches, the more "surplus" will be generated by implementing it. Relative to the status quo ex ante, when the program does not exist, there are many Pareto-improving outcomes available for a popular program. Any of these outcomes generates a surplus—benefits relative to the status quo—that can be distributed among the relevant players, here the legislature and the executive.

Any exchange relationship that generates a surplus thus presents the potential for a battle over its distribution. If the executive and legislature are in entire agreement about the specific characteristics of the program, no battle will occur. But this is an extreme and highly unusual case. Instead, it is nearly always true that a number of interested parties will have different ideas over the specific characteristics of the program and will be willing to fight to see these preferences reflected in the final legislation. Even on very popular programs we can therefore expect to see intense debates, threats of holding up legislation, and other maneuvers typical of legislative activity in democracies. Such debates are about the distribution of the surplus generated by a new program.

This discussion may be clarified with an example. Figure 5.1 presents a simplified version of the debate over a food-aid program. It shows the debate having two dimensions, the total level of aid provided and the ability to direct it for political purposes. These two dimensions reflect the exchange relationship between the branches, as for example when in 1975 Senator Humphrey offered

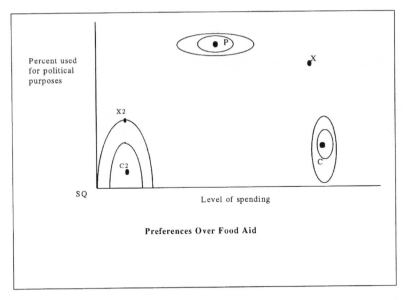

Figure 5.1. An exchange model of food-aid institutions.

the administration a deal in which Congress linked the ability to allocate aid for foreign-policy purposes to higher expenditures (Destler 1978, 63).

In this figure, the status quo (assumed to be the reversion point if no program is approved) is zero spending on food aid. The program shown here has two dimensions over which the branches of government have some disagreement. The first, on the horizontal axis, is the level of aid. In this figure, Congress prefers a higher level of spending than does the president. The vertical dimension shows the percent of food aid that will be spent for purely political purposes, such as supporting the military programs of allies. This figure shows the president wishing to spend a higher percent of aid on political purposes than does Congress. The president's ideal point is "P," and that of the swing voter in Congress "C."

As shown here, a large number of programs potentially could be approved. Because there is strong support for having *some* food-aid program, many outcomes make both actors happier than the status quo, that is, they are Pareto-improving. The question is exactly which outcome will result from the legislative process. This debate generates a classic bargaining problem, with players attempting to pull the eventual outcome as close to their ideal point as possible. The predicted outcome depends on a large number of factors: bargaining skill, institutional details, ability to link to other issues, ability to make credible threats, discount rates (i.e., patience), for example. All of these fall into the general category of "bargaining power," and make precise predictions of outcomes a hazardous endeavor. In the case of food aid, however, as in other cases of multiple-dimension issues, one factor is consistently important: differing preference intensities across the dimensions.

Different preference intensities create potential for mutually advantageous exchanges, and exemplify situations where heterogeneity of actors facilitates cooperation, rather than hindering it (Martin 1994). Preference intensities refer to the degree to which an actor is willing to trade off one good in exchange for another. If two goods are valued equally, only one-for-one exchanges maintain the same payoff. But if one good is valued more highly than the other, then an actor will be willing to trade off more than one of the latter in exchange for one of the former. In a spatial diagram such as that in figure 5.1, an actor that valued both goods—ability to use aid for political purposes and the overall level of aid—with the same intensity would have circular indifference curves. An actor that valued one more highly than the other, in contrast, would have elongated indifference curves, illustrating the willingness to exchange a number of units on one dimension in exchange for smaller movement on the other.

In figure 5.1, the sample indifference curves are drawn to show that Congress cares more intensely about the level of spending than about the political uses of aid. A small change in the level of spending creates the same change in C's utility as a relatively large change in the use of aid for political purposes. This characterization of congressional preferences seems likely, given the origins of food aid as a surplus-disposal program and its dominance by the agricultural committees for the first couple of decades of its existence. P, on the other hand, cares more intensely about the political purposes of aid than about spending. This characterization also seems uncontroversial.

Different preference intensities, rather than creating irreconcilable differences, create scope for mutually beneficial bargains. The president, as portrayed here, is willing to make relatively large concessions on the level of aid, but will play tough on the issue of being able to use aid for political purposes. Congress, in contrast, is quite happy to make concessions on the political uses of aid, but not willing to do so on the overall level of aid. This leads us to expect that the outcome of bargaining will tend to reflect congressional preferences on the level of aid and executive preferences on how it will be used. We should therefore expect the outcome to fall somewhere near the point marked "X" in figure 5.1.

The analysis summarized in figure 5.1 is not intended to make a precise prediction, which would require much more detailed information about executive and legislative preferences than we have. The point is general and robust: actors will be most willing to make concessions on those issues of least consequence to themselves, and the outcome of bargaining will reflect these preferences. Arriving at mutually advantageous deals creates potential conflict over the distribution of the surplus the deals generate. If the actors have differing

preference intensities, we have a strong clue as to how these distributional conflicts will be resolved. In the case of food aid, it seems unproblematic to claim
that the nature of the program meant that Congress cared most intensely about
shipping high levels of agricultural products overseas, while the executive
branch was more sensitive to the foreign-policy and political implications of aid.

This line of analysis leads us to an answer to the puzzle of why the president
was able to gain such a high level of flexibility on how aid was to be used. The
primary congressional concern was to put a surplus-disposal program into
place, and the strong desire to do so created the potential for the executive
branch to get its way on other dimensions of the program, such as how this aid
was to be used. If Congress had not been so enthusiastic about the program, we
would expect a very different outcome in terms of the level of delegation. If
food aid were not popular, Congress would not have been so willing to make
concessions on other dimensions for the sake of institutionalizing a program,
and we should expect to see a lower level of delegation with more stringent conditions for the use of aid written into the legislation and greater legislative oversight. In fact, this is what we see on aid for development, which does not have
the benefit of a large, enthusiastic constituency that food aid does. On development assistance, in contrast to food aid, Congress has been more willing to
micromanage, write in stringent conditions, and generally frustrate the executive's desire for flexibility in the use of aid.

In figure 5.1, the points C2 and X2 illustrate the outcome we would expect
if Congress were not supportive of high levels of spending on food aid. I have
assumed here similar kinds of preference intensities as in the former example,
but a Congress that is more reluctant to spend money on an aid program. Because Congress is reluctant, the set of points that are Pareto-improving relative
to zero spending is significantly reduced, giving Congress enhanced bargaining power. Now, Congress is only willing to approve programs that fall within
the area enclosed by the indifference curve that goes through the SQ point. Assuming that the president does the best possible job bargaining, we would still
expect to see a reduction in the level of discretion allowed him, relative to the
X outcome. Instead, we might expect an outcome like X2. X2 leaves Congress
indifferent between approving the aid program and zero spending, while it gives
the president the maximum possible level of discretion, which is the dimension
that matters the most to him. For an aid program with widespread support, but
below that illustrated by point C, we would expect an outcome somewhere
between X and X2. This is likely the situation that arose on PL 480 in 1974,
discussed below.

The general point that I wish to make here is one that should be familiar to
anyone who has been in the position of buying a car, a house, or any other good
that involves bargaining with the seller over the price. One of the biggest mistakes a potential buyer can make is to signal a high level of enthusiasm for mak-

Figure 5.2. Total grain surplus.

ing a deal to the seller. The buyer who falls in love with a house, and allows the seller to see this, is unlikely to get as good a deal as one who plays hard to get. The intense desire to complete a deal puts the other player in a stronger bargaining position, allowing her to acquire most of the surplus generated by the deal. In the case of food aid, Congress was an enthusiastic, motivated "buyer" that did not conceal this information from the executive. The executive branch took advantage of the situation to get its way on the specific characteristics of the food-aid program, particularly the level of delegation to the executive.

If this explanation of the high level of executive discretion is correct, it suggests a hypothesis about how the level of delegation will change over time. If delegation results from strong congressional support for an ambitious surplus-disposal program, we should see the level of delegation decreasing when surplus disposal is less important. For example, in years where agricultural output is low and prices high, we should see the level of delegation being questioned. When Congress is no longer so anxious to dispose of agricultural surpluses, it is in the position of a reluctant buyer rather than an enthusiastic one and so better positioned to get its way on other issues.

In fact, the correlation between small agricultural surpluses and rethinking the level of delegation appears to be strong. For the first decade of the PL 480 program, surpluses were large and we saw no change in the high level of delegation to the executive. But bad harvests and increased demand for exports

Figure 5.3. Wheat surplus.

meant that in 1964–66 there was little need for surplus disposal. This coincides with the first substantial reforms to the program, put into place in 1966. Figure 5.2 shows the total grain surplus for 1962 (the earliest year for which data are available) through 1976.[3] This figure clearly shows the rapid drop in surpluses from 1962 through 1966. In order to provide more background, figure 5.3 shows the surplus figures for wheat, figures which go back to the 1950s. Here we see a similar pattern of declining surpluses, beginning in 1960.

In 1973–74 we once again see no problem of surpluses, as figure 5.2 shows surpluses again declining rapidly from 1971 to 1974. In fact, the situation at this time was one of rapidly rising domestic prices for food (Wallensteen 1976, 286). Figure 5.4 shows the prices received by American farmers for food and feed grains, indexed so that the average price in 1910 to 1914 is set at 100. This figure shows a dramatic escalation in 1971 to 1974. Food prices shot up from an index level of 166 in 1971 to 529 in 1974, more than a threefold increase. The rapid rise in prices coincides with the most significant changes in PL 480, the imposition of the requirement that 75 percent of Title I sales go to poor countries. This requirement represented a major decline in the level of delegation to the executive, one that was fiercely resisted. Arthur Mead, a former sales man-

[3] The data for figures 5.2, 5.3, and 5.4 are all obtained from U.S. Department of Agriculture, *Agricultural Statistics,* various years.

Figure 5.4. Prices for food and feed grains.

ager for PL 480, went so far as to suggest that these stringent legislative conditions led him to think that USDA would be happy to get rid of the program
altogether (Hopkins and Puchala 1980, 93).

However, changing surplus and price levels do not fully explain the observed
delegation. The level of delegation changed more significantly in 1974 than in
1966. This variation appears to be accounted for in part by factors discussed
further elsewhere in this book. In 1966, Democratic President Johnson faced a
Democratic Congress generally supportive of his foreign-policy goals. In 1974,
in contrast, a Republican president faced a Democratic Congress incensed
about abuse of executive power and at odds with his foreign policy, particularly
in Southeast Asia. Divided government and incompatible goals led to a much
more substantial reclamation of authority in 1974 than in 1966. But common
to both instances of reform was the fact of declining agricultural surpluses, thus
a decrease in congressional enthusiasm for PL 480. The price changes in 1972–
74 were more substantial than in 1966, also contributing to greater congressional activism in the later period. Overall, common interests, in this case a
function of the need to dispose of agricultural surpluses and divided government, are a direct predictor of the level of delegation that we see. The pattern
of delegation on food aid firmly supports the Delegation Hypothesis, as agricultural surpluses and unified government led to common interests and so a high
level of delegation; their absence led to a declining level of delegation.

The Consequences of Delegation

The next question is to ask whether changes in delegation have any impact on the nature and uses of food aid. In particular, we are interested in the ways that changing levels of delegation influence patterns of international cooperation. High levels of delegation can have the consequence of undermining the credibility of commitments. In the case of food aid, we need to determine whether credibility is an important issue, then examine how it has been influenced by delegation patterns.

Food aid is a highly fungible resource. Particularly as Title I was originally fashioned, it provided the executive branch with a tool that appeared designed for political manipulation. Title I sales provided the recipient government with a source of local currency, a budget resource raised without imposing any immediate costs on society in the form of taxes.[4] This money could be used to cover military expenditures, provide social services, or otherwise meet pressing demands of developing countries. Thus, while some states balked at having to accept the large quantity of goods being pressed on them by the United States, or at the specific commodities they were asked to accept, recipient governments generally saw food aid as a valuable political resource. This fact, plus the great leeway allowed the administration in the distribution of PL 480 appropriations, led the president to see it as a valuable political resource, one that could be used strategically to meet shifting foreign-policy demands (Garst and Barry 1990, 9).

As discussed above, various agencies had qualms about some aspects of PL 480, including its negative effects on other agricultural exporters or the potential competition it would create for U.S. exports. The major benefit PL 480 would provide for the executive branch was precisely its political value. While other sources of foreign aid were subject to congressional constraints, food aid was not. From the beginning, presidents used food aid to meet foreign-policy goals, rewarding friends, punishing enemies, and enticing those states sitting on the fence. We can see the effects of this strategic use of aid in the patterns shown in table 5.1. First, we notice that the top recipients of PL 480–Title I sales have been states of great political importance to the United States at some time in the post–World War II era. Second, we notice that the distribution of food aid to these states does not follow the pattern of consistent disbursements we would expect from an institutionalized program. Instead, the numbers exhibit great variability. A state may get a huge amount of food aid in one year, little or none the next. This is the pattern we should expect if food aid is being manipulated strategically to serve short-term foreign-policy goals, as a reward or punishment for recipients' behavior.

As noted above, observers saw in the early years of the program that food aid was being used to provide "common defense" benefits for U.S. allies such as

---

[4] There has been much debate about longer-term costs of these aid programs, particularly about whether they inhibit the development of domestic agriculture. See Ruttan (1993, 65–127).

Iran and Greece. During the Eisenhower administration, leaks from the State Department indicated that Title I sales were used to twist the arms of Ecuador and Colombia in various foreign-policy disputes (Peterson 1979, 61). In the 1960s, a major political use of food aid involved relations with India, which will be discussed in more depth later in this chapter. The Kennedy administration used PL 480 to punish Indonesia for its conflict with Malaysia in 1963, while Nixon tied it to restraint of textile exports from South Korea. Ford followed the pattern by cutting food aid to punish Tanzania and Guyana for votes in the UN (Cohen 1988, 4). In Chile, the United States cut off food aid after President Allende took office, then quickly reinstated it after his overthrow in 1973 (Hopkins and Puchala 1980, 86; Wallerstein 1980, 156–60).

Food aid thus proved to be a valuable resource with which to pursue short-term goals, as many observers have noted. In many cases, credibility was not much of an issue. The United States was not looking, in these situations, for a long-term commitment of specific investments in exchange for food aid. The exchange of political benefits and receipt of aid were nearly simultaneous, not creating the opportunities for reneging that would occur if exchanges were spread out over time. However, as time went on, the objectives pursued by the United States became more ambitious and so created more serious credibility problems.

Under what conditions is credibility an important consideration in bilateral aid programs? Credibility concerns would arise if the United States were looking for the recipient to sink investments into areas such as agricultural development (Waltz 1967, 197; J. Nelson 1968, 73). Once such investments are made, they cannot be shifted easily into other uses, creating problems of irreversibility, as discussed in figure 2.1. Once the investment is made, the donor would have little reason to carry through on its commitment to provide aid in the future. This is a typical problem of investing assets in ways that exhibit irreversibility, very similar to the situation of firms deciding whether to make specific investments that have been studied in the theory of the firm and transaction-costs economics (Williamson 1985). Unless the donor can establish a credible commitment to continue providing aid in the future, recipients will be unwilling to make the necessary shift of resources into specific investments.

A similar problem arises if the donor is asking the recipient to undertake difficult policy reforms that will need to be implemented over a number of years. Unless the recipient is fairly sure that aid will indeed be forthcoming in future years, there will be little incentive to implement in a sincere manner the reforms being demanded (U.S. Senate 1974b, 32). Another situation of this type arises if food aid is being used to begin a durable relationship that will provide benefits to both parties into the future. Credibility matters if the offer of aid is intended as a signal of a desire to establish a long-term cooperative relationship. From the U.S. perspective, such a relationship requires establishing its willingness to provide regular aid in order to maintain its utility as a mechanism of influence in the future. To give one example of this motivation at work, in the late 1960s the executive branch was anxious to continue providing food aid to India in spite of the disappearance of domestic agricultural surpluses. In response, the Secretary of Agriculture actually approved sowing more ground to produce wheat in order to meet the expected demand from India. The desire to maintain a means with which to influence Indian policy in the future lay behind this decision (as did the Indian decision to move toward self-reliance in the agricultural sphere) (Krupadanam 1985, 114).

A conditional commitment to continue providing aid in the future is necessary in all of these cases. However, as structured and implemented, PL 480 was not designed to provide the necessary reassurances in cases that required long-term conditional commitments. The executive branch had the scope to act as arbitrarily as it liked with this program, and made only short-term agreements with recipients in order to keep its flexibility high. We have already mentioned how the distribution of aid shows large fluctuations from year to year, giving recipients little reason to find U.S. commitments dependable. In addition, recipients were well aware that PL 480 was a surplus-disposal program. This suggested to them that commitments from the executive branch might not be credible. If harvests in the United States were poor, appropriations for PL 480 would fall and the temptation would be high to renege on promises of providing aid. On the other hand, when surpluses were large, the administration was under intense pressure to move grain overseas. This meant that threats to cut off aid if recipients reneged on their part of the deal also lacked credibility.

All in all, the structure of the PL 480 program meant that while it was a valuable tool for pursuing relatively easy, one-shot political arm-twisting, it was a poor tool for pursuing more ambitious foreign-policy strategies that would require longer-term credible commitments. Such uses of food aid would require steps to assure recipients that the United States would carry through on its threats and promises. In the case study later in this chapter on food aid to India, we see these credibility dynamics in action. First, we notice that when India begins to see food aid as part of an overall economic-reform program, it asks the United States for long-term commitments, not just emergency shipments of food. Second, we see that President Johnson takes steps such as working to put together a supportive congressional coalition to enhance the credibility of his commitments. In the case of aid to Egypt also discussed below, because the United States in the late 1970s was promising a long-term commitment of high continuing levels of aid, President Carter needed to take the even more substantial step of institutionalizing the PL 480 commitment (as well as other aid commitments) to Egypt.

As the Credibility Hypothesis proposes, on food aid logic suggests that executive flexibility may not be the great benefit in the pursuit of foreign policy that traditional analyses suggest. Once we begin considering the conditions necessary to convince recipients to undertake significant policy adjustments that might involve multiyear commitments or specific investments, the lack of institutionalization inherent in high levels of executive discretion can present real obstacles to effective international cooperation. On these more ambitious attempts to engage recipients, the success of executive efforts will be constrained by the ability to make credible commitments. Commitments can gain credibility if there is obvious widespread legislative support for the president's efforts, or if they are institutionalized. In the presence of questionable legislative support for the president's foreign-policy goals, for example as we often see under divided government, it is unlikely that an ad hoc use of food aid to pressure recipients to undertake difficult reforms will be successful. The rest of this chapter explores issues raised here about the causes and consequences of delegation by looking at three specific cases: the use of food aid to provide military support for Cambodia and South Vietnam in 1973–74; Johnson's use of food aid to manipulate Indian policies in 1964–66; and the tying of food aid to political developments in the Middle East in the late 1970s.

Changes in Delegation: The "Food for War" Debate

Throughout its history PL 480 aid, particularly Title I, has been used to pursue the foreign-policy objectives of the president. Such uses of aid were recognized explicitly in the initial PL 480 legislation and are clear when we look at the history of the program. Following in this tradition, Presidents Nixon and Ford took advantage of food aid to shift resources to the governments of Cambodia and South Vietnam in 1973–74, once other sources of financial support had been cut by Congress (Destler 1980, 78). This particular use of aid was extremely unpopular and poorly timed to coincide with declining levels of agricultural surpluses in the United States. It led to the largest reclaiming of authority seen in the history of the food-aid program, consistent with the Delegation Hypothesis.

The concern over the redirection of food aid to Vietnam became an issue during the consideration of food aid legislation in 1973. PL 480 programming showed a large increase in Title I sales-agreements with South Vietnam. They rose from $108 million in 1972 to $177 million in 1973, making South Vietnam the largest single recipient. Sales to Cambodia were also climbing rapidly, at a time when small surpluses meant that the total size of the PL 480 program was falling. Cambodia received almost no PL 480 support prior to 1971. By fiscal year 1973, it received $25.8 million (U.S. House 1974, 390). Food aid provided military assistance to the South Vietnamese government, as it used the proceeds from Title I sales to contribute to its military budget under the common-defense provisions of PL 480 agreements (U.S. Senate 1973b, 147). Wallerstein (1980, 46) calculates that by 1973 nearly half of total food aid was going to just South Vietnam and Cambodia, at a time when the world food situation was bleaker than it had been for years. Widespread food shortages in 1973 meant that world prices were climbing rapidly. Because PL 480 appropriations took the form of dollars rather than tons of commodities, rising prices meant that smaller amounts of agricultural products were actually shipped. A report by a Senate Select Committee on Nutrition and Human Needs (U.S. Senate, 1974a, 26) found that these factors led to a "drastic" decline in the amount of food shipped in 1973, at the same time large amounts were being redirected to Southeast Asia. (See also U.S. Senate 1974a, 9.)

In addition to the diversion of Title I sales, Nixon took the even more unpopular step of introducing political criteria into the disbursement of Title II funds. Previously, these funds had been channeled solely through voluntary agencies and so were relatively insulated from political pressure. The introduction of political considerations led voluntary agencies and the multilateral World Food Program to protest loudly (Wallerstein 1980, 47). The diversion of resources to Southeast Asia coincided with a major shift in the bureaucratic structure for administering food aid. The Agriculture Department and the Agency for International Development (AID) were marginalized, with the National Security Council (NSC) playing a much larger role (U.S. House 1974, 392). The secretary of agriculture, Earl Butz, reacted to this marginalization, resulting congressional constraints on food aid, and low surpluses by developing a "zero" request for PL 480 funds for fiscal year 1975 (U.S. House 1974, 392). The attempt to circumvent congressional limitations on direct military assistance was obvious, and led to an outcry on the Hill (Wallerstein 1980, 48). Congress, in the Foreign Assistance Act of 1973, terminated the use of local currencies generated from Title I sales for common-defense purposes unless it specifically approved such use (Cohen 1988, 7).

However, given the high level of fungibility of the proceeds from Title I sales, simply putting this restriction on the use of local currencies into legislation had little impact. Proceeds went directly into the budget of the recipient government, and so tracing them was impossible. Even if the proceeds could not be used directly for military support, they allowed other budgetary resources to be shifted in this direction (U.S. House 1974, 387). The figures for fiscal year 1974 show the failure of this modest reform, as Title I assistance to South Vietnam again grew at a rapid pace, reaching $234 million. In Cambodia, where the administration had projected $30 million in Title I sales in 1974, levels instead skyrocketed to $194 million (U.S. House 1974, 390). Cohen (1988, 7–8) finds that in fiscal year 1974, 70 percent of the total concessional-sales budget, or 48 percent of all food-aid funds, went to just South Vietnam and Cambodia.

Congress responded to the failure of its first attempt to reclaim authority by taking measures that could not be so easily circumvented by a determined executive. For fiscal year 1975, the food aid legislation required that a minimum of 70 percent of Title I sales go to countries designated by the UN as those "most seriously affected" by economic distress (Wallerstein 1980, 48). In 1975 legislation, this figure was changed to 75 percent, and the criterion shifted to countries with a maximum per-capita income of $300 in order to assure better executive compliance (Udell 1976, 64; Wallerstein 1980, 49; Cohen 1988, 9). The income limit was raised in 1977 to $520, as the lower level had created problems when inflation led countries to "graduate" and no longer be eligible for food aid. In contrast to efforts in the 1950s and 1960s on the part of Senator Humphrey to direct food aid to poor countries, in the face of executive abuse of discretion real constraints were written into the 1975 legislation (Ruttan 1993, 27). The 1975 measures still allowed the president substantial flexibility to distribute food aid for political purposes. Twenty-five percent of Title I could be used as the president desired, and within the 75 percent going to poor countries he or she could pick and choose recipients at will. However, the measures constituted a comprehensive restructuring of the food-aid program and did have the effect of ending the massive redirection of food aid to replace military aid, sending a signal that Congress was able and willing to respond to executive actions by rewriting legislation. Title I sales to South Vietnam declined to $22.6 million for fiscal year 1975.

Taking a longer view, these attempts to impose conditions on the use of food aid and provide some institutional structure appear to have had a substantial impact. In contrast to the wild ups and downs of food-aid distributions in the first two decades of the program, since the mid-1970s we see more stable patterns of distribution (see table 5.1). Part of this stability is accounted for by the special case of Egypt, discussed below. However, even outside Egypt we see consistent flows to countries such as Pakistan and Bangladesh. Political motives are still central. But the political use of aid now takes place within a more regulated, constrained policy environment, providing a degree of stability and predictability missing when the distribution of funds was the sole prerogative of the executive branch.

As long as Congress strongly supported food aid as a means to dispose of large agricultural surpluses, and the president did not blatantly direct these funds to pursue objectives at odds with expressed congressional will, the level of delegation of authority to the executive on food aid was extraordinarily high. As food aid remains a popular program in comparison to other kinds of foreign aid, the level of delegation remains high. But the coincidence of declining surpluses, divided government, and large executive missteps in the early 1970s led to substantial changes in PL 480. These changes have narrowed the scope of its utility for controversial foreign-policy goals and that created more predictable commitments to other goals, such as encouraging agricultural development in poor countries (Weinbaum 1986, 16). The days when the president could send 70 percent of total concessional food sales to just two countries in opposition to congressional preferences have come to an end.

FOOD AID AND CONDITIONAL COMMITMENTS: PL 480 IN INDIA AND EGYPT

The flexibility delegated the executive on the distribution of food aid made it more readily available as a presidential tool to link to policy changes in recipients than were other forms of aid. However, the logic of delegation developed in this book suggests that the ability of the president to use aid effectively as a political lever will be constrained by the ability to make credible conditional commitments. The necessary conditions include a credible commitment to cut food aid if policy changes are not forthcoming, even if Congress is pushing for rapid disposal of agricultural surpluses, and a commitment to continue providing aid, even if Congress is not wholly behind the specific foreign policies being pursued by the president. Such credibility is difficult to achieve in an environment with the low level of institutionalization of most PL 480 programs. On the one hand, the high level of presidential discretion creates scope for arbitrariness. On the other, the fact that Congress retains the power to override presidential actions as it did in the 1970s means that commitments can only be credible if there is some minimal level of support in the legislature for presidential actions. Two cases that allow us to examine the limits of the ability to use PL 480 for strategic purposes and the role of institutionalization in making commitments credible are the histories of food aid to India and to Egypt.

India: The Short Tether and Self-Help

U.S. food aid to India followed a tumultuous path in the 1950s to 1960s. In 1951, responding to failed harvests, India requested and received emergency food-assistance from the United States. Since the United States had large supplies of agricultural products and ocean transport, it was the only reasonable source of emergency assistance on the scale required. At this time, the United States was not facing an agricultural-surplus problem because of the effects of the Korean War. However, President Truman saw the Indian request for assistance as an opportunity to establish a potentially profitable relationship and was sympathetic to it. While India had asked for soft loans, Truman asked Congress instead for a grant of $190 million. Given the lack of agricultural surpluses and public hostility to India for its recent recognition of China and criticism of U.S. actions in Korea, Congress was not highly sympathetic to this request and refused to approve a grant. It did nevertheless approve a loan of $190 million in the India Emergency Food Assistance Act of 1951 (Krupadanam 1985, 101–103).

India did not receive any food aid under PL 480 Title I during its first two years (1955 and 1956), but received over half a billion dollars under this program in 1957, far more than any other recipient. Over the next two decades, levels of food aid fluctuated wildly. In 1961 Title I agreements with India reached a maximum level of $1.7 billion, more than the total yearly appropriations for PL 480 during most of the 1970s and 1980s. An agreement reached in 1960 committed the United States to send India more than a fifth of its entire wheat crop over the next four years. In 1962, PL 480 shipments fell to just $53 million, but climbed again to $601 million in 1964. (See table 5.1 for details.) In the 1970s the level of food aid to India was much smaller, and India removed itself entirely from Title I by 1979.

The political, economic, and social interests of India and the United States in the 1960s created a situation where both recognized large potential "mutual advantage" available through PL 480 (Krupadanam 1985, 15–17). For the United States, food aid to India provided humanitarian and surplus-disposal benefits, as well as potential strategic advantages if the conditions on the release of aid could be made credible and manipulated. Of course, given the first two motives, consistently following the third would prove difficult. India did not see any strategic advantages, given the country's strong desire to establish an independent foreign policy, including the right to criticize U.S. actions abroad (especially in Southeast Asia). However, disastrous economic conditions in India made the possibility of forgoing U.S. food aid out of the question, for domestic political reasons as well as the simple and overwhelming need to feed people. The possibility of massive starvation and widespread famine threatened in the mid-1960s. Any Indian government that neglected to take advantage of the American food aid on offer would not only be cruel but would create such domestic instability that its survival would be highly questionable.

The food-aid relationship between India and the United States began in the early 1950s and peaked in 1965–67 as a result of two successive failed harvests in India. As discussed above, in spite of major congressional overhauls of the PL 480 program in 1964 and 1966, during this period the president retained a high level of discretion to distribute food-aid funds as he wished. President Johnson took advantage of this situation in the mid-1960s to push India to pursue policy changes on both the foreign-policy and economic fronts, through the mechanism of putting a "short tether" on the release of aid shipments. On foreign policy, Johnson used food aid to punish India for criticism of U.S. actions abroad, particularly in Southeast Asia, and for Indian resistance to concluding a settlement with Pakistan over Kashmir. On economic policy, Johnson tied food aid to giving high priority to programs of agricultural development. The latter linkage was supported by Congress, as it was consistent with the emphasis on self-help that appeared in the revisions to PL 480 legislation in the 1960s.

The stage for Johnson's short-tether policy was set by the decline of U.S. surpluses by the end of 1961, due to poor harvests and the implementation of domestic agricultural policies, combined with India's desperate need for food aid. The low level of surpluses meant that threats to cut off aid suddenly gained credibility they would not have had previously. John Kenneth Galbraith, the U.S. ambassador to India, noted that the low surpluses "enabled changes in the style of diplomacy" (Prasad 1980, 82). Recipients were well aware of the agricultural situation in the United States, acknowledging that the anxiety to quickly ship surpluses overseas had largely disappeared by the mid-1960s. The situation was further tightened by the beginning of commercial sales to the Soviet Union in 1963. One of the first signs of the shift in American policy came in 1964, when the agreement to extend food aid to India was extended for only two years, rather than the five that India had requested. Anticipating the need to undertake domestic agricultural reforms, India preferred a long-term commitment from the United States that would provide the necessary breathing space to put reforms into place. But low surpluses and continuing congressional criticism of India, for example for its plans to buy military aircraft from the Soviet Union, made a long-term extension unacceptable. Congress also made clear in 1964 that it wanted the self-help measures written into legislation to be applied to India (Prasad 1980, 88; 113). India's plans for economic development had focused on the industrial sector to the exclusion of the agricultural, contributing to the desperate situation in which it found itself.

The short-tether policy was Johnson's own invention, opposed by some in his administration (Prasad 1980, 121; Paarlberg 1985, 151, 154). It consisted of his personal oversight of the release of grain shipments to India, as well as negotiations for each installment. At each stage, Johnson would hold up delivery until the last possible minute as a means of generating pressure on Indian policies. This tactic meant that sufficient grain for only one or two months at a time was actually shipped. When the Indian government gave in to U.S. demands, large shipments of grain were completed quickly. The short-tether procedure was effective in gaining concrete concessions from the Indian government, such as an agreement to allow foreign investment in fertilizer plants and decreased state control of the agricultural sector (Krupadanam 1985, 115). However, it created huge problems for the Indian government in adopting long-range plans, since it could never be certain that U.S. aid would be delivered as expected (Paarlberg 1985, 156, 167). Thus while the short-tether policy was an effective negotiating tool, its long-run effects may be judged less positively (Mellor 1976, 46).[5]

Johnson undertook his pressure on self-help policies in India with the support of Congress. Indeed, Secretary of Agriculture Orville Freeman suggested that the large level of aid flowing to India during this period, which required very large appropriations for PL 480 as a whole, would never have received the necessary congressional authorization if commitments to take self-help measures had not been forthcoming (Prasad 1980, 123). Congressional interest in pushing self-help measures was not entirely motivated by an interest in development in India. More narrowly self-interested motives were present as well. For one, some members of Congress became worried that, now that surpluses were low, the United States had created a situation of dependence on U.S. food

---

[5] Paarlberg (1985, 161–69), is more skeptical of the impact of U.S. measures than other authors. He notes that even in the areas that showed apparent short-term successes there were some in the Indian government, such as Minister of Agriculture Chidambara Subramaniam, who favored the policies being advocated by the United States. Their preferences, rather than U.S. pressure, may account for policy change. However, Paarlberg's argument is not fully convincing since the existence of divisions within the Indian government does not contradict the argument that U.S. pressure encouraged policy change. In fact, U.S. pressure was designed to increase the influence of Subramaniam within the Indian government and appears to have been effective at doing so.

aid and created expectations that they were not willing to honor indefinitely. This concern also led Congress to push for more burden-sharing through the establishment of multilateral food-assistance programs. Another dimension of congressional interest centered around the practical meaning of "self-help measures." Many of the steps Congress had in mind would not only benefit agricultural producers in places like India, but American exporters and investors as well. In the Indian case, opening parts of the agricultural sector to foreign investment was of great interest in Congress, as was increasing the potential for exports of agricultural technology and machinery (Krupadanam 1985, 64). The emphasis on self-help was thus seen as entirely consistent with the constant refrain of "market development" that runs through discussions of PL 480.

The president took steps to assure continuing congressional support for his actions, such as meeting frequently with key members of Congress and asking specifically for approval to ship 6.5 million tons of grain, following a meeting with Prime Minister Indira Gandhi. As another step to mobilize congressional support, Johnson requested that a congressional committee visit India to assess the situation there. The visit took place in December 1966, and led to confirmation that India had taken the kinds of steps it promised on self-help measures and continued to have an intense need for U.S. aid (Prasad 1980, 126–27). While the president thus had a high level of discretion, his techniques for cooperating with Congress are typical of what we see under unified government. There was some resistance to his policies in Congress, particularly from those who felt that the level of aid going to India was too high to be justified during this period of low surpluses. However, rather than going around Congress or adopting a confrontational approach, he worked with sympathizers there to generate support for his preferred policies.

In a careful study of this episode, Krupadanam (1985, 6, 118–20) concludes that U.S. pressure on self-help measures did achieve clear results, at least in the short term. The Indian government allowed foreign investment in the fertilizer industry and agreed to reduce the level of government participation in these projects. It also devalued the rupee and increased spending on agriculture. To this extent, economic coercion was successful, an "effective inducement to the government of India to reallocate both foreign and domestic resources toward the agricultural sector" (Ruttan 1993, 19). In the longer run, however, the verdict must be more mixed. This episode convinced India that it needed to reduce its reliance on American aid, as it created the potential for too much arm-twisting. Thus India moved as rapidly as possible to remove itself from the PL 480 program, achieving this goal by the end of the 1970s.

The most public uses of the short-tether policy were in the service of pushing agricultural development. However, this was not the only kind of pressure Johnson put on India. In addition, he attempted to use food aid to push India to come to some kind of accommodation with Pakistan over Kashmir and as punishment for its criticism of U.S. actions in Vietnam (Krupadanam 1985, 105).

While there was likely not much congressional resistance to these particular measures, Congress was generally worried that the president was putting too much emphasis on foreign-policy goals. Johnson did not take steps to round up congressional support on these issues as he had on self-help measures, where widespread legislative support already existed. All analyses conclude that these political pressures did not achieve any of their aims, in contrast to the progress on agricultural development. Krupadanam (1985, 121) finds that aid had no impact in forcing a resolution to the conflict with Pakistan. Paarlberg (1985, 161) concludes that "the short-tether demands that were placed on India *beyond* the agricultural and economic policy realm—particularly those in the diplomatic realm—were rejected entirely" (emphasis in original; see also Gilmore 1982, 154). The difference in political dynamics in the United States created doubts about credibility of the threats on diplomatic issues, while cooperation between Congress and the president made threats on agricultural issues highly credible. Without this interbranch cooperation, efforts on agricultural reform could well have been as fruitless as those on foreign policy.

The pattern of U.S. linkage of food aid to Indian policy-reforms in the 1960s illuminates a number of arguments about the consequences of delegation to the executive. First, we see that delegation leads to strategic manipulation of aid. More generally, it creates scope for executive arbitrariness, as Johnson made a "changing variety of demands" the condition for receiving each tranche of food aid (Paarlberg 1985, 144). Under conditions of substantial delegation like this, the executive must be worried about the credibility of threats and promises, a necessary condition for linkage to work. Johnson recognized this fact, and took the necessary steps to signal strong congressional support for his linkage to agricultural reform. A key example of such action was Johnson's request for congressional approval of increased food-aid shipments in March 1966 (U.S. Senate 1966, 1). While such a step was not legally necessary, it was practically necessary to signal congressional support for his policies. Similarly, in July 1966 he demanded that groups of interested senators and representatives provide him with a unanimous endorsement for continuation of the short-tether policy (Paarlberg 1985, 153). Congressional delegation of authority created the potential for strategic linkage of food aid, but the application of this policy could take place only within the constraints of credible commitments created by executive-legislative relations.

The instance of U.S. food aid to India provides evidence for the proposition that delegation is a function of common interests between the branches. The Delegation Hypothesis proposes that institutionalized legislative participation in processes of international cooperation increases when conflicts of interest arise between the branches. Food aid to India supports this hypothesis, as strong common interests led to minimal legislative participation. The evidence here also supports the hypotheses that credibility and cooperation increase when the legislature is involved in a regular, institutionalized manner in negotiations with other countries—the Credibility and Cooperation Hypotheses. Presidential actions to bring legislators into the process enhanced the credibility of U.S. threats and promises associated with food aid, and so led to an increased level of realized cooperation. This dynamic allowed for the partial success of U.S. efforts to promote agricultural development, where shifting Indian investments required a credible commitment from the United States. Where institutionalized collaboration between the president and Congress was lacking (on the foreign-policy dimension), U.S. efforts lacked credibility and had no impact. One additional interesting aspect of the Indian food-aid case is that moves to enhance legislative participation frequently originated in the executive branch, suggesting that at least some presidents are aware of the dynamics of credibility proposed in this book.

Egypt: From Nasser to Camp David

Egypt began participating in the PL 480 program early, with agreements totaling $36 million in 1955. But the strings attached to this assistance quickly became obvious, as aid for 1956 was frozen in retaliation for the Suez Canal incident and in response to congressional pressure (Wallerstein 1980, 125; Burns 1985, 76, 94). Aid resumed the next year, and in 1962–63 Egypt was the largest recipient of Title I sales, in spite of some opposition in Congress to this scale of aid to Egypt. President Eisenhower recognized that congressional support for PL 480 meant that he would have the leeway to use it as he pleased that was lacking in other programs, and therefore saw food aid as a valuable political tool and used it as a tool to improve relations between the two countries (Burns 1985, 114). President Kennedy continued the pattern of using his discretion to manipulate food aid to Egypt for strategic purposes, calling the Food for Peace program a "great unseen weapon" in policy toward developing countries (Burns 1985, 121). At the same time, the executive remained aware that congressional support for linkage between aid and Egyptian policy was necessary and took steps to demonstrate the nature of congressional power. John Badeau, an ambassador to Egypt, noted that the size and duration of the food-aid program to Egypt was constructed so as to make clear the nature of American political demands and congressional pressure, through tactics of "continuous negotiation" (Burns 1985, 127).

Over time, the local-currency provisions for the large PL 480 sales to Egypt created a problem. As mentioned above, proceeds from local-currency sales were placed into a special account for the use of the local government. However, in Egypt local-currency accounts became very large, leading Congress to become concerned about the uses of this "excess currency" (Merriam 1979, 90). The presence of such excess-currency countries eventually led Congress to substitute long-term dollar-credit sales for the use of local currency.

In September 1962, Egypt became involved in a conflict in Yemen, leading to an end to U.S. economic and technical aid. Congress reacted by passing bills that suspended food aid to Egypt. However, the Kennedy administration lobbied heavily against this reduction in executive discretion and managed to maintain an escape clause that allowed PL 480 funds to flow (Wallerstein 1980, 127). Following this strong show of congressional willingness to cut aid, President Johnson attempted to link further PL 480 funds to policy changes, leading Nasser to react negatively.

As the political situation in Egypt deteriorated, riots in Cairo in November 1964 destroyed U.S. government property, including a number of buildings. The next month an American oil-company plane, allegedly violating military airspace near Alexandria, was shot down, killing the pilot and co-pilot (Merriam 1979, 95). By early 1965 the situation had deteriorated to the point that Congress attempted to halt further PL 480 funds to Egypt (Gilmore 1982, 154). An amendment to a routine bill passed in the House, cutting aid to Egypt after June 1965 (Merriam 1979, 96). However, the Senate responded to heavy administration pressure and left the final decision up to presidential discretion. The debate in the Senate focused on "party loyalty," with many references to contradicting State Department policy and infringing on presidential prerogatives (Merriam 1979, 97). This appeal to party unity, along with a presidential commitment to take actions to cut aid if Egypt did not become more cooperative, had the intended effect of maintaining presidential flexibility (Burns 1985, 162).[6] A separate proposal to require explicit congressional approval of shipments of food aid was defeated by the wide margin of 73–7 (Merriam 1979, 98). The Johnson administration continued to use the threat of congressional action to increase the pressure on Egypt.

Egypt was quite anxious to receive aid in late 1965, and Nasser made some concessions to American demands by ending arms shipments to the Belgian Congo and compensating the United States for the burned buildings. Concerned that a total end to assistance would eliminate the chance of moving toward more amicable relations in the future, the administration decided to provide a modest sum of aid in 1966, but on only a six-month basis (Merriam 1979, 98). However, the Johnson administration at this point put Nasser on notice that Congress was in no mood to continue funding PL 480 sales to Egypt unless Nasser toned down his anti-U.S. rhetoric. In this case, the threat did not work, and the United States refused new requests for aid beginning in 1967. There appeared to be widespread support for the linkage of food aid to reforms in Egypt, as in the Indian short-tether policy case. Low surpluses and unified government facilitated linkage of food aid to Egyptian policies. However, the effort to apply pressure was not as well coordinated or planned as in the Indian situation, and Egypt would not make the necessary gestures to accommodate American de-

---

[6] O'Leary (1967, 64) finds that party unity is a major factor explaining congressional action on foreign aid generally.

mands. PL 480 sales to Egypt did not resume until 1975, and once again they were linked closely to foreign-policy initiatives.

In 1974, Henry Kissinger decided to use offers of food aid to sweeten the pot in negotiating with Egypt to resolve conflicts with Israel (Gilmore 1982, 155). A new PL 480 program was signed in June of that year, tied to a peace agreement between Egypt and Israel. By this time, administration of PL 480 had moved from USDA to the State Department and NSC. The reinstatement of food aid to Egypt gained momentum, and the linkage between politics in the Middle East and food aid eventually became institutionalized, signaling a major departure from the pattern of executive discretion and short-term agreements that characterized other food aid programs. After the Camp David agreements in 1978 Egypt became established as the largest recipient of Title I sales (Paarlberg 1985, 118), receiving 23 percent of the entire volume of PL 480 sales by 1980 (Gilmore 1982, 163). In contrast to congressional reaction to the use of PL 480 in Vietnam, Congress approved of and endorsed the institutionalization of food aid to Egypt.

As table 5.1 shows, not only are the levels of food aid to Egypt high, in recent years they show a remarkable degree of consistency. The Camp David accords required Egypt to make a number of extremely difficult, long-term revisions to its foreign policy. The promise of one-shot food aid, still subject to executive discretion, was not sufficient to solidify the complex bargains. Instead, Egypt received a regular commitment to high levels of food aid, valuable because of the desperate economic situation and demand for food imports in Egypt (Stein 1993, 86; Weinbaum 1986, 37). Egypt's domestic problems, and Sadat's plans to solve them through economic reforms, required a predictable commitment to U.S. food aid (Burns 1985, 190; Weinbaum 1986, 11). Such a commitment was made on discretion of the president. However, it succeeded and became institutionalized because it was supported by Congress. In this case, the problem of establishing the necessary credible commitments to provide aid to persuade the recipient to undertake significant long-term reforms was solved by establishing an institutionalized bilateral mechanism for providing food aid.

As in the case of India, food aid to Egypt sheds light on the connection between institutionalized legislative participation and the credibility of commitments. During negotiations with Nasser, Congress was involved, although not in a particularly formal, institutionalized capacity. In this case, the U.S. threat to cut aid turned out to be credible, but was not sufficient to induce cooperation. The pattern of institutionalized aid-flows at Camp David is especially intriguing for the thesis of this book. It supports the proposition that deep cooperation, that which requires states to take steps that would be costly to reverse, demands credible commitments, and that credibility is enhanced through institutionalized legislative participation. As the Credibility and Cooperation Hypotheses suggest, involving Congress in a regularized manner increased the credibility of U.S. commitments to aid to Egypt, and so allowed for deeper cooperation.

CONCLUSION

Food aid has proven to be a tool that presidents use to pursue foreign-policy objectives at the same time that it satisfies the demands of numerous domestic constituencies, especially agricultural producers. The history of the food-aid program allows us to examine variation in levels of executive discretion as well as the impact of this variation on the U.S. capacity to interact strategically with other countries. The lessons of this case support and extend those found in the other empirical chapters of this book, and once again show the power of using models of legislative-executive interaction to understand the domestic sources of international cooperation in democracies.

The level of legislative delegation to the executive on food aid is very high, especially if we compare it to other forms of foreign aid (Destler 1978, 59). The major puzzle about delegation in this chapter is to explain this high level of delegation. I have argued that Congress has been willing to allow the president a great deal of discretion on food aid because food aid is such a popular program. The popularity is explained in part by the humanitarian nature of food aid, but more important is the fact that it allows the United States to maintain price supports for agriculture by providing an efficient means to ship excess produce overseas. If this proposition is correct, we should find that Congress reconsiders the level of delegation when surplus disposal becomes a less important objective. The expected pattern shows up clearly in the legislative history, with periods of high prices and low surpluses coinciding with legislative revisions that put constraints on the executive.

However, not all such revisions lead to substantial increases in constraints. Presidents facing a Congress controlled by their own party, and who have not shown a propensity to run roughshod over congressional preferences in using PL 480 as a foreign-policy tool, can convince Congress to make only minor modifications. Presidents facing an opposition Congress, and who have blatantly violated the expressed policy preferences of Congress, will in a similar situation find that they lose substantial discretion. Thus, both President Johnson and President Nixon faced major reviews of PL 480, but under Johnson the review resulted in minor changes compared to what we find in the early 1970s. Overall, variation in the level of delegation strongly supports the Delegation Hypothesis. The food-aid case allowed us to think about the problem of common interests when the issue at stake involves more than one dimension, in this instance the level of aid disbursed and the ability to use it for foreign-policy purposes. It extends and clarifies the exchange model of executive-legislative relations.

Executive discretion leads to strategic manipulation of food aid to pressure recipients to change their policies. In some instances, where the president is only looking for a short-term policy change, credibility is not much of an issue. But when presidents are looking for major reforms, they need to establish a longer-term commitment to aid levels. When Johnson faced this situation in India, he made sure to work with Congress in such a way as to establish a credible commitment. In the case of Egypt, President Carter was promising over a long term an extraordinarily high level of continuing aid. To make this commitment credible, he turned to institutionalization that has led to consistent high levels of food aid to Egypt, in contrast to the usual pattern of substantial fluctuations. Without congressional support, attempts to use food aid in ways that require long-term commitments have not been successful. The case studies in this chapter thus support the Credibility and Cooperation Hypotheses. They also show that executives are often aware of these incentives and are sometimes willing to sacrifice flexibility in order to gain credibility.

CHAPTER 6

National Parliaments and European Integration: Institutional Choice in EU Member States

THIS BOOK makes general arguments about the role of legislatures in stable democracies. The analytical framework used draws on models primarily developed in the U.S. context, and the previous three empirical chapters have focused on the U.S. Congress. To what extent does this framework help us to understand the dynamics of legislative involvement in international cooperation outside the United States, particularly in a parliamentary context? To answer this question, this chapter and the next turn to examining the member states of the European Union. They focus on the influence that national parliaments have on the process of European integration. In the first couple of chapters of this book, I proposed that a similar logic of legislative influence should apply to the United States and the member states of the European Union. Although presidential and parliamentary systems differ in many respects, legislatures in stable democracies are similar in many ways. They possess similar tools with which they can attempt to influence processes of international cooperation, such as forming powerful legislative committees that constrain negotiators or refusing to implement international agreements of which they do not approve. Incentives to use these tools do differ across systems, as stronger party discipline can make parliaments more reluctant than the U.S. Congress to exercise their authority. However, a difference in degree is not a difference in kind. I propose that the same general hypotheses about influence and credibility apply to Europe as to the United States, and test this proposition in the following two chapters.

This chapter treats parliamentary institutions that structure interaction with the executive branch and negotiations within the EU as the dependent variable, focusing on the Delegation Hypothesis. It finds strong support for the proposition that as executive-legislative conflict increases, legislatures move to institutionalize their participation in the process of international cooperation, even in a parliamentary setting. The next chapter turns to the more controversial question of whether the creation of parliamentary institutions matters for the course of European integration, concentrating on implementation of the single market within the EU.

The study of European parliaments is important from the perspective of generalizing theories of legislatures, as it shows that the same framework can provide analytical leverage in parliamentary as well as presidential systems. It is also important from the perspective of understanding European integration, since it challenges the widely held view that national parliaments have abdicated their capacity to influence the course of integration. The first section of this chapter discusses how the logic of delegation should lead us to question the conventional wisdom about the liabilities of parliamentary democracy in the EU. It contrasts abdication and delegation models of legislative-executive relations. The Abdication Hypothesis is the equivalent of the Evasion Hypothesis in chapter 3. It is the null hypothesis, the key alternative to the Delegation Hypothesis. The second section develops observable implications of the Delegation Hypothesis in the EU context. The third presents evidence showing that as conflict over European integration has grown more intense, parliaments have begun playing a more active role, forcing governments to take their preferences into account. A major argument of this chapter is that the ways in which parliaments influence the process of integration over time can be understood with a consistent model, rather than having to rely on one model of "parliamentary impotence" for earlier periods and "parliamentary activism" for the current period. The Delegation Hypothesis allows us to explain change over time, rather than simply taking it as determined exogenously.

THE NULL HYPOTHESIS: PARLIAMENTARY ABDICATION

Parliamentary-abdication models have dominated the study of politics in Western Europe, and more specifically of European integration. The Abdication Hypothesis claims that parliaments have abdicated their policymaking authority to governments, leaving themselves with no means by which to influence policy. The Abdication Hypothesis contrasts to the Delegation Hypothesis, which sees the process of delegation as a mechanism of legislative influence, not as the abdication of influence. Many parliamentary scholars have written of the "decline of parliaments," referring to some unspecified previous era in which parliaments constrained governments and strongly influenced policy (Loewenberg 1971). The belief that parliaments play little role in making policy has led to a body of work that analyzes other "functions" of parliaments, such as providing legitimacy for government actions. Huber (1996, 11–12) rightly criticizes these studies of parliamentary functions for lacking microfoundations that explain how and why parliaments might perform functions such as legitimacy if they have no influence on policy. While some studies have recently suggested that parliaments are becoming more active (Mezey 1995), we still find little study of parliamentary influence on policy.

I find evidence in this chapter and next disputing the Abdication Hypothesis. However, this hypothesis rests on logical foundations that are not totally without merit. As the nature of issues with which governments must contend becomes more complex, the informational demands on policymakers increase hugely. MPs thus find it difficult to keep close tabs on what the government, with its higher level of technical expertise, is doing. Other demands on MPs' resources, including time, also grow, so that MPs lack the time to pay attention to any but the most pressing, immediate concerns. Beyond these structural changes that tend to enhance the role of government in the modern political world, governments have developed mechanisms to increase their freedom from tight legislative constraints, according to the Abdication Hypothesis. The various mechanisms of party discipline are key to the logic of government evasion. If members of a party are not able to challenge government actions or to demand that the government reveal information about policies, there is little they can do to influence policy. Politicians in Europe tend not to have the individual electoral resources that are available to their American counterparts, making European politicians more dependent on the party and therefore poorly placed to challenge governments. These arguments apply with special force to foreign policy, which beyond its complexity has traditionally been an area that parliaments recognize as the proper domain of executives.

A difficulty with the Abdication Hypothesis, persuasive as it may seem at first glance, is that it treats as exogenous many factors that are, in practice, endogenous. Party discipline and MPs' ability to extract information from the government, or to acquire independent sources of information, are variables that change over time in response to more fundamental political and economic forces. The Abdication Hypothesis treats these variables as fixed and exogenous, and so predicts little change in them over time. Delegation models, as elaborated below, instead predict systematic variation in the institutional structures that allow parliaments to exercise influence over government actions. Thus a powerful test for abdication versus delegation models lies in their ability to explain observed changes in institutions. While parties continue to be the major structuring force in European politics, channeling demands and ordering political life, the degree to which parties encourage executive dominance and make MPs irrelevant to policy changes over time in a way that delegation models can help us understand.

If parliamentary-abdication models dominate the study of domestic policy in Europe, they are even more strongly held in studies of foreign policy or European integration. These models suggest that national parliaments do not and cannot influence EU policy. Because the process of integration is highly technical, and because the realm of foreign policy in general is an area of executive dominance, parliaments have been marginalized in EU policymaking. Most analysts have portrayed the development of the EU as a process of national governments using international agreements to assert control over policymaking, thereby weakening national parliaments (Milward 1992; for a critique see Marks, Hooghe, and Blank 1996). Because only executives are represented in the European Council, and Council proceedings have been kept secret until recently, the process left national parliaments without a means by which to influence integration, according to the Abdication Hypothesis. The founders of the EU saw integration as an elite-driven process and so designed institutions such as the Council of Ministers and Commission to provide governments with insulation from public pressures (Featherstone 1994). Executives welcomed this design, since it allowed them to escape parliamentary constraints. As a result, "national governments are able to take initiatives and reach bargains in Council negotiations with relatively little constraint" (Moravcsik 1993, 515). Governments designed EU institutions, particularly the powers of the Council, to allow them to overcome potential domestic opposition to specific policies. Abdication models argue that this lack of democratic accountability has been a necessary condition for European integration, assuming a tension between democracy and efficiency. The next chapter scrutinizes this proposition, asking whether such a tension in fact exists to any substantial degree.

Studies focusing on the role of national parliaments concur that they have had little influence on EU agreements. EU business has been characterized as "predominantly an executive process," (Wallace 1973, 13), with the impact of parliaments "slight and intermittent" (Niblock 1971, 16). Analyses of the powers of the Council have concluded that the chains of accountability between the Council and national parliaments are weak (Herman and van Schendelen 1979; Marquand 1981). Lodge (1991, 10–11) asserts that national parliaments cannot apply effective sanctions against governments in the EU context, and that the process of joining the EU meant that they "signed away" their authority to influence policy. A special issue of the *Journal of Legislative Studies* (Norton 1995a) on national parliaments and the European Union scrutinized parliamentary attempts to influence EU policy. It found that parliaments "ultimately lacked any formal power to say 'aye' or 'nay' to a measure enacted by the institutions of the EC under the provisions of Community treaties" (Norton 1995b, 3–4). The picture that emerged showed that parliaments "have been marginal actors in the process. They have been unable and, in many respects, unwilling to play a significant role in European law making" (Norton 1995c, 187).

Studies that found national parliaments to have abdicated their powers inferred a lack of constraints on the government from a lack of parliamentary activity during EU negotiations. Minimal parliamentary activity was attributed, early on, to lack of interest on the part of national parliaments in EU business, combined with national practices by which parliaments had already abdicated their ability to exercise much influence over what governments did, especially in foreign policy. More recently, analysts have introduced the further factor of intentional actions on the part of governments, such as the procedures used in the Council, to exacerbate parliaments' lack of capacity. If the Abdication Hypothesis is correct, parliaments should be able to do little to constrain executives or otherwise influence policy. Their lack of interest, expertise, and subservience to governments and parties should render them ineffective in the EU policymaking context. In the next section, I contrast this view to the Delegation Hypothesis, which predicts systematic variation in the institutional structures that regulate interaction between parliaments and governments.

THE DELEGATION HYPOTHESIS: AN INTEGRATED FRAMEWORK

Events since 1992 have called the Abdication Hypothesis into question. Parliaments throughout the EU have moved to create committees and other structures to constrain government ministers in their negotiations in the EU, as described in more detail below. Some analysts, noting this trend, conclude that a new era has arisen, one in which the decline of parliaments has, for a variety of reasons, been reversed (Mezey 1995). They imply that, in order to understand the role of parliaments in European integration, we need to rely on two separate models. One model, that of parliamentary abdication, characterizes the period before the Single European Act (SEA), or perhaps before the Treaty on European Union (TEU, or Maastricht Treaty). A new model, one of parliamentary activism, characterizes the post-Maastricht period. This approach relies on two separate models that do not share common assumptions about actors. It assumes that parliaments have different capacities, interests, and accountability relations with the government in different time periods. The difficulty with such an approach is that we are left without a general theory that can help us understand when to use one model and when the other. If parliaments had in fact abdicated their powers, how have they managed to reclaim them? How can we tell which model is appropriate without inferring it from looking at parliamentary activity—which leaves us unable to develop refutable propositions about parliamentary influence? If we are in a situation of multiple equilibria, one that involves parliamentary acquiescence and one that involves parliamentary activism, how can we explain the shift from one equilibrium to another? Relying on two separate models, rather than an integrated one, is highly unsatisfactory, because it cannot answer such questions.

Models of delegation provide an integrated method for making sense of parliaments' role in European integration, allowing us to explain both the earlier period of apparent parliamentary acquiescence and the more recent one of apparent parliamentary importance. Increasingly, it appears that what analysts took to be parliamentary abdication to executives was in fact a more subtle form of delegation, one that allowed parliaments to reassert their prerogatives if governments moved too far, too fast. Prior to the SEA, the issues that governments dealt with on the EU level were either quite technical or stayed within the boundaries of domestic political consensus, such as agricultural subsidies. Executives may have *appeared* unconstrained during this period not because parliaments were unable to constrain them but because the domestic consensus about issues being negotiated on the EU level meant that parliaments rarely had to step in to exercise constraints. Parliamentary inactivity during the earlier period, from a delegation perspective, could reflect a pattern of delegation that worked reasonably well, not a failure of parliaments to hold governments accountable. Well-functioning delegation patterns mean that parliaments can exercise influence, defined as having their preferences reflected in international agreements, without much overt oversight or other activity.

The situation of EU-level agreements being confined to technical or consensual issues changed substantially in 1985, and even more dramatically in the 1990s (Bocquet 1995, 40). Major commitments to integration took place in the SEA of 1985 and the TEU, signed at Maastricht in 1991. In the SEA, governments committed themselves to complete the internal market, meaning that they would remove all barriers to the exchange of goods and services within the EU. Explicit border measures that interfered with trade, such as tariffs and quotas, would be removed. More significantly, governments agreed to eliminate more subtle barriers to exchange, such as differing standards for product safety, training in the service professions, and so on.[1] The SEA also included important institutional reforms, such as the acceptance of qualified-majority voting in the Council, that have had wide-reaching effects (Pierson 1996). The single-market measures, examined more directly in the next chapter, were bound to cause economic dislocation in member states and moved policymaking on many issues that traditionally remained on the domestic level to the EU level. The SEA's institutional reforms also created consternation as MPs and domestic publics came to understand them, since they often transferred authority away from individual member states to supranational institutions or the vagaries of majoritarian, rather than unit-veto, procedures.

The SEA required ratification in all states, as do all changes to the Treaty of Rome, the founding document of the EU. It ran into difficulties only in Denmark, where the government called a popular referendum to overcome partisan opposition in the parliament. The ease of ratification was interpreted as yet another indication that governments were largely unconstrained, further support for the Abdication Hypothesis. However, as the implications of SEA commitments became known, anti-EU feeling and organized opposition to the new, rapid pace of European integration arose.

The TEU took a number of significant steps beyond the SEA, and is in many ways a far more ambitious document. In fact, it is so ambitious that governments found it difficult to carry through on the promises they made at Maastricht, particularly to move to the use of a single currency in Europe by 1999 at the latest. The TEU's provisions for monetary union are perhaps the most important of the substantive measures in this treaty, and have received a great deal of analysis. Monetary union removes a key aspect of sovereignty, national currencies. To assure that the new currency (the Euro) will be strong on world markets and not undermine low-inflation policies, negotiators agreed to a strict set of convergence criteria, including stringent controls on government spending,

[1] The literature on the SEA and TEU is enormous. For a few examples, see Moravcsik (1998); Keohane and Hoffmann (1991); Eichengreen and Frieden (1994); Eichengreen, Frieden, and von Hagen (1995); Sbragia (1992); Adams (1993).

that have caused deep economic pain in member states. Attempts to enforce the austerity policies necessitated by the convergence criteria during a period of high, intractable unemployment even contributed to an unexpected and consequential electoral loss by the conservative French government in 1997. Clearly, EU-level negotiations now engage issues far more conflictual and of immediate importance to citizens than at an earlier stage of European integration.

Beyond agreements to deep cooperation on a number of issues such as monetary union, the TEU introduced additional institutional reforms. The powers of the European Parliament were increased, as they had been in the SEA (Tsebelis 1994, 1995a; Martin 1993b). The powers of the Commission were reduced somewhat, the Council agreed to introduce more transparency in its proceedings, and more issues were made subject to qualified-majority voting in the Council. The scope of cooperation extended beyond economic issues to foreign policy and defense, although the implementation of commitments in those areas remains problematic. In addition, the way in which the TEU was negotiated revealed quite extraordinary efforts by governments to minimize parliamentary or popular participation (Bocquet 1995, 50). As discussed below, the TEU ran into many more difficulties during the ratification process than had the SEA.

Chapter 2 outlined the general proposition that legislatures move to reclaim authority, creating stronger institutions to structure relations with the executive, when conflicts of interest exist between the branches. In the context of the EU, the Delegation Hypothesis leads to a straightforward implication: as conflicts arise between the government and parliament, parliaments will move to create more stringent oversight mechanisms, appearing more activist than when little conflict exists. Three sources of conflict of interest appear most relevant in the case of European integration, and give rise to observable hypotheses. These key sources of conflict are: EU negotiations that deal with more conflictual issues, executives that overstep the implied bounds of delegated authority, and minority government.

Issues being negotiated on the international level are a major source of potential conflicts of interest among political actors at the domestic level. When the issues being negotiated are highly technical, so that they will have little impact on the well-being of constituents, there is little reason to expect serious conflicts of interest. Similarly, when the issues being negotiated are those on which a domestic consensus exists, we should find little conflict of interest. However, as the issues being negotiated move into more sensitive realms, where winners and losers are identifiable, the impact on constituents' welfare more immediate, and disagreement exists about the appropriate course of action, more conflict of interest emerges. As the theories of delegation reviewed in chapter 2 implied, greater conflicts of interest between negotiators and those they represent should lead to lower levels of delegation. When the issues being negotiated are more contentious, legislators will be less willing to allow negotiators a free hand.

Thus, in the EU context, we can predict that *as the issues being negotiated on the EU level become more conflictual and have more immediate impact on constituents' welfare, parliaments should act to create structures to constrain the governments' actions in EU negotiations.* As discussed above, with the SEA and, especially, the TEU, EU policymaking moved into areas that lacked domestic consensus, created clear winners and losers, and infringed on citizens' daily lives in an unprecedented manner. Thus, models of delegation lead us to expect that MPs would reclaim authority over EU affairs from governments, by creating committees to oversee EU policymaking and devoting more resources to gaining information about EU activities. In contrast, abdication models that see parliaments as not capable of constraining governments would predict no systematic relation between the nature of issues being negotiated and parliamentary creation of institutional structures to constrain governments.

A second source of conflict between parliaments and governments is behavior by governments that exceeds the implicit (or explicit) bounds of delegated authority. As long as governments properly anticipate what parliaments are willing to accept, and remain within these constraints, MPs have little reason to expend resources overseeing and reining in government negotiators. However, when negotiators make commitments that fall outside the bounds of delegated authority, we should see MPs become more willing to expend these resources. In the case of the EU, this logic implies that we should see MPs acting in an apparently acquiescent manner as long as governments do not make commitments to integration that move too quickly, going beyond the expectations of MPs. But when governments overstep these bounds, agreeing to plans for integration that are too ambitious, parliaments should react by creating structures to put more explicit constraints on negotiators. Overall, *government commitments that go beyond the bounds of delegated authority should lead parliaments to create stricter mechanisms to constrain negotiators.*

A third important source of conflict lies in domestic politics rather than activities on the EU level. In parliamentary democracies, political struggles are mediated through political parties. Party discipline tends to be high, relative to that in the United States, although it varies over time, across countries, and across issues. Thus, party control of government is a good indicator of conflicts of interest. Laver and Shepsle (1994, 294) have argued that minority government in parliamentary systems is in many respects analogous to divided government in the U.S. system. Without automatic support from a party that has majority control of parliament, minority governments must pay more attention to the demands and interests of MPs. Relying on the analogy between minority and divided government, we should expect to see less willingness to delegate to minority governments. Thus, we can expect to find *stronger structures to constrain negotiators in minority governments.*

Delegation models differ from abdication models in a number of important respects. They explain government freedom of maneuver not by parliamentary inability to constrain governments but by rational decisions on the part of MPs to delegate authority to the government. Delegation models thus provide, in contrast to abdication models, systematic expectations about variation in parliamentary efforts to constrain governments. They lead to testable predictions about the conditions under which MPs will create institutional structures to oversee governments in the negotiations on the EU level and to gain information about EU negotiations. In general, the Delegation Hypothesis leads us to expect that parliaments will create oversight institutions, such as powerful committees to deal with EU affairs, when there exist conflicts of interest between MPs and governments. The next section presents evidence testing this expectation.

EVIDENCE: PARLIAMENTARY INSTITUTIONS FOR THE EU

The Delegation Hypothesis predicts that increased conflicts of interest should lead legislators to create institutions to more tightly constrain executives. In the context of parliamentary government and the EU, these conflicts of interest should give rise to institutions such as parliamentary committees to oversee EU business. Three factors that seem particularly important as sources of conflicts of interest are: having controversial issues on the negotiating table; government behavior that oversteps the bounds of delegated authority; and minority government. Looking at the history of European integration, especially the recent history, we find strong support for the Delegation Hypothesis, suggesting that claims that parliaments have abdicated their powers are misguided.

Delegation models predict an outcry and backlash among parliaments, with attempts to rein governments back in, when negotiations move to more controversial policies. In fact, this is precisely what we observe after the TEU was signed. The Maastricht Treaty moved decision-making authority to the EU on a far wider range of issues than the SEA, moving well beyond the bounds of domestic consensus. Suddenly, concerns about a "democratic deficit" that had been confined to a few politicians became widespread (Williams 1991; Boyce 1993; Lodge 1994). The TEU did not pass ratification processes with the ease of the SEA, but encountered debilitating resistance in Denmark and just barely scraped by in a French referendum and a messy British ratification process. This situation contrasts strongly to earlier eras, where "a large measure of consensus between the executive and parliamentary branches" prevailed (Niblock 1971, 50). "In an era of 'euro-sclerosis' intra-party and intra-parliamentary divisions could be subsumed within a common defence of national interests within a static Community" (Judge 1995, 95).

National parliaments that had barely bothered to set up or empower committees to oversee EU business began to take these structures seriously in the late 1980s, to study how the parliaments of other member states attempted to control their governments, and to develop mechanisms to confer with one another and with members of the EP (MEPs). Fitzmaurice (1996, 89) finds that "[a]fter Maastricht, many national parliaments came to the issue [of the democratic deficit] with the zeal of the late convert." Judge (1995, 80) observes that "events since the signing of the Treaty on European Union by Heads of Government and States in December 1991 suggest that national parliaments have used the uncertainties surrounding ratification to bargain increased powers of scrutiny over EC legislation." A report prepared by the Commission's Directorate-General for Information, Communication, Culture, and Audiovisual Media in preparation for the 1996 Intergovernmental Conference claimed that "[t]he difficulties experienced in ratifying the Treaty [TEU] in certain countries showed how important it is to involve the national parliaments in the work of European integration" (European Commission 1995, 26).

If parliaments have latent influence over EU policy, we would only expect to see them take action once governments fail to anticipate parliamentary preferences. In fact, it was not until 1990 that all chambers of the member states' national parliaments set up bodies specializing in EU affairs (European Centre for Parliamentary Research and Documentation, 1990, 1; see table 6.1). "Only with considerable delay did parliaments start to think about specific internal structures which could help them to fulfil their role" (Neunreither 1994, 303). In 1989 and 1990 alone, parliaments created five new specialized bodies (in Luxembourg, Greece, the *Bundesrat* in Germany, the Senate in Belgium, and the *Camera dei Deputati* in Italy). An Interparliamentary Conference of these bodies began meeting twice annually, together with MEPs, in November 1989 (Govaere and Hélin 1990). This conference, known as COSAC, gained access to greater information about Council proceedings and a consultative role in EU legislative procedures in the Amsterdam Treaty of 1996.[2]

The TEU includes two declarations on the role of national parliaments, and the Amsterdam Treaty includes a Protocol on this topic. In response to outcry about the secrecy of Council proceedings, the Council agreed to publicize its activities and voting records (European Commission 1995). This reform responds to the demands of national parliaments by promising to provide information necessary to allow more effective national control of negotiators. Of course, using such information to influence government behavior depends on the success of parliaments in organizing themselves and their relations with governments.

A number of recent studies have taken note of the substantial increase in parliamentary activity and creation of stronger parliamentary institutions in the 1990s (Mezey 1995). These steps are apparent even in member states with the strongest traditions of executive dominance and parliamentary acquiescence, such as France (Vedel 1994; Rizutto 1995). Fitzmaurice (1996, 89) cites France and Germany as examples of national parliaments being driven "to enact new

---

[2] See "The Amsterdam Treaty: A Comprehensive Guide," http://europa.eu.int/.

TABLE 6.1
Bodies in National Parliaments Dealing with EU Affairs

Country	Parliamentary Body	EU Committee	Date Established	Frequency of Meetings	Number of Members
Austria	Nationalrat	Hauptausschuss/Ständiger Unterausschuss in Angelegenheiten der Europäischen Union	1920	Twice a month	29 members
	Bundesrat	EU-Ausschuss	February 8, 1995	At chair's discretion	16 members, 16 substitutes
Belgium	Chambre des Représentants/ Sénat	Comité d'avis fédéral chargé de Questions européennes/ Federaal Adviescomité voor Europese aangelegenheden	October 1995 (date when EU committees in the Chamber of Representatives, formed 1985, and in the Senate, formed 1990, merged)	Once a month (while Parliament is in session)	30 members
Denmark	Folketing	Europaudvalget	October 11, 1972	Once a week	17 members, 11 substitutes
Finland	Eduskunta	Suuri valiokunta/Stora utskottet	1906	Twice a week	25 members, 13 alternate members
France	Assemblée Nationale	Délégation de l'Assemblée Nationale pour l'Union européenne	July 6, 1979	Once a week	36 members

(continued)

TABLE 6.1 (Continued)

Country	Parliamentary Body	EU Committee	Date Established	Frequency of Meetings	Number of Members
	Sénat	Délégation du Sénat pour l'Union européenne	July 6, 1979	About 35 meetings a year	36 members
Germany	Bundestag	Ausschuss für die Angelegen-heiten der Europäischen Union	December 14, 1994 (replaces former committees established in 1987 and 1991)	Once a week during Bundestag committee weeks (about 21 meetings a year)	39 members and 11 German members of the European Parliament (MEPs)
	Bundesrat	Ausschuss für Fragen der Europäischen Union	December 20, 1957	Every three weeks	18 members
Greece	Vouli ton Ellinon	Epitropi Evropaikon Ypothesseon	June 13, 1990	Irregular intervals	31 members
Ireland	Dail Éireann/Seanad Éireann	Joint Committee on European Affairs	November 1997 (separate EU committees of Dail and Seanad merged in 1983, and again in 1997)	Every two weeks	19 members (14 from Dail, 5 from Seanad)
Italy	Camera dei Deputati	Commissione Politiche dell'Europea	1990	Two–three times a week	48 members
	Senato della Repubblica	Giunta per gli Affari delle Comunità europee	July 17, 1968	Irregular intervals	24 members

Country	Chamber	Committee	Date established	Frequency of meeting	Membership
Luxembourg	Chambre des Députés	Commission des Affaires étrangères et communautaires	December 6, 1989	Committee itself decides	11 members
Netherlands	Tweede Kamer der Staten-Generaal	Algemene commissie voor EU-zaken	May 18, 1994 (replacing an EU committee formed in 1986)	Once a week in public, once a month in private	25 members, 25 substitutes
	Eerste Kamer der Staten-Generaal	Vaste Commissie voor Europese Samenwerkings organisaties	June 1970	Twenty times a year	11 members, 11 substitutes
Portugal	Assembleia da Republica	Commissão de Assuntos Europeus	October 29, 1987	Once a week	27 members
Spain	Congreso de los Diputados/Senado	Comisión Mixta para la Unión Europea	December 17, 1985	Roughly once a month	Membership established at the start of each parliamentary term. Current membership is 39
Sweden	Riksdagen	EU Advisory Committee	December 16, 1994	Once a week	17 members, 25 substitutes
United Kingdom	House of Commons	Select Committee on European Legislation	May 7, 1974	Once a week	16 members
	House of Lords	Select Committee on the European Communities	April 10, 1974	Twice a month (although its subcommittees meet once a week)	20 members (and 36 sub-committee members)

Source: Directorate General for Committees and Delegations, *The Specialised Committees on European Affairs in the Parliaments of the Members States and the Applicant Countries*, September 1998 brochure.

and considerably more binding constitutional provisions for involving the national parliament in the EU decision-making process at the national level."[3] "National parliaments responded to the patent danger of their further residualisation by becoming more active on EC issues" (Judge 1995, 87). The most ambitious step toward integration in Europe, monetary union, required specific acts of approval in a number of national parliaments, including Germany's and Sweden's (*Economist,* 30 September 1995, 58). National parliaments are attempting to gain information about policies of the European Central Bank (ECB) by instituting requirements that national central-bank governors appear before them regularly for questioning about ECB policies. This requirement has been put into law in Belgium as the result of rewriting its central-bank legislation, and is being discussed in Britain (not yet a member of EMU) and France.

Torbjörn Bergman (1997) has undertaken a comprehensive survey of European Affairs Committees in all fifteen current member states. He finds that all member states have active EU committees, although the degree to which they can bind government ministers varies widely. The most binding committees are in Austria (Kaiser 1995), Denmark (Fitzmaurice 1996), and the Bundesrat in Germany (Goetz 1995; Saalfeld 1995). Even committees that have historically been quite weak and inactive, as in Belgium, are moving to improve their ability to constrain the government (De Winter and Laurent 1995). One of Bergman's findings is that while there is some correlation between the strength of the EU committee and national parliamentary committees generally—member states with stronger committees in general also tend to have a strong EU committee—this correlation is not perfect. An interesting exception, relevant to the discussion of Denmark in the next chapter, is the comparison between Sweden and Denmark (Bergman 1997, 385 n. 7). While Denmark's committee system is in general weaker than Sweden's, the Danish EU committee has greater powers than does Sweden's (Hegeland and Mattson 1996).

The history of parliamentary institutions thus conforms closely to that predicted by delegation models. Another expectation about parliamentary institutions is that they will be strongest in cases of minority government. This expectation is strikingly met in the case of Denmark, discussed in more detail in the next chapter. A tradition of majority government in Denmark collapsed at just about the same time Denmark entered the EU (then EC), leading to a consistent pattern of minority or coalition government (Mezey 1995, 197; Strom 1990). Hegeland and Mattson (1996, 202) conclude that "[a]n important reason for both the establishment of the Danish European Committee and its relatively strong position, [*sic*] is the fact that Denmark has seldom been ruled by majority governments."[4] Overall, they conclude that European Committees generally become stronger when governments have less support in parliaments, and that

---

[3] Judge (1995, 91) calls the strengthening in scrutiny procedures in France "dramatic."
[4] See also Jacobs, Corbett, and Shackleton (1995, 286).

the desire to maintain "unity" in foreign policy is in part responsible for this pattern. In Sweden, in contrast to Denmark, a history of strong majority governments has led to a weaker European Committee.

Denmark also stands out as being skeptical about the idea of rapid European integration. Not surprisingly, given this skepticism combined with minority governments, for years Denmark was the only member state with strong parliamentary institutions to constrain government representatives in EU negotiations. In states with stronger support for European integration, the demand to create a strong parliamentary committee to oversee EU affairs is reduced. Hegeland and Mattson (1996, 205), for example, find that current Swedish support for participation in the EU has contributed to a somewhat weaker committee than that in Denmark. Overall, in "those states in which a fundamental consensus existed around the cause of integration, the need for national parliamentary control of their respective executives in EC deliberations appeared, initially at least, less pressing than in those states more sceptical about the national advantage to be gained from closer cooperation" (Judge 1995, 84). Given the increasing conflicts over European integration in other countries, Denmark is becoming less and less unique within the EU, as other states move in the direction of stronger parliamentary control. But for years the Danish experience provided strong support for the proposition that conflict of interest and minority government lead to the creation of strong parliamentary institutions for the EU.

The trend toward greater explicit parliamentary involvement in EU affairs is unmistakable. We do not only observe consistent, public moves among the twelve members of the EU who signed the TEU. The latest enlargement of the EU has brought in Austria, Sweden, and Finland (Granell 1995). In the Scandinavian states, in particular, the commitment to parliamentary democracy and institutionalized legislative influence over executive actions is strong. These new member states have studied the "Danish model" closely, determining how to adapt it to their own political systems. The parliament of Finland has entrusted oversight of EU affairs to its Grand Committee. The Grand Committee meets twice a week to consider ongoing EU negotiations. The views of the Grand Committee are explicitly considered to be binding on the government, and the government's activities during negotiations are closely monitored.[5] The Swedish parliament has created an Advisory Committee on EU Affairs, which meets once weekly with cabinet ministers who are involved in EU negotiations.[6] The possibility that governments can continue to behave as if they have a free hand in determining the course of European integration is now remote, if indeed it was ever realistic at all.

[5] See "The Parliament of Finland and the European Union," http://www.eduskunta.fi/fakta/opas/tiedotus/esiteen7.htm.
[6] See "The Swedish Parliament: The Parliament and EU," http://www.riksdagen.se/eu/fab_k_en.htm.

CONCLUSION

Legislative behavior of the type we observe in the EU—apparently acquiescent, then activist—is entirely consistent with that predicted by modern theories of legislative organization that see legislators as having significant leverage over executive decisions (Kiewiet and McCubbins 1991; Weingast and Moran 1983; Huber 1992; Krehbiel 1991). Leverage can be exercised through the mechanism of anticipated reactions, rather than explicit legislative activity. That is, executives have incentives to anticipate the reactions of legislatures when they are making policy. If governments can anticipate opposition that will jeopardize agreed policies, they will take steps to avoid it. Thus, apparent legislative inactivity may simply reflect acquiescence in the executive's policies and good executive anticipation of the limits of their flexibility. Active legislative involvement and attempts to restrain the executive are a sign of a failure of institutions of executive accountability, not the only indications that the legislature is making any difference. The most effective legislature is perhaps one that works quietly, putting *ex ante* constraints on the executive that avoid public *ex post* embarrassments such as failure to implement agreed policies.

According to the Delegation Hypothesis, we should expect to see parliaments moving to create stronger institutions to structure EU negotiations and provide information about these negotiations when the issues being negotiated are more contentious, when governments have overstepped the bounds of delegated authority, and under conditions of minority government. The history of parliamentary institutions on EU issues in the 1990s provides strong support for the first two of these propositions. Support for the third is important in the Danish case, considered in more detail in the next chapter. Overall, it appears that delegation models provide significant explanatory leverage when attempting to understand the development of parliamentary institutions in the EU. The internal structure of parliaments determines the level of delegation to the executive, and is itself determined by conflicts over the process of European integration (Hegeland and Mattson 1996). The Abdication Hypothesis cannot explain these developments.

As long as the government properly anticipates legislative reactions when reaching international agreements, we should expect to see minimal legislative activity in parliaments if the delegation logic of chapter 2 is correct. However, a pattern of "behind-the-scenes" influence creates the potential to infer mistakenly that parliaments have been closed out of the process and that governments do not have to take their preferences into account. "In studying policymaking it is natural to focus on the units making the actual decisions. However, concentrating on *acts* of decision making rather than on *influences* over decision making is a kind of myopia that can lead to false conclusions about where the responsibility for policies lies" (Calvert, McCubbins, and Weingast 1989, 590). Most member-state governments seem to have believed until quite recently that their parliaments could not influence EU policymaking. Thus, the new consternation and activity within national parliaments caught executives by surprise, reminding them in a most unwelcome way of the limits of their powers. The next chapter turns to consider the implications of the fact that parliaments are now less willing to let governments exercise a free hand in EU negotiations, having reclaimed some of the powers they had earlier delegated.

CHAPTER 7

Implementing the EU's Internal Market: The Influence of National Parliaments

CHAPTER 6 demonstrated that the institutions created by national parliaments to structure their interactions with governments on EU business respond in a regular manner to incentives to constrain government negotiators. As conflict over European integration has increased in the 1990s, parliaments have developed stronger institutions in an attempt to more tightly constrain governments. In addition, parliamentary committees are strongest in those states with the most conflict of interest about European integration. The Delegation Hypothesis is supported in the member states of the EU. However, the previous chapter did not turn to the next, probably more important, question of whether stronger parliamentary institutions make any difference for the course of European integration. This chapter looks at the effects of parliamentary institutions. It considers the Credibility Hypothesis: institutionalized legislative participation in the process of international cooperation enhances the credibility of states' commitments.

Debates about the role of national parliaments in European Union policymaking usually are framed as regarding a choice *between* democracy and efficiency (e.g., see *Economist,* 7 July 1990, survey 34; House of Commons 1995). Studies of European integration claim that national parliaments are uninterested, uninvolved, and unable to influence the course of European integration. Proponents of integration have generally considered this supposed parliamentary incompetence a good thing, since parliamentary involvement would only slow down integration, perhaps leading to paralysis (Fitzmaurice 1996, 880). However, if we consider the entire process of European integration—implementation as well as negotiation—we gain a new perspective on processes that allow regular parliamentary influence. Because parliaments retain significant authority at the implementation stage of integration, failure to involve them in the negotiation stage can pose severe obstacles to effective adjustment of policies. But where parliaments play an acknowledged and transparent role in EU business, implementation proceeds smoothly. Thus, the apparent conflict between parliamentary democracy and integration disappears on fuller inspection of the cooperation process, since democracy enhances rates of implementation, an important aspect of integration. Closing parliaments out of EU negotiations can only enhance the prospects for cooperation if the credibility of commitments is irrelevant.

This chapter considers the implementation of international agreements in the context of the EU, using implementation rates as a measure of credibility. While the name "European Union" implies a form of political organization that goes beyond an international institution, reflecting the aspirations of the EU's founders and some contemporary policymakers, in many respects the process of reaching and implementing agreements within the Union is like that in any international institution.

Member states have retained influence through their responsibility for implementation of directives adopted through the EU legislative process. The Commission monitors the process of implementation, identifying laggard states and publishing reports on their implementation records. The European Court of Justice (ECJ) also figures in implementation, primarily as a dispute-resolution and standard-setting mechanism. But national governments, in the Treaties of Rome and in practice, are responsible for changing domestic law to conform to European law, a fact that has been reinforced in a series of ECJ judgments. The process of implementation remains the same as that assumed in political theories of international cooperation. While supranational institutions perform monitoring and dispute-resolution functions, states themselves must change their policies.

I argue that parliamentary involvement is not a liability in the process of integration. A well-organized, well-informed parliament, with clear relations of accountability to its government, can play a constructive role by enhancing the credibility of state commitments. Governments constrained by accountability to a parliament are, indeed, more difficult negotiating partners than those free to agree to any deals they like. However, this difficulty at the negotiation stage is offset by an expeditious implementation process, leading to fewer problems of reneging and renegotiation than we find in governments without transparent parliamentary constraints.

This chapter brings empirical evidence to bear on the connection between institutions and credibility. Here, we see that Denmark stands out in having an excellent implementation record in spite of a well-deserved reputation as a "reluctant European" (Ingebritsen 1997). I argue that this pattern is explained by Denmark's stringent system of parliamentary control of government ministers. Parliamentary control accounts for a good record of cooperation in spite of Denmark's reticence about rushing ahead with European integration; it may also give Denmark advantages at the bargaining stage. Thus, in this case, parliamentary democracy does not seriously impair international cooperation. Evidence from the newest member states, who also have relatively strong parliamentary committees and good implementation records, supports the pattern found in Denmark.

I then consider extensions of the analytical framework to explain further variation in implementation rates and alternative explanations. Since Denmark's system has been unique until recent years, parliamentary involvement cannot explain all observed variation. The autonomy of regional governments appears to be another major influence on implementation. Unless regional governments with responsibilities for implementation are well-integrated into the negotiation process, as in Germany, they become hindrances to implementation. Thus, the regional story supports the analytical framework developed here, in that institutions that will be involved at the implementation stage are best integrated into the negotiation process as well. Integration of domestic players can happen directly, for example with regional representatives at the international bargaining table, although such a process is cumbersome; it may best occur through domestic institutionalization of accountability. Unless such integration takes place, negotiators will fail to anticipate properly the difficulties of implementation, making them more liable to renege on agreements and threatening the success of European integration.

Domestic Institutions and Implementation

Not all legislatures are created equal in their ability to put effective constraints on executives. The U.S. Congress marks one end of a continuum in stable democracies, one where the division of powers between the executive and legislative branches of government gives Congress more direct influence than that typically enjoyed by European parliaments. However, recent attempts to apply a similar logic of delegation to parliamentary systems suggest that, while the details and mechanisms of control are different, similar lessons about needing to understand the nature and limits of executive power apply (Huber 1992, 1996). The ability of a parliament to influence policymaking depends in large part on the way in which it is organized; that is, on the institutional structure it has created for itself. An unorganized parliament—today's Russian *Duma* is an extreme example, recent Italian parliaments perhaps more relevant—may influence policy in only a negative way, by placing impediments in the way of governments. For parliaments and governments to work together effectively, the internal organization of the parliament and its mechanisms for calling the government to account are extremely important. These institutional features, such as organized and authoritative committees and oversight procedures, will have a substantial impact on a state's ability to cooperate effectively in international settings, including European integration.

The nature of legislative-executive interaction in parliamentary systems is the focus of a new body of work on parliamentary government. A model of parliamentary government that assumed that legislators dictate policy would have executives, i.e., the cabinet, simply implementing policy determined by parliament. Studies have found no evidence to support such a model (Laver and Shepsle 1994) and I do not wish to make that kind of argument here. Instead, as argued in chapter 1, legislative-executive interaction can be understood as an exchange process, one in which both executives and legislatures can benefit from certain institutional arrangements and in which the level of executive discretion to make policy becomes a central variable. As Laver and Shepsle (1994, 289) argue, executives in parliamentary systems are "constrained optimizers" who interact strategically with parliaments. The analytical task is to understand the nature of the constraints on executives and how they influence executive behavior both toward parliaments and, in this study, other states.[1] The Credibility Hypothesis, consistent with the constrained-optimization approach, posits that without consistent appreciation of parliamentary powers, the commitments that governments make to one another lack credibility. Formal engagement of parliaments may thus prove an asset in international cooperation.

The constrained-optimization approach stands in direct contrast to most work on European integration. Most studies argue that a lack of parliamentary constraints is an asset for integration, allowing it to proceed relatively rapidly. Moravcsik (1993, 515) argues that "ironically, the EC's 'democratic deficit' may be a fundamental source of its success." The logic of abdication models is that needing to convince parliaments to agree to commitments and to take parliamentary concerns into account, rather than simply circumventing them, would put significant obstacles in the way of pro-integration executives and supranational bureaucrats. The EU has been lucky, according to this perspective, in having "parliamentary democracies" that were largely a fiction, a euphemism for "cabinet government." Parliaments may have some influence over the makeup of cabinets. But once a cabinet is in place, there is little parliaments can do to control its policymaking, particularly EU policymaking.

Designing empirical research to elucidate parliamentary influence is not a trivial problem. If influence is exercised through nonobvious mechanisms such as anticipated reactions, the usual case-study approaches are likely to be misleading, since they are better designed to identify action than influence. However, the empirical problem is not intractable. Often, discovering patterns of influence requires that we search for patterned variation in outcomes. Emphasizing systematic variation allows us to identify evidence that may be obscured if we instead trace individual negotiation processes. Here, I argue that evidence for the Credibility Hypothesis lies in a positive correlation between formal parliamentary enmeshment in negotiations and efficient implementation

---

[1] Laver and Shepsle (1994, 294) point out that the cabinet in parliamentary systems has generally gained a great deal of control over the legislative agenda, constituting a major source of influence over policy that presidents lack. However, it is unclear how much this agenda-setting power extends to EU business, except in some circumstances in the most powerful member-states. For smaller states, and for all members most of the time, the agenda of EU business is established by a complicated set of negotiations and prior commitments. Governments do not have the power, as on domestic policy, of refusing to open the legislative gates if they anticipate that the outcome of the legislative process will leave them worse off than the status quo. Thus one of the most significant sources of cabinet power in parliamentary systems is substantially attenuated when we consider EU legislation.

of EU legislation. Abdication models, in contrast, give us no reason to expect any consistent correlation between the formal role of parliament and rates of implementation.

The credibility of the commitments that governments make during EU negotiations is at stake in the implementation process. I consider the implementation of EU agreements a key dependent variable, as a measure of credibility. Mechanisms of parliamentary influence often appear during implementation of agreements, especially if no direct avenue of influence is available earlier in the negotiation process. If governments' commitments are credible, we should see little reneging or foot-dragging at the implementation stage. Thus, the features that encourage credible commitments should lead to good implementation records, even if these features seem to make a state a tough bargaining partner during the negotiation stage (Allen 1992, 244). Theories of credible commitments and policy studies of implementation are thus closely tied to one another. Considering the logic of delegated authority and legislative-executive interaction, I suggest three factors that go into creating a process by which parliamentary involvement increases the credibility of a state's commitments. These three factors are early parliamentary involvement, government accountability, and transparency.[2]

Early parliamentary involvement is essential if governments are to be able to anticipate the level and nature of opposition to agreements they reach with other countries. The content of agreements that governments reach is typically quite detailed and technical, especially in the EU. The costs of agreements will fall unevenly on different districts back home. Information about the potential difficulties involved in implementation is therefore valuable. Legislative representatives are well placed to provide such information, as well as other information about potential implementation problems. The precise way in which such representatives should be involved during the negotiation process depends on the organization of a state's political system. For example, a system with strong party discipline may meet the requirement of early parliamentary involvement in a fairly simple manner by involving party leaders in the negotiation process. Systems without strong party discipline, such as the United States, are likely to have to rely on other mechanisms for early legislative involvement, such as interaction between the executive and senior members of relevant congressional committees. In either case, if executives fail to avail themselves of the opportunity to consult with the legislature during the negotiation process, they are likely to find themselves surprised by the extent or nature of opposition during implementation. The anticipated relation between early parliamentary engagement and efficiency of implementation repeats a common public-

---

[2] These criteria for parliamentary influence are similar to those Neunreither (1994, 304) identifies: early information, governmental obligation to consult parliament, and the binding nature of parliamentary decisions.

policy lesson, that those involved in implementing policies should also be involved in designing them (Wallace 1984).

However, parliamentary involvement alone will do only modest good if government ministers are not *accountable* to parliamentary representatives. One of the key problems national parliaments have faced in EU business, as in foreign policy more generally, is holding negotiators accountable. That is, parliaments have found it difficult to punish ministers who disregard parliamentary preferences by giving assent to international agreements to which parliaments object. They may still undermine the credibility of the government's commitment by refusing to implement agreements. But unless negotiators feel that they will have to pay some penalty for committing the state to an agreement that will not be implemented efficaciously, the risk of involuntary defection remains.

Domestic accountability may have another effect, by encouraging ministers to invest the necessary time and energy to master the details of European legislation. The substance of EU directives and other bargains is complex and full of details. Busy ministers, unless they have clear incentives to study the details, may not fully understand the implications of any specific piece of proposed legislation. The potential for such lack of understanding to hinder implementation back home, as the implications of legislation become clear, is high. In addition, a relatively uninformed minister is unlikely to be a particularly skillful bargainer, and so will not be able to exert much leverage to modify EU legislation in the directions that constituents desire. In states where domestic accountability is strong and transparent, as Danish ministers have noted, the incentives to master the details of complex EU bargaining and legislation process on individual issues are strong. If ministers are later found by interested MPs to have been derelict in their responsibilities to represent Danish interests at the EU table, which requires investing in information about EU legislation, they will pay a political price. In states without such clear mechanisms of accountability, ministers can more easily evade blame and so are less likely to gain the necessary expertise to either bargain well or assure rapid implementation.

Third, ratification processes that are *transparent* are more likely to lead to credible commitments. By transparent, I mean that the steps for implementation, and identification of those who will be involved or have veto power, should be obvious.[3] Transparency makes it less likely that negotiators will be able to fool themselves—and others—into thinking that they can circumvent opposition later. Most EU members have not until recently developed a clear system of responsibility for EU business within their parliaments. This failure has led to a great deal of uncertainty about which committees, if any, will be involved

---

[3] I do not mean to imply that all discussions between the legislature and executive should be made public. Such publicity has a number of drawbacks, including potential undermining of strategic advantages that flow from keeping one's reservation point private knowledge. Transparency inheres in the process by which ratification takes place, and is often facilitated by clear, formalized procedures.

in implementation, whether a policy will be treated as "domestic" or "foreign" policy, which interest groups will have access to politicians, etc. These types of uncertainty, while perhaps allowing the government a freer hand during negotiations, will come back to haunt a state when it attempts to put into practice the policies to which the government has committed it.

In sum, a focus on negotiation rather than implementation of agreements has led, in the European context, to downplaying the role of national parliaments in the integration process. Successful achievement of the goals of European integration, such as a "level playing field" for businesses across member states, requires that the bargains to which governments commit themselves are put into place on the domestic level. Once we consider the implementation stage of the cooperation process, we find that parliaments can reassert themselves. Governments' commitments are more likely to be credible, and so implementation records better, if parliaments are involved at an early stage in the negotiation process, if clear patterns of accountability between governments and parliaments are established, and if the implementation process is transparent. As theories of legislative-executive interaction suggest, indirect mechanisms of legislative influence arise at the implementation stage. This chapter looks directly at the implementation stage. The next section turns to Denmark as an example of how parliamentary democracy can facilitate implementation of EU bargains.

EXPLAINING IMPLEMENTATION RATES

Responsibility for transforming agreed measures for European integration into the necessary changes in domestic law lies with national governments. EU legislation takes two primary forms: *regulations* and *directives* (Nugent 1991, 168–71). Regulations have "direct effect," meaning that they supersede national legislation and so do not require explicit domestic action in order to be incorporated into domestic law. Direct effect may be an efficient process, but it leaves governments no flexibility to modify legislation to take account of specific characteristics of their own domestic situations. Governments may therefore tend to favor directives, many of which do not have direct effect. Directives must be incorporated into domestic legislation through whatever process is specified in domestic law (Duina 1997).

Incorporation brings in national parliaments, directly or indirectly. Often parliaments must pass the necessary legislation themselves. In another common procedure, governments may use delegated powers to treat EU directives as secondary legislation, so that they can be incorporated through executive action. However, even indirect procedures require parliamentary delegation of the authority to use secondary legislation. Attempts to circumvent usual domestic legislative mechanisms when implementing directives have been found unacceptable in a number of cases brought before the European Court of Justice (ECJ), for example in Ireland, Italy, and Belgium. Parliaments retain at least the formal capacity to influence the implementation of EU legislation, suggesting that mechanisms exist to create variation in implementation rates. I focus on directives, as they are central to the process of integration and because we have good data available on their implementation.

Implementation Records

Governments' implementation performance in the EU is monitored through the use of both police patrols and fire alarms (McCubbins and Schwartz 1984). Citizens, businesses, and other member states can ring fire alarms by notifying the Commission of perceived failures to implement EU legislation. This method of monitoring is quite effective, with hundreds of complaints coming in every year. The Commission supplements the fire alarm system of monitoring with its own equivalent of police patrols: investigations and public reports on member states' performance. The Commission thus provides two types of information: regular reports on the number of directives implemented on the national level and publication of violations it discovers. I concentrate here on the former, as they provide a systematic and simple measure of the rate of implementation.[4]

Prior to the 1992 program to complete the internal market, data on implementation were sporadic, at best. Governments resist providing information on their implementation records and the Commission lacked a standard by which to compare governments to one another. Occasional studies by academics and lawyers indicated which member states had a good or bad reputation for implementation, although these findings were not backed up with hard numbers (Ciavarini Azzi 1985). However, the early studies pointed to one trend that has been confirmed more recently: Denmark has an unusually good implementation record, in spite of its reputation as a reluctant participant in European integration. This observation poses a puzzle that provides insight into the role of national parliaments more generally.

The process of completing the internal market, the major project of the SEA, was spurred on by the adoption of a white paper outlining nearly three hundred specific measures that states should take to remove barriers to the flow of people, goods, and services across borders within the EU. The white paper greatly facilitated agreement and implementation of the internal market by providing transparency and standardization. Its directives made clear what each government committed itself to do, thus reducing fears that some states would be doing more than others. The Commission, under direction from the Council and the

---

[4] There may be a regular bias inherent in using the Commission reports as indicators of implementation rates. It is likely that this measure systematically overstates the level of implementation, since it does not ask whether these laws are actually enforced. However, as discussed below, more direct examination of enforcement difficulties suggests similar patterns to those we find with the Commission data. In addition, there is little reason to expect that the level of overestimation of implementation varies much across countries. As long as the bias toward overestimating rates is consistent across countries, we can comfortably use these data to compare countries to one another.

EP, contributed to the transparency of the process by agreeing to publish semi-annual reports on the progress of the white-paper directives. These Commission reports specify exactly which white-paper directives each member state has incorporated into domestic law. They thus allow us to answer a number of questions about the progress of different types of directives and of the success of each government in living up to its commitments. While these measures may not be a complete measure of implementation—they ask only whether domestic law has been changed appropriately, not whether it is being enforced—they provide a systematic survey of each state's behavior.

Through 1991, businesses and other observers expressed a great deal of concern that states were not implementing the white-paper directives on schedule, and that this failure would in practice lead to failure of the single market (Bronckers 1989). Scholars worried about an "implementation deficit." Colchester and Buchan (1990) noted that by the end of 1989, only 14 of the 88 directives that should have been put into national legislation had in fact completed this process in all member states. They worried that "here is where doubts arise about 1992" (p. 131). Following the standard logic about problems of international cooperation, they argued that "uneven implementation of EC rules could distort competition across the market quite as much as having no rules at all" (p. 132), leading to a backlash among the "virtuous" states and potentially escalating into a tit-for-tat, foot-dragging battle. And the situation was only likely to get worse: "The temptation will mount for member states to renege on EC commitments that multiply and become more onerous as project 1992 and its manifold directives bite more deeply into their affairs" (p. 138). In Denmark, which has an excellent implementation record, the failure of other member states to follow suit leads to frequent public complaints, as academic worries about the consequences of nonimplementation would predict (Knudsen 1992, 291).

As of the end of 1989, Colchester and Buchan identified Italy as having a very poor implementation reputation, with a government willing to agree to ambitious integration directives without considering its ability to get them through the bureaucracy and parliament back home. At this point, Italy had converted into national law only 35 of the 88 directives it should have by that time. In part, Italy's poor record was due to constant changes of government, leading to gridlock not only in implementation of EU directives but in the entire national legislative process. Italy also had the most letters of complaint issued against it in 1988: 107, compared to 64 for Greece, the next highest. These findings continue a long, consistent history of Italy dragging its feet until prodded to take action by the Commission.

Following the Commission's reports through time, we can see that the performance of states seems, in general, to vary considerably from year to year. Figure 7.1 traces implementation rates from 1989 to 1992.

Many states seem to pass legislation in spurts, quickly bringing them from a poor record to a good one. For example, as of the end of 1989 Portugal had an

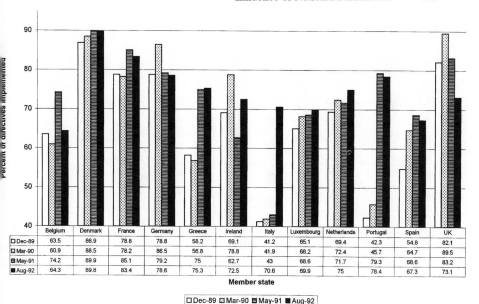

Figure 7.1. Implementation rates, 1989–1992.

implementation record at the bottom of the scale, along with Italy. However, by August 1992 it was in a virtual tie with Germany for the third *best* record in the EU. Between March and October 1990, according to Commission records, Portugal jumped from implementing less than 50% of directives to implementing over 80%, controlling for the deadlines by which directives should have been implemented (Commission of the European Communities 1992, annex 8). In 1989, an apparent inability of the southern members of the EU to pass legislation made arguments about "political culture" an attractive explanation for performance, as the three new entrants (Greece, Spain, and Portugal), plus Italy, had the worst records.

But all this changed by August 1992. Then, Belgium had the worst record; Portugal and Greece had dramatically improved theirs, moving into the top half of the EU. Germany, with a good record early on, fell to ninth place by March 1993, perhaps reflecting the strains and distractions of unification. Figure 7.2 shows implementation records as of August 15, 1992, a date as representative as any and at which we see substantial variation in performance. Figure 7.3 shows average implementation rates for 1990–1997, showing that many patterns observed in 1992 extend to the rest of the 1990s, with very good performance by Denmark. Figure 7.3 also includes data on the three new member states, which began implementing directives in 1995.

Through all this variation and inconstancy, one consistent fact stands out:

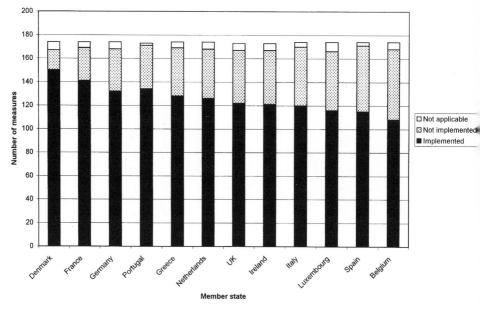

Figure 7.2. Measures implemented as of 15 August 1992.

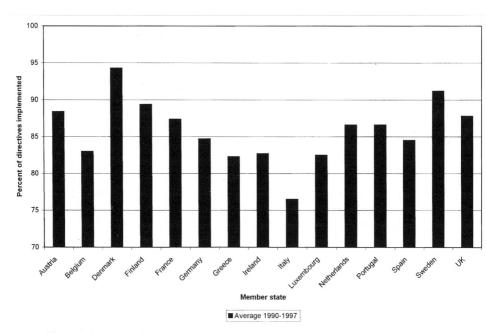

Figure 7.3. Average implementation rate, 1990–1997.

Denmark has the best implementation record. It had the best record in 1989, having incorporated over 70 of 88 directives. As of August 1992, it had implemented 89.8% of the directives it should have (150 of 167), compared to an EU average of 74.8%, and a rate of 64.3% for Belgium at the bottom of the scale. The Commission's figures are supported by Denmark's record on being taken to court for infringements of EU law, which show that Denmark has one of the best enforcement records. It has rarely been taken to court, and the ECJ has rarely decided against Denmark. For example, from 1981–1988 Denmark had 189 letters of complaint filed with the Commission, compared to 376 for Belgium and 253 for the Netherlands (Colchester and Buchan 1990, 140).[5] During the same period, Denmark was faced with only 13 court cases, compared to 90 for Belgium and 23 for the Netherlands. Audretsch (1986, 356) also finds very few judgments against Denmark. (See also Ciavarini Azzi 1988, 194.)

A report in 1997 found a similar pattern with almost no prosecutions against Denmark in the ECJ, while Belgium headed the list (*Economist,* 17 May 1997, 60). Commission infringement statistics for the mid-to-late-1990s show continuing good performance by Denmark, with the lowest number of letters of formal notice filed against it.[6] While these data are subject to more difficulties of interpretation than those collected by the Commission on incorporation of European law, they do suggest that Denmark not only transposes European law into domestic law quickly, it also lives up to the commitments expressed in these laws. Thus data on transposition appear to be an accurate indicator of implementation.

The Danish Parliamentary Solution

If one were to suggest the intuitive notion that states' performance in living up to their commitments was a straightforward function of their liking for those commitments, the implementation figures for Denmark would be quite surprising. An explanation based on preferences alone cannot help us understand why Denmark's performance is held up as an example to other member states. Denmark has become known as a reluctant member of the EU, a "footnote country" that is not enthusiastic about ambitious integration schemes and frequently demands (and receives) special treatment in EU agreements. Danish negotiators bargain hard, unlike their counterparts from some of the other small northern member states. Denmark did not join the EU until Britain did in 1973. The initial Danish rejection of the TEU, due to a "no" vote in the first referen-

---

[5] The number of complaints is, of course, positively correlated with the size of a state, so I chose other small states for comparison. France, for example, had 606 complaints filed during this period.

[6] "Single Market: New Scoreboard Reflects Significant Progress," http://europa.eu.int/comm/dg15/en/update/score/score2.htm, 12 October 1998.

dum in 1992, symbolized and confirmed continuing Danish skepticism about the process of integration that many Danes perceived to be racing ahead too swiftly.[7] While by 1992 EU membership had come to be accepted and seen as advantageous by the Danish public, there remained a strong reluctance to more ahead rapidly with extensive transfer of authority to EU bodies (Schou 1992; Branner 1992). It is simply implausible to suggest that Denmark implements EU agreements efficaciously because there is a consistent domestic consensus in favor of EU membership and deep integration. We must turn to other factors to explain the observed pattern.

The Danish political system has always put tight constraints on the government's ability to commit to international agreements. Ratification procedures are stringent, involving either large parliamentary majorities or popular referenda. The Danish constitution specifies that ratification of treaties requires a five-sixths supermajority in the *Folketing,* the Danish parliament. If a treaty is not able to gain this high level of parliamentary support, it can only be ratified by a majority vote in a national referendum in which at least 30 percent of the electorate is participating (Elklit and Petersen 1973, 198). These procedures have influenced the major Danish decisions about EU membership. In 1972, Denmark held a referendum to decide about joining the EC. The accession treaty passed with over 63 percent of the popular vote (Borre 1986, 191). Ratification of the SEA also went to a referendum, since the necessary majority did not materialize in the Folketing for partisan reasons. The procedure in 1986 was slightly different than that specified in the constitution, since the referendum was merely a consultative one, not binding. The voters approved the SEA by a vote of 56 percent in favor (Worre 1988). Following the vote, the parliament dropped its opposition and gave the necessary supermajority approval of the SEA.

The Credibility Hypothesis relates legislative institutions to the credibility of states' commitments. Following this logic, the highly activist participation of the Folketing in EU business suggests a solution to the puzzle of Danish performance. The Danish example suggests that parliamentary democracy and European integration are not at all contradictory; in fact, they may support one another. States without strong parliamentary control may have governments that are willing to commit themselves readily to ambitious integration schemes. However, these governments will find themselves handicapped at the implementation stage, presenting at least as significant a block to integration as tough negotiating behavior.

Considering institutional constraints helps unravel a paradox noted by students of European integration. Surprisingly, there seems to be little correlation between the general support a member state expresses for the EU and its implementation record. In a comprehensive study of implementation, Ciavarini Azzi (1988, 196) finds that "the Member States which pose basic problems during the

---

[7] For analysis of the Danish vote, see Nielsen (1992) and Worre (1995).

negotiations are not necessarily the ones which will create problems during the implementation." Toonen (1992, 111–12) supports Ciavarini Azzi's view:

> Italy has been constantly one of the frontrunners where the high politics of institutional reform and "deepened" integration of the European Community is concerned. The country is, however, notoriously lagging behind where the transposition and actual implementation of Community directives are concerned. Denmark, in contrast, is renowned as being one of the most critical members of the Community. . . . A look at the transposition and the actual implementation of EC directives in the national legal and administrative system shows, however, that Denmark is among the countries with the "best" compliance records.

Earlier studies of implementation have found that Italy's consistently poor record is in part due to the "quasiabsence" of parliament, leaving the government to act unilaterally (Guizzi and Leanza 1985, 62). At least in Italy, government flexibility does not appear to encourage cooperative behavior in any deep sense.

Lack of enthusiasm in the Folketing for European integration, which reflects popular skepticism more widely, has led to the development of a structure whereby Danish ministers' ability to make concessions in EU negotiations is constrained tightly by a mandate from parliament. Williams (1991, 159) points out that only Denmark "has managed to retain significant leverage over the Council by dint of closely controlling its own national representatives at Council meetings." Even before formal entry into the EU, the Folketing set up a Market Relations Committee (MRC), charged with oversight of EU activities.[8] The MRC endeavored to constrain government negotiators to agree to bargains only after receiving a mandate from the committee and to keep itself informed about all ongoing business of any importance in the Council. At one point just after Danish entry into the EU, a government minister was perceived to have gone beyond his MRC mandate during Council negotiations. This led to a crisis that threatened to bring down the minority government, which the government resolved by making guarantees to negotiate only within the parameters set by the MRC. The system of consultation and constraint has now been institutionalized, leading to Danish ministers having little flexibility and negotiating with tied hands (Fitzmaurice 1976; Hegeland and Mattson 1996, 210). The system that Denmark has developed characterizes a "strong state" in the revised sense discussed in chapter 2, a state that has a kind of institutionalized decentralism that allows the government to get things done. One analyst describes the Danish state in these terms, noting that it is highly rule-bound and that the center has fairly low powers, but arguing that it has the legitimacy necessary to implement decisions (Knudsen 1992, 275, 284).

In contrast to most other member states, the making of EU policy in Den-

---

[8] The MRC was renamed the European Affairs Committee after the TEU.

mark is highly politicized and the Folketing is the focus of political activity. The Danish system assures extensive consultation with the legislature throughout the negotiation process. The MRC acts as if it has a binding mandate on its ministers and threatens government viability if ministers neglect the constraints it imposes (Rasmussen 1988, 96). Representation on the MRC is proportional to party representation in the Folketing and representatives are prominent members of their parties (Hagel-Sørenson and Rasmussen 1985; Fitzmaurice 1981, 138). Their assent to negotiating positions thus assures majority support in the Folketing, in spite of the fact that Denmark has in recent years had perpetual minority governments (Marquand 1981, 235). Danish ministers see the credibility that the MRC arrangement gives them as an important asset in EU-level bargaining (Møller 1983). The MRC is in nearly constant session, not meeting sporadically as have EU-responsible committees in other member states. The government provides the MRC with a constant flow of information on proposed legislation and changes that occur during the negotiation process in the Council (European Centre for Parliamentary Research and Documentation 1990, 8–9). Overall, parliamentary institutions allow for a high degree of parliamentary influence. "The Danish committee members also state that they expect, and see it as natural, to exert influence over governmental policy" (Hegeland and Mattson 1996, 204).

Why does this institutionalized mandate procedure matter? Because it assures the three components that were identified above as necessary to effective commitment strategies. The Folketing is involved at an early stage, assuring that potential opposition to policies is anticipated properly by the government. The government is accountable to parliamentary representatives, in this case through the mechanism of MRC oversight. And the procedure is transparent, so that negotiating partners and those affected by the laws have a good understanding of who has leverage in the policymaking process. MRC proceedings and discussions with ministers are not published, for fear that publication would compromise Denmark's bargaining leverage in the Council. However, the process is transparent in that there is little uncertainty about the process that will be used to determine negotiating positions and to whom the government is accountable.

Domestic institutions thus provide Denmark with twofold advantages. They increase Danish bargaining leverage over that possessed by other small member states as well as improving implementation performance. It is not possible to show conclusively that Denmark has received "more" concessions than it merits, based on its size and economic power. However, a great deal of circumstantial evidence, beginning with the results of the "no" vote on the TEU in 1992, shows Denmark to be an unusually effective negotiator. After the "no" vote, Denmark won a number of opt-outs, allowing it to decide unilaterally not to participate in a single currency, security arrangements, and European citizenship (Worre 1995, 256; Gjørtler 1993, 359; Martin 1993b). Another indicator of Denmark's strong bargaining power is its ability to transfer EU resources in its direction. Denmark is the only EU member state in the top eight with respect to GNP per capita (with the exception of Luxembourg) that had a positive balance of net receipts in 1994, receiving more from the EU budget than it paid in (Baldwin, Francois, and Portes 1997, 163). In 1994 it ranked third in GNP per capita, behind Luxembourg and Belgium. If receipts from the EU budget responded solely to incentives to offset differences in wealth, this should have put Denmark near the bottom of the net receipt chart. Instead, it ranks sixth in the net receipt chart, receiving more than poorer countries including Italy, Germany, and the UK.

In addition to these statistical indicators, the Danish government has come to see its good reputation for implementation as extremely valuable and takes steps to protect it. According to Siedentopf and Hauschild (1988, 41), the "Danish government would rather sacrifice even important local policy-interests than jeopardize its good compliance record. This is an important factor in the Danish process of EC policy-making and interest groups expect the Danish government to live up to this." Widespread support for subsuming particularistic interests to maintain a good compliance record suggests that the record itself is an asset for the government. Møller (1983, 258), having been involved in EU negotiations, affirms this impression that the credibility of Danish negotiators provides them with additional leverage and is worth making sacrifices to maintain.

Members of national parliaments interested in EU affairs, as well as the European Commission, have begun to recognize the importance of engaging those parties responsible for implementation at an early stage in the negotiation process. A conference held to study implementation in 1989 concluded that "in fact, the tendency to speed up the decision making through avoiding preliminary negotiations with those ultimately concerned leads to the slowing down of the actual implementation through post-factum 're-negotiations' and a reluctance to put the measures into practice" (Govaere and Hélin 1990, 687). Participants tied implementation failures directly to the "democratic deficit" existing procedures created in most member states. "In contrast, it seems that where the decision making at E.C. level is preceeded [sic] by consistent and well prepared negotiations at national level, implementation is less cumbersome. . . . It is now well established that a direct relationship exists between participation in the rule-making and the application of those rules" (emphasis added).

As other states appreciate the potential advantages of parliamentary involvement, and as parliaments organize to exert influence more consistently on the nature of EU bargains, other states are beginning on occasion to receive some of the benefits Denmark always has had from its domestic arrangements. For example, in discussions about admitting the new Alpine and Nordic members of the EU in 1994, the Spanish parliament held up ratification of the accession treaty, demanding and receiving compromises on provisions for access to fisheries, an issue of constant contention and high politicization within the EU (Granell 1995, 131). The recognition that parliamentary institutions were intimately linked to credibility showed up in Swedish deliberations. The commission that prepared the way for accession argued "that, as in Denmark, prior control will ensure that the government always has adequate parliamentary backing, enabling it to implement Community decisions" (Fitzmaurice 1996, 93).

Until the mid-1990s, since Denmark was the only member state with a strong EU committee, there was little point in looking at the overall pattern of implementation rates across the EU, except to ask whether Denmark stood out. However, as the previous chapter related, the early-to-mid-1990s saw a burst of activity within most national parliaments. In addition, the newest member states carefully crafted parliamentary mechanisms to provide them with some control over government activities. As a result, there is now enough variation in the strength of parliamentary committees to begin asking whether we can find a correlation between their strength and their implementation records.

Table 7.1 summarizes evidence on implementation records and the strength of member-state EU committees. The implementation rates included here are the average rate from 1990 through 1997, the same data found in figure 7.3. States are ranked from the best record (Denmark) to the worst (Italy). The third column of the table is a measure of the strength of the EU committee. The measure used is the "degree of binding" from Bergman (1997). Bergman based his

TABLE 7.1

Average Implementation Rate and Parliamentary Oversight, 1990–1997

Member State	Implementation Rate	"Degree of Binding"
Denmark	94.3	3
Sweden	91.2	2
Finland	89.4	2
Austria	88.4	3
UK	87.8	2
France	87.4	1
Netherlands	86.6	1
Portugal	86.6	1
Germany	84.7	3
Spain	84.5	1
Belgium	83.0	1
Ireland	82.5	1
Luxembourg	82.5	1
Greece	82.3	1
Italy	76.5	1

Sources: Implementation rates obtained from European Commission Directorate General XV; rating of parliamentary oversight from Bergman (1997), 377.

calculations of the extent to which committees could bind their governments on a thorough examination of the constitutional and practical powers of parliaments to gain information about negotiations, give ministers a mandate, and enforce their instructions to ministers. He ranked the committees from a high of three, achieved only by Denmark, Austria, and Germany, to a low of one, still the most common ranking.

This table shows a high positive correlation between the strength of the committee and a good implementation record, as the Credibility Hypothesis leads us to expect. With the notable exception of Germany, all states with a ranking of two or three are at the top of the implementation ranks; those with weak committees are at the bottom. The correlation between the implementation rate and the degree of binding is 0.62. The German exception is somewhat surprising, since German implementation rates were good in the 1980s. A number of factors may account for its relatively poor performance in the 1990s. The difficulties of unification, and incorporation of the eastern *Länder* into the consultation system, may have caused unanticipated problems. This could especially be the case in a federal system where the Länder have responsibilities for implementation, as discussed below. Another possibility is that a unified Germany, the monetary powerhouse of the EU, feels less pressure to keep up with implementation than the smaller, poorer member states. However, even taking into account the German exception, table 7.1 shows that the pattern begun by Denmark can be generalized across the EU. As member states create more powerful committees to oversee EU affairs, which gain the power to bind their governments, their record of implementation improves.

Overall, evidence on implementation rates bears out the expectations developed from considering the impact of legislative involvement and delegation. If abdication models are correct, we should see no correlation between formal parliamentary involvement and implementation. The Credibility Hypothesis, on the other hand, suggests a positive correlation. The Danish Folketing, which has a more powerful position domestically than other parliaments of EU member states, has organized itself to exercise tight control over government ministers in their dealings with other member states. Far from making Denmark an unwieldy partner in cooperation, the institutionalized involvement of the parliament has led to Denmark's excellent record in implementing EU-level agreements. Because negotiators have consulted with representatives of interested parties beforehand, they do not commit themselves to agreements that will be difficult to force through back home, and Denmark does not find it necessary to renege on or renegotiate agreements in spite of the potential handicaps of minority government. The Danish experience bears out one of the primary lessons of public policy studies, that early involvement in the negotiation process by those parties who will have to implement agreements assures more efficient implementation (Siedentopf 1988, 171). However, the implications of parliamentary structure and enmeshment go well beyond a technical administrative viewpoint, suggesting that European integration is consistent with, and perhaps even supported by, well-organized parliamentary involvement in EU negotiations. It is not surprising, and should not be troubling, that other national parliaments are becoming more deeply involved in EU business.

ALTERNATIVE EXPLANATIONS AND EXTENSIONS

Parliamentary structure is not the only factor that explains rates of implementation. Of the models that could potentially explain further variation in rates, some are extensions of the basic analytical framework developed in this book, while others are best seen as alternative explanations. In this section, I briefly consider other explanations for impediments to implementation of EU agreements. Two extensions that seem particularly promising concentrate on the role of regional governments and the transparency of directives themselves.

The evidence discussed thus far allows us to reject some alternative explanations of rates of implementation. For example, consider what we would expect to see if executive-dominance models were correct. These would lead us to predict one of two patterns. One possibility is that we would expect little relation between domestic institutions and rates, since the formalities of domestic institutions merely disguise the fact of executive dominance. Since we do find significant variation in rates of implementation, and that these are connected predictably to domestic structures, this particular executive-dominance hypothesis does not hold up. An alternative implication of executive dominance, perhaps more consistent with usual treatments of European integration, might lead us to expect that implementation would be *fastest* in those states where domestic institutions clearly delegated authority for implementation to the executive, excluding the national parliament. If there is a marked trade-off between democracy and efficiency, and if European integration is genuinely a process dominated by and responsive only to elites, we should expect a positive correlation between executive discretion and rapid implementation. Of course, we have discovered just the opposite, leading us to reject this hypothesis as well.

Another vast body of work on European integration falls under the label of neofunctionalism (Haas 1958). To simplify drastically a complex and rich literature, the neofunctionalist approach sees integration as a gradual process of transfer of authority to the supranational level. Through a process of spillover, in which supranational policymaking on one issue creates pressures to extend the scope of supranational institutions to other issues, these institutions and supranational decision-makers gain authority at the expense of national decision-makers. Some of this neofunctionalist logic is apparent in the linked pressures for completion of the internal market and monetary union. As other barriers to the free movement of goods and services within the EU fall, the persistence of separate currencies and independent national monetary policies emerges as an impediment to realization of the full benefits of the internal market. Thus pressures arise to coordinate monetary policies, even to the extent of creating a single currency and a European central bank. According to neofunctionalist logic, as individuals realize that supranational institutions can better protect their interests than national representatives, they will transfer their political loyalties to supranational institutions, leading to the creation of a European political identity.

Neofunctionalism leads to its own predictions about patterns of implementation, predictions that are not as easy to dismiss as those from the executive-dominance perspective. If functions and loyalties are indeed being transferred to the European level, we would expect to see convergence in national implementation rates over time. Domestic structures would come to have little impact on rates of implementation, since important political functions and decisions would take place at the European, not the national, level. Table 7.1 provides some evidence to support this neofunctionalist prediction. In 1989, we see high variance in implementation rates, ranging from a low of 41.2% in Italy to a high of 86.9% in Denmark. At this point, Denmark was outperforming the slowest member by a factor of more than two. By 1992, the variance has dropped. Now, Belgium holds the low position, at 64.3%, while Denmark remains the highest, with 89.8%. In 1989, the standard deviation in implementation rates was 14.8; by 1992, it had dropped to 7.03. It fell further, to 2.14, by 1997, in spite of the addition of three new members. In addition, the neofunctionalist model might lead us to expect a gradual improvement in implementation rates. This pattern also shows up in the SEA data, with a mean rate of 65.9% in 1989, 74.9% in 1992, and 93.8% in 1997.

These results suggest that we should take seriously the possibility that neofunctionalism tells us something important about implementation, at least with respect to the completion of the internal market. The proposition that functions are gradually being transferred from the national to the supranational level has empirical support. However, two observations should suggest caution before substituting a neofunctionalist model for one that considers the domestic characteristics of states. First, it is important to keep in mind that we are indeed examining data on the one issue on which the most authority has been transferred to Brussels. The extent of delegation of policymaking authority away from states has gone much further in the quest to complete the internal market than on any other issue. To provide a more rigorous test of neofunctionalism, we would need to examine a range of different issues, to see if similar patterns of convergence hold. Given the extent of variation remaining on even the internal market, it does not appear that the time has yet arrived to abandon analysis of domestic institutions in Europe. Second, convergence and improvement of implementation rates over time are also consistent with the Credibility Hypothesis. As discussed in the previous chapter, national parliaments have been strengthening their oversight mechanisms in the 1990s. This domestic-level process predicts the same trend in implementation rates as does neofunctionalism, and provides a strong alternative explanation.

Regionalism and Federalism

The experience of federal systems (as in Germany), or political systems that give significant autonomy to regional governments (like Spain and Belgium), suggests lessons that support the Credibility Hypothesis. States where those responsible for implementing agreements, whether in the national parliament or regional governments, are involved in the negotiation process have better records of implementation. In some systems regional governments are the key actors at the implementation stage. While the role of the national parliament set Denmark apart from the rest of the EU, other features of domestic political institutions are likely to have their own effects on the implementation of international agreements. In particular, studies have suggested that federal systems and, similarly, those that give significant autonomy to regional governments, are likely to have difficulties implementing directives efficaciously (From and Stava 1993). The reasons are similar to those for the logic of parliamentary involvement. Under a federal system, subnational governments have responsibility for much implementation of legislation. In Germany, the Länder actually implement most EU directives, rather than the federal government (Goetz 1995; *Economist,* 21 June 1997, 52). In Spain and Belgium, regional governments have acquired authority for much implementation. Following the logic developed above, we can expect that unless these regional governments are integrated into negotiations early and have a clearly specified role in the entire integration process, problems would arise during the implementation stage.

In fact, this seems to be the case. Belgium, although an original member of the EU, a strong supporter of integration, and home to the major EU institutions, has a very poor implementation record. As of August 1992, it had the worst in the Union. Earlier studies found that implementation deficits were a long-standing Belgian problem, and noted that since ministers did not consult the regions, the regions did not feel bound by the results of EU-level negotiations (Defalque 1985, 19). Spain's performance, like that of other new members, started out quite weakly. It is not surprising that new members, particularly those just going through processes of democratic consolidation such as Spain and Portugal, find it difficult to adapt quickly to the slew of major changes in domestic legislation required by EU membership. However, over the last few years Portugal and Greece have dramatically improved their records. Portugal, in particular, is striking for its rapid adoption of the internal market, considering its backward economic structure and lowest per-capita GDP in the EU. The completion of the internal market was seen by both the prime minister, Aníbal Cavaco Silva, and the president, Mário Soares, as an opportunity to force modernization of the Portuguese economy. The fact that these two leaders represented the two major parties meant that support for modernization and consultation with affected groups was widespread. By 1992, Portugal's performance at implementing directives was exemplary, the third best in the EU.

Spain, in contrast, has continued to be a laggard in spite of starting from a stronger economic position than Portugal and having similar economic goals. As in Belgium, regional autonomy without consultation greatly complicates the implementation process. The Spanish court system recently considered whether regional authority to implement legislation might be circumvented by the national government in the case of EU law, but determined that the procedures specified domestically remained in place in spite of the demands of EU membership (Santacruz 1991). The ECJ reached a similar decision for Belgium, going on to argue that these difficulties did not excuse the national government from its responsibility to assure implementation of directives. Responsibility without authority creates severe obstacles: "As there is no coercitive [*sic*] power of the Government *vis-à-vis* the 'Regions' or 'Communities,' quite a number of Community directives remain unimplemented" (Lenaerts and Coppenholle 1992, 452). Belgium is considering a number of measures to improve its implementation capacity, including the creation of a "European cell" within the Council of State. "This substitute for full parliamentary democracy within the Community itself would at the same time facilitate the later implementation of the outcome of the Community's legislative process at national level" (p. 453).

Germany, at least up until 1993, does not appear to have been so handicapped by its federal structure as Spain and Belgium, although the German Länder have responsibility for implementation of EU directives (Goetz 1995, 95). Perhaps this record is not surprising, as Germany is one of the three most influential states within the EU and generally pro-integration. However, another distinction stands out that helps to explain how Germany overcomes the potential obstacles posed by federalism. In contrast to Spain and Belgium, where the subnational governments are closed out of the legislative process until the implementation stage, the Länder have gained a seat for themselves at the negotiating table and the ability to constrain the federal government (Hrbek 1992; Neunreither 1994, 306). The points at which the Länder have influence have increased over time (Goetz 1995, 105). Constant institutionalized interaction, at the federal level and in Brussels, allows information to flow in both directions, from the Länder to the national executive and back again. In Germany, constraints on the government flow more directly from regional representatives than from the parliament. Because the Länder are involved in the negotiating process early on, the government can anticipate and bargain around potential implementation difficulties. The Länder are also warned about upcoming directives, allowing for more efficient implementation (Goetz 1995, 103).[9]

[9] For a detailed study of the contrast between Belgium and Germany, see the analysis of implementation of directives on the quality of bathing waters in Ciavarini Azzi (1985, 148–71). In Belgium, the decentralization of power created great difficulties. In Germany, the Länder were consulted from the beginning, leading to a smooth implementation process. However, it is worth noting

The regional story thus fits closely the logic of the parliamentary account. Those with authority for implementation, whether national parliaments or regional governments, should be involved in the integration process early. The alternative is to allow governments to behave as if they are unconstrained and to deprive them of information about potential difficulties of implementation, leaving them to confront serious domestic resistance to implementing EU directives and making them unreliable partners in international cooperation.

Transparency of Directives

The substance of directives is likely to provide additional leverage to explain patterns of implementation. The delegation framework implies that transparency will improve implementation. Transparency inheres in the characteristics of directives themselves, as well as the procedures by which they are ratified. In its reports to the Council and EP on the implementation of the white-paper directives, the Commission divides the directives into three major categories: removal of physical barriers, removal of technical barriers, and removal of tax barriers. Of the directives states were to have implemented by 15 August 1992, only five fell in the tax category. Three of these had been implemented in all member states on time (Commission 1992).

Turning to the first two categories, the Commission considered 77 directives to regard physical barriers and 124 to regard technical barriers. The technical-barriers category can be further broken down. The majority, 73 of these directives, involved the free movement of goods, and included directives on transportation and health standards for foodstuffs. The rest of the technical-barrier directives dealt with less observable barriers than those to the free movement of goods, involving public procurement, a common market for services, industrial cooperation, etc. We can thus divide the nontax directives into three groups: physical barriers (77), technical barriers to the movement of goods (73), and other technical barriers (51).

Table 7.2 shows the number of directives that had been incorporated into domestic law in all member states by 15 August 1992, broken down by the substance of each measure. A clear pattern emerges, one that is tied to the discussion of transparency. Directives dealing with physical barriers and those dealing with technical barriers to the movement of goods were implemented at nearly the same rate, 35.1% and 38.4%, respectively. Other technical barriers, however, were implemented at a much lower rate, 15.7%. These data suggest that rates of implementation are tied to the transparency of the issues that the directives involve. Physical barriers are easily observable, involving explicit con-

---

that the German implementation record has declined relative to other states since the mid-1990s, suggesting that the process of coordination is working less smoothly than it did previously.

TABLE 7.2
Implementation of White-Paper Directives by 15 August 1992

	Total	Number of Measures in Place in All Member States	Percent Implemented
Removal of physical barriers			
Controls on goods			
Miscellaneous controls	2	1	50.0
Veterinary and plant health controls	69	23	33.3
Controls on individuals	6	3	50.0
Removal of technical barriers			
Free movement of goods			
Technical harmonization and standards	10	1	10.0
Motor vehicles	11	5	45.5
Agricultural machinery	3	3	100.0
Foodstuffs	18	7	38.9
Pharmaceuticals	14	5	35.7
Chemical products	6	4	66.7
Construction products	2	1	50.0
Other items	9	2	22.2
Other technical barriers			
Public procurement	4	0	0.0
Labor and the professions	8	1	12.5
Common market for services	26	4	15.4
Capital movements	1	1	100.0
Industrial cooperation	12	2	16.7
Removal of tax barriers			
VAT	4	3	75.0
Excise duties	1	0	0.0
Physical barriers	77	27	35.1
Technical barriers to flow of goods	73	28	38.4
Other technical barriers	51	8	15.7
Tax barriers	5	3	60.0

Source: European Commission (1992).

trols on the movement of goods and individuals such as customs charges or restrictions on importing personal effects. Technical barriers to the movement of goods are also quite visible, often taking the form of conflicting standards or restrictions on the means used to move goods, such as product-safety standards or regulations on the capacities of trucks. The very visibility of these measures may explain why they are removed rather quickly once a directive is negotiated requiring states to dismantle them.

Other technical barriers are less transparent, however. These include, for example, coordinating procedures on public-procurement contracts or vocational-training qualifications. Lack of transparency means that it is either more difficult for states to implement these directives or that they are more tempting targets for cheating. Either way, we would expect to see lower implementation rates, and do. Technical barriers are harder to identify, being buried within domestic legislation on the treatment of labor, banking regulation, etc. Until they are clearly identified and their impact on the internal market assessed, it is easier for states to overlook their implementation, either intentionally or through lack of information. The pattern suggests that a promising area for further research on the implementation stage of international cooperation lies in consideration of the impact of the transparency of the agreed measures for cooperation.

CONCLUSION

The Credibility Hypothesis posits that institutionalized legislative participation increases the credibility of states' commitments. This chapter provides a direct test, using implementation rates as a measure of credibility. With the TEU, the EU took a major step toward making policy in areas of daily concern to businesses and individuals in all the member states. With this development, national parliaments have rediscovered their latent powers to influence the activities of governments in European integration, as initially argued in the last chapter. What appeared to be a lack of parliamentary interest and/or capacity to constrain governments earlier now appears more likely a case of congruent interests between parliaments and their governments. But once governments began to commit themselves to making more controversial policies at the European level, parliaments found their voice once again and are now organizing themselves to influence the course of European integration.

Many students of European integration find this development troubling, leading them to minimize the consequences of the democratic deficit. Their legitimate concern is that reassertion of direct parliamentary involvement in EU affairs would greatly impede, if not halt, the integration process. However, examination of the records of the member states when it comes to implementing EU directives suggests that parliamentary democracy need not be such a threat, after all. The benefits of high levels of executive flexibility are short-term and illusory. Parliaments matter *ex post,* since they have not relinquished implementation authority. Therefore, governments are well-advised to take account of potential parliamentary opposition *ex ante.*

Major negotiations in the EU have always been an elite-driven, closed process. Only recently have governments been forced to begin breaking open this insularity. Negotiations on the SEA involved very few private or domestic actors; those on European Monetary Union excluded all but finance ministers and central bankers. The evidence presented here should lead us to wonder whether such intentional creation of a democratic deficit has been a shortsighted strategy on the part of governments. It has increased their autonomy, but at the cost of decreasing their ability to implement agreements effectively. Correction of the democratic deficit through organized integration of national parliaments will force governments to change their negotiating styles, but is probably a necessary condition for further integration.

The Danish experience in particular bears out this logic. Denmark's parliament, the Folketing, is deeply involved in every step of the integration process. It holds government negotiators to account for their actions, handing down a negotiating mandate to them. And everyone, including other member states, recognizes the nature of this process. This puts Denmark in an excellent position to make credible commitments. The credibility asset shows up in increased bargaining leverage, at least according to anecdotal evidence, and robustly in the best implementation record in the EU. If parliaments had indeed abdicated to governments their ability to influence policy, we should see no correlation between implementation records and formal provisions for consultation with parliament. Instead, we find a positive correlation, suggesting that national parliaments have delegated rather than abdicated their powers and continue to influence realized levels of cooperation. Both across countries and over time, parliamentary mechanisms that are more binding on executives lead to better implementation records.

International cooperation does not stop when governments commit themselves to a particular agreement. They must always concern themselves with the potential for others to renege on these agreements, voluntarily or not; thus the implementation process is as essential a component of integration as is negotiation. Economic actors in the EU appreciate this fact, since they care about the policies governments actually adopt, not only those they promise to adopt. An implementation deficit thus threatens integration. Beyond problematic executive-legislative relations, obstacles to implementation arise from lack of transparency in directives and from regional governments with authority to implement directives but which are closed out of the negotiation process. The power of parliaments, even if exercised through subtle patterns of accountability rather than direct legislation, should become a more prominent part of studies of European integration as well as other forms of international cooperation. Within the EU, institutionalized parliamentary engagement leads to more credible government commitments.

CHAPTER 8

Conclusion

STATES that wish to cooperate with one another must be able to make credible commitments. While studies of international cooperation have focused on the systemic conditions for commitment, scholars also believe that domestic factors have an impact on the capacity for credible commitments. But few studies have attempted to generalize about the domestic conditions for commitment. This book has concentrated on how variation in the role of the legislature in stable democracies influences patterns of commitment and cooperation.

Legislatures come to our attention since they often seem to interfere with states' attempts to reach and implement reliable, predictable international agreements. Parliaments may put obstacles in the path of economic integration; Congress may refuse to ratify treaties or to appropriate funds for foreign assistance. Such observations lead many to disparage the role that legislatures can or should play in international politics, calling instead for strong, centralized state structures as a necessary condition for efficient and effective international interaction. Yet executive-dominance arguments create a puzzle, since in spite of legislative interference it appears that democracies are perfectly capable of coping with, and in fact succeeding in, the international system. Our analysis of legislatures needs to move beyond the notion that they needlessly and harmfully complicate international bargaining, and needs to discount persistent executive complaints about legislative interference.

Modern theories of legislative organization, legislative-executive interaction, and credible commitments lead in the necessary direction, suggesting that casual observations of conflict can easily mask underlying patterns of structured influence. Legislatures possess many indirect, subtle means by which to influence processes of international cooperation. If executives respect these mechanisms and so take them into account during international bargaining, legislative influence on international cooperation turns into a democratic asset. Unorganized, post hoc legislative reaction to executives who believe legislators have no legitimate role in foreign policy will indeed bring the credibility of democracies' commitments into question. But the logic of consistent, institutionalized legislative influence bears little resemblance to that picture.

To gain insight into the logic and consequences of legislative influence on international cooperation, this book has examined a diverse set of issues. Numerous other studies have examined, and are continuing to explore, the role of legislatures in international trade. I apply modern legislative theories to a different set of cases, including economic integration in Europe, the use of executive agreements and treaties in the United States, and the American politics of economic sanctions and food aid. I find results that are consistent with applications to international trade issues, and that suggest that modern theories of legislatures can be applied powerfully to foreign as well as domestic policy. Foreign policy is not an executive prerogative, nor should it be. The outcomes of international negotiations affect legislators' constituents, and legislators are capable of making constructive contributions to international cooperation if they are brought into the process in an organized manner.

The key propositions about the role of legislatures in international cooperation were summarized in four central hypotheses, which were operationalized and tested in the empirical chapters. These four hypotheses, stated again, are the Influence Hypothesis, the Delegation Hypothesis, the Credibility Hypothesis, and the Cooperation Hypothesis. These propositions follow directly from models of legislative organization and legislative-executive interaction as applied to the problem of international cooperation. They apply to presidential as well as parliamentary systems, and draw our attention to the factors that explain variation in influence, delegation, credibility, and cooperation.

By way of conclusion, this chapter stresses the major themes that have emerged from the diverse set of applications in this book. I consider what these cases have to tell us about the logic of legislative influence, how legislative influence varies, and the effect of legislative engagement on credibility and cooperation. On some issues we can draw firm conclusions; on others we find intriguing patterns and puzzles for future research.

THE LOGIC OF LEGISLATIVE INFLUENCE IN THE UNITED STATES AND EUROPEAN UNION

As outside analysts, we cannot observe influence directly. We can observe activity, and too easily mistake activity for influence. We see executives negotiating international agreements, intervening in markets to achieve desired economic outcomes, making decisions about military commitments, etc., and infer that executives must be the actors most able to influence such processes. Legislatures, on the other hand, rarely meet with representatives of other states and often have to scramble to follow what the executive branch has been doing after the fact, by holding hearings or otherwise registering protests. The pattern of activity in the two branches easily leads the unwary observer to believe that legislators are either uninterested in or unable to influence executive actions on foreign policy.

But such an inference is logically unsound, and the evidence in this book suggests that it is empirically inaccurate as well. We cannot determine how rules influence actors' behavior simply by counting up cases where rules are invoked, as long as players are rational and sophisticated. They anticipate rules, taking them into account when developing strategies. Thus invocation of a rule—for example, holding a congressional hearing to investigate charges of executive misdirection of funds—does not indicate much about the actual influence of that rule. In fact, rules and institutions likely have the most influence when they are least visible. When we observe them publicly displayed, with actors referring to rules to protest others' behavior, we can infer that someone has miscalculated or been unlucky, not that this is a rare case where the rule actually matters.

If this kind of equilibrium, anticipated-reaction logic led to the conclusion that all models of influence were observationally equivalent, it would be worse than useless for generating a framework for understanding politics. But, happily, this is not the case. *Processes* may indeed become observationally equivalent: legislative acceptance of a treaty can imply either that legislatures are merely a rubber stamp for the executive or that the executive has taken legislative preferences into account when negotiating the treaty. But equivalent predictions about processes do not imply equivalence of *outcomes*. If the legislature's and the executive's preferences for the treaty differ, we can determine the degree to which the legislature has influence by investigating whether the treaty reflects its desires. Determining influence, and how it varies over time, suggests that we need to focus more on outcomes, less on processes.

When attempting to sort out influence on international cooperation, the logic of influence and anticipated reactions means that we have to look at the actual realization of cooperation, not just the process of negotiating international agreements. International bargaining is fascinating and important, but it is not all there is to international cooperation. We need to look beyond the process of bargaining, with its retinue of media coverage and the ceremony of state, to whether international agreements actually lead to the mutual adjustment of state policies that is the heart of international cooperation. We have to consider the implementation of agreements, not just their conclusion. Once we turn our attention to implementation, the potential for legislative influence suddenly looms larger than those who focus only on negotiation might realize.

The empirical studies in this book have taken seriously the advice of looking at outcomes, trying not to be too distracted by the typically messy processes of international cooperation that result when legislatures have the potential to exert influence. Processes are not irrelevant: to make a causal argument about legislative influence, we need to explore the mechanisms through which it can be exercised. So in studying the use of executive agreements and treaties, we consider the mechanisms by which Congress can influence the implementation of informal agreements; in studying European integration, we need to consider the varying institutions for engaging national parliaments.

But we need to turn, in the end, to whether variation in processes makes much of a difference on outcomes. Essentially, this is a question of whether domestic institutions have any regular impact on patterns of international cooperation. The studies here suggest that they do. The way that national parliaments engage negotiations within the EU influences the quality of cooperation among member states down the road. Executive agreements and treaties respond to the demands of domestic politics and international commitment. Economic sanctions that are initiated by Congress differ from those that are initiated by the president, but are still under specified conditions able to generate international support. The distribution of food aid depends on legislative provisions for its use. The outcomes of international cooperation vary in ways that make sense from the perspective of legislative organization; they do not vary in the ways we would expect if the executive branch dominated foreign policy.

The outcomes of attempts to cooperate with other states depend on the nature of legislative-executive interaction. This book has argued that legislatures possess mechanisms by which to hold executives accountable. These mechanisms are not perfectly effective; legislatures do not "dominate" the process of international cooperation. But neither can executives afford to ignore the constraints that legislatures place on them, if they have any interest in being able to live up to promises to cooperate with other states. Rather than arguing about legislative-executive interaction in terms of who has the most power, which branch dominates policymaking, or whether we are observing the decline of either branch, we should conceive of legislative-executive interaction as an exchange relationship. Focusing on the distribution of power between branches, beyond drawing our attention to a variable that is impossible to measure with any accuracy, obscures the potential for legislatures and executives to arrange their relations in such a way that both benefit. Just as states can reap mutual benefits through cooperation, so can the branches of government in democracies. In spite of persistent "struggles for power" reflecting distributional conflict between the branches, they often find ways to institutionalize their relations such that they can achieve mutual gains.

The mechanisms and institutions of legislative-executive interaction vary immensely from one country to another. When we contrast presidential and parliamentary systems, the mechanisms of interaction are considerably different. Variation among parliamentary systems is also substantial and of great significance. One of the contributions of the set of studies in this book is to extend the logic of legislative-executive interaction on problems of international cooperation to parliamentary systems. This is not to argue that interaction is the same in presidential and parliamentary systems. But it is to argue that mechanisms assuring executive accountability and legislative influence exist in both types of systems, and that developing models of how executive discretion varies over time and across issues is of great importance. The fundamental logic of legislative-executive interaction, the factors that determine how much discretion the executive branch has and how discretion influences international cooperation, can be applied to both parliamentary and presidential systems. In parliaments, the executive is drawn from the legislature and responsible to it; in presidential systems, it is not. In response to the complexities of modern governance, parliamentary systems have developed strong party institutions and high levels of delegation to the executive. But these are factors that vary in intelligible ways among different types of systems.

This book has developed both an understanding of how and why legislative-executive interaction varies and how this variation impacts patterns of international cooperation. The following sections will highlight some of the themes that have emerged from this theoretical and empirical analysis, emphasizing the empirical support found for hypotheses about variation in legislative influence, credibility of commitments, and realized level of cooperation.

VARIATION IN LEGISLATIVE INFLUENCE

The models used in this book assume that the rules that determine legislative influence and executive discretion vary in response to the incentives facing rational legislators. Legislators want to achieve certain foreign-policy goals, and find that allowing the executive branch discretion to interact with other states is sometimes necessary in order to do so. Legislatures are not organized to bargain with other states, and they face their own internal collective-action problems. Creating structured interaction with the executive branch, in which some degree of discretion is allowed but mechanisms of accountability remain, is a common approach to solving these problems, as well as other dilemmas that face legislators. To understand how and why legislative influence varies, I consider the incentives facing legislators. The empirical studies in this book suggest that three factors exert consistent effects on the nature of legislative influence: political parties, the level of support for and trust of the executive branch, and the level of legislative support for particular programs.

Chapter 2 developed two general hypotheses about variation in legislative influence: the Influence Hypothesis, positing that executives cannot choose institutional procedures that allow them to evade legislative influence; and the Delegation Hypothesis, stating that legislatures will institutionalize their participation in international cooperation when substantial conflict of interest exists with the executive branch or when executives have recently violated the bounds of legislative delegation. The alternative hypotheses, drawn from an executive-dominance perspective, are that executives can manipulate institutions so as to evade legislative influence (the Evasion Hypothesis); and that legislatures abdicate their ability to influence policy when they delegate (the Abdication Hypothesis). The study of executive agreements and treaties in chapter 3 provided strong support in favor of the Influence Hypothesis, while the Delegation Hypothesis was found powerful in the studies of economic sanctions, food aid, and the legislative procedures that govern European integration.

Political Parties

In parliamentary systems, there is little doubt about the importance of political parties. The structure of political parties and the importance of their role in parliamentary decision-making and parliamentary relations with the government mean that most policy battles are fought within parties, behind closed doors, rather than on the floor of the legislature, as we often see in the United States. The importance of parties also gives rise to substantial differences between majority-party systems, as in Britain, and systems where minority or coalition government is more common, as in Denmark. Coalition or minority government can generate dynamics that are quite similar to those we see during periods of divided government in the United States (Laver and Shepsle 1994, 301). For example, Denmark's tradition of minority government accounts in part for its adoption of institutions that constrain government ministers more tightly than in most other EU member states.

The role of parties in the policymaking process in parliamentary systems is well established and needs little elaboration. But just as models of legislative organization can produce insights into parliamentary government as well as into the U.S. Congress, developing an understanding of the role of political parties helps us to understand the nature of legislative-executive relations in both. The cases studied in this book have suggested that political parties exercise marked influence on these relations in the United States, even during periods such as the 1970s when party discipline is understood to be low.

The clearest evidence of party effects in the United States arises in chapter 4, when we consider the domestic politics of economic sanctions. Here we find predictable, substantial, and significant differences in legislative behavior depending on the structure of party control of government. When control of the two houses of Congress is split between the parties, we find that Congress rarely takes the initiative and imposes sanctions. In the key exception to this rule, the Comprehensive Anti-Apartheid Act of 1986, we find that extremely high levels of organized resistance to the administration's policy, along with deep divisions in policy preferences among the agencies of the executive branch, allowed Congress to overcome the hurdles imposed by split party control.[1] When the executive branch is controlled by the same party as Congress—i.e., under unified government—we also find that Congress is reluctant to take the initiative on sanctions. In contrast, when control of the branches is divided, we see Congress more frequently choosing to impose sanctions in defiance of the executive branch.

When we turn to food-aid policy, we find that party control of government correlates with congressional actions to restrict executive discretion during reviews of food-aid legislation. We see more substantial retraction of discretion under divided than unified government, consistent with the pattern of legislative activism we see on sanctions. However, in the food-aid case, party control

[1] The analytical framework used in this book assumed that the executive branch was a unitary actor, obviously a major simplification of reality. In a number of cases, such as sanctions against South Africa, we found that anomalous outcomes were explained by the presence of deep divisions within the executive branch. Further work on legislative-executive interaction and international cooperation may benefit by building in the possibility of such executive divisions more rigorously.

is highly correlated with the variable we will turn to next, legislative trust of the executive branch, so that it is not possible to sort out with much confidence its independent impact. Consistent with the Delegation Hypothesis, under minority or divided government we see legislatures that are less willing to allow the executive a free hand in international cooperation.

Legislative Trust of the Executive

When a legislature grants the executive a large degree of discretion, it is showing that it trusts the executive to carry out policy in a way preferred by the legislature, at least within acceptable bounds. When reasons exist to distrust the executive, we would expect the legislature to take steps to reduce the level of discretion allowed. Distrust may arise from a number of sources. It may simply result from divided party control, thus subsuming the effect of parties just discussed. It may result, even more directly, from clear evidence that the executive has abused discretion in the past. It is these abuses of executive discretion, especially when they are followed by no actions to restore legislative confidence in the executive, that give rise to the most dramatic observed changes in the level of executive discretion.

Executives in the EU may be learning this painful fact now, as they see their plans for monetary union and the rest of the Maastricht Treaty agenda stimulate efforts by national parliaments to constrain and oversee the activities of government ministers in EU negotiations. The Maastricht agenda was negotiated by executives with little consideration of legislative and public willingness to accept the deep, wide changes it would bring to political and economic life in the member states. Not only are parliaments showing that they have the capacity to impede implementation of such executive agreements, they are establishing institutions that will more tightly bind executives and enhance predictable legislative influence on EU business in the future, as the Delegation Hypothesis would suggest.

The most obvious example of the results of executive abuse of authority, and one that had an impact on a wide range of issues, was the Nixon administration's actions in Southeast Asia. Combined with the Watergate revelations and other administration missteps, legislative levels of trust in the executive fell to new lows. As a result, we saw a massive reclaiming of authority by Congress, including on the foreign-policy issues examined here. On food-aid policy, in 1973 and 1974 we saw the most substantial change in discretion allowed the executive. Although discretion remains high relative to other foreign-aid programs, in 1974 Congress for the first time put constraints that actually bit into food-aid legislation by specifying that a certain percentage of total PL 480 spending go to poor countries.

Similarly, our examination of executive agreements and treaties showed that the most effective institutional revisions came in the mid-1970s. In this instance the Case Act has forced the executive branch to provide Congress with good information on the negotiation of executive agreements, thus more efficiently and consistently bringing legislators into the process, even if they often are brought in through indirect means.[2] Executive-branch actors do sometimes step outside the bounds of legislative consent; the process of consultation and discussion does not work perfectly to prevent such mistakes. But when they occur, mistakes have the anticipated effect on executive discretion, leading legislatures to take steps to reduce it.

Legislative Preferences and Preference Intensities

The level of discretion that a legislature is willing to allow the executive also depends on how much legislators care about a particular program. Perhaps counterintuitively, they will allow the executive more discretion to manipulate and determine the details of programs that are popular and have widespread support in the legislature. When a policy is popular, there are many specific programs that would generate benefits for both the legislative and executive branches. In a situation like this, debate over the details of the program becomes a matter of distributional bargaining between the two branches. If support for the policy is high, legislators will not be in a good position to prevail in this struggle, leading to a program whose details reflect the preferences of the executive branch in many respects. The underlying reason for this pattern follows from conceiving of interbranch relations as an exchange process, in which actors are willing to make concessions on those dimensions of a program of least interest to themselves. Preference intensities give us insight into how the shape of a program will reflect the interests of the legislative and executive branches.

The study of U.S. food aid allowed us to develop this exchange model of interbranch bargaining. Food aid is a popular program, which explains why on average it allows for a substantially higher level of executive discretion than we find on other, much less popular, foreign-aid programs. But within these bounds, the popularity of food aid has changed over time as the levels of agricultural surpluses in the United States and associated price levels change. When surpluses are low and prices high, Congress is less interested in a large food-aid program to dispose of goods overseas. Congress will then reexamine the level of discretion it has allowed the executive branch. We found that the results of these reexaminations reflected the interaction of a number of variables in addition to surplus levels, particularly legislative trust of the executive. But underlying congressional attitudes and attention to executive discretion are motivated by the general demand for a food-aid program.

---

[2] Why the executive branch sometimes abuses its authority in ways that lead to such reassertion of legislative prerogatives is an important question not addressed in this book. For some speculation along these lines, see the discussion of executive use of institutionalization to enhance credibility later in this chapter.

Overall, the cases considered in this book suggest that legislative influence and choice of rules that determine executive discretion vary regularly. It is not necessary to resort to ad hoc invocation of the decline of parliaments, the resurgence of Congress, and similar devices to understand why on occasion we see executive-branch actors making commitments to other states without much apparent constraint from the legislature, while at other times legislative oversight verges on micromanagement. Instead, party control of government, legislative trust of the executive branch, and legislative support for programs explain variation in the level of executive discretion across issues and through time. Executives cannot freely choose institutional procedures that allow them to evade legislative constraints; and legislatures will respond to conflict of interest with the executive or evidence of executive abuse of discretion by institutionalizing their participation in processes of international cooperation.

CREDIBILITY OF COMMITMENTS AND COOPERATION

The central issue motivating this study has been an exploration of the sources of democratic capacity to make commitments to other states. A complete answer to this question will require a variety of approaches, including attention to the role of an independent judiciary and direct comparisons between democracies, nondemocracies of various sorts, and states in transition to and from democracy. This study has concentrated on a fraction of the problem, considering the role of legislatures with the capacity to influence policy in stable democracies. In contrast to most foreign-policy analysis, I argue that organized legislative engagement in processes of international cooperation can enhance the credibility of democracies' commitments and therefore the level of cooperation achieved, as summarized in the Credibility and Cooperation Hypotheses. Celebrated instances of legislative action undermining state commitments result from attempts to ignore or circumvent the legislature's role, not from institutionalized procedures of legislative engagement.

As long as legislatures have the capacity to impede implementation of international agreements, closing them out of the initial stages of international cooperation and attempting to prevent their preferences from influencing the course of negotiations has the potential to cause severe commitment dilemmas. Insulated executives are not, in the final analysis, strong executives, because they find it difficult to implement international agreements. In contrast, bringing legislators into the cooperation process in a formalized, regular manner allows states to bargain more effectively and to assure others that agreements signed at the international table will in fact be put in place at the domestic level. Within the democracies studied we find that institutionalized legislative engagement enhances credibility. Chapter 2 developed two general hypotheses about credibility and cooperation. The Credibility Hypothesis claims that institutionalized legislative participation in international bargaining increases the credibility of state commitments. The Cooperation Hypothesis proposes that institutionalized legislative participation increases the level of international cooperation realized.

The clearest demonstration of enhanced credibility comes from comparing rates of implementation of EU legislation, examined in chapter 7. Although all EU member states have some form of parliamentary democracy, they vary substantially in the degree to which parliament plays a role in overseeing ministers' activities on the EU level. The standard stories about the role of national parliaments in the EU see them as potentially destructive to the course of economic integration, or at best unable to influence it. Such logic would lead us to expect that states that bargain without effective, *ex ante* parliamentary constraints would either have the best records of cooperation within the EU, or that we would see no correlation between the role of parliament and implementation. Instead, we find that the state with the most institutionalized parliamentary oversight of EU bargaining, Denmark, consistently has the best record of implementing EU legislation. Overall, the degree to which the parliament binds government ministers is strongly, and positively, correlated with implementation rates. Because strong parliamentary institutions allow for accountability, transparency, and regular involvement in bargaining of those responsible for implementation, they allow the state to make credible commitments to implement EU legislation.

Within the United States, we also find that credibility varies depending on the role of Congress. On food aid, we see that when Congress puts few constraints on the uses of aid, the president is tempted to manipulate it to gain policy concessions from recipients. But unless the desired policy concessions can be achieved in the short term so that U.S. credibility is not an issue, or Congress supports particular political uses of food aid, the strategic manipulation of aid has little impact. When the president wishes to engage in tying aid to more extensive reform programs, which require commitments that will persist for at least a few years, he needs to gain the express support of Congress. This may be accomplished by engaging Congress in the process of determining how food aid is to be used, as Johnson did with aid to India; alternatively, the commitment can be formalized, as in the Camp David accords with Egypt. This formal congressional participation in policymaking on food aid leads to higher levels of international cooperation.

Within the United States, another key question about Congress and credibility is whether Congress has the capacity to make credible commitments on its own and gain international cooperation without presidential support. Chapter 4, on economic sanctions, allowed us to examine this problem. We find that on average, Congress is indeed less able than the president to establish the commitments necessary to support extensive international cooperation. However, we also find that the ability of either branch to establish commitments depends on divided government. The president's superior ability to generate international cooperation turns out to exist only during periods of unified government, when Congress has few incentives to undermine the president's commitments. But under divided government, Congress becomes significantly better at establishing independent commitments, achieving levels of international cooperation that match those of the president. Thus, the capacity of the legislature to establish the commitments necessary for international cooperation depends on the partisan incentives facing legislators. When the circumstances are right, Congress can become an effective international actor. Table 8.1 summarizes the major empirical findings of this book.

The evidence and logic of commitment presented in this book leave us with one puzzle that I can only speculate on here. If institutionalized legislative involvement is necessary for substantial international cooperation in democracies, and if executives value the capacity to make credible commitments to other states, we should see executives welcoming formalized legislative participation in international cooperation (see Milner 1997). In fact, we do observe such a dynamic in some instances. President Johnson worked with Congress to

TABLE 8.1
Empirical Results

Influence Hypothesis	· The executive cannot choose between executive agreements and treaties to evade Senate opposition.
Delegation Hypothesis	· Reporting requirements on executive agreements increase after executive abuse of authority, during divided government.
	· Congress more often imposes economic sanctions under divided government.
	· High levels of executive discretion on food aid result from its popularity relative to other foreign-aid programs.
	· Congress decreases the level of delegation on food aid when low surpluses are combined with executive abuse of authority.
	· European parliaments increase constraints on the executive as the process of integration becomes more contentious.
Credibility Hypothesis	· Tighter parliamentary constraints on the executive lead to improved implementation records.
Cooperation Hypothesis	· The number of treaties concluded decreases when congressional support for the president declines.
	· Congressional cooperation on economic sanctions increases under divided government.
	· Cooperation on food aid increases when the president engages Congress.

make commitments on food aid; President Carter institutionalized the aid commitment to Egypt at Camp David; executives sometimes choose to use treaties rather than informal agreements. However, at other times we see executives attempting to work around and close out the legislature, protecting their prerogatives and trying to maximize their freedom of maneuver. Members of the executive branch frequently lobby against reductions in their discretion in the United States; executives in the EU do not welcome, for the most part, increased parliamentary oversight.

Why is this the case? Why are executives so jealous of their prerogatives, if in fact these prerogatives increase the scope for arbitrariness and decrease their capacity to make credible commitments? I would speculate that the answer lies in incentives facing the executive that have not been considered adequately here. The empirical problem is to explain variation in executive behavior: when executives welcome legislative constraints, and when they resist them. The fact that executive behavior varies suggests that executives are trading off costs and benefits of legislative engagement in making calculations about how to deal with the legislature. I have concentrated on the benefits of legislative engagement. But the capacity to make credible international commitments is not the only value in an executive's utility function. On the international level, there is most likely a trade-off between credibility and flexibility. Bringing a legislature into the process may make a commitment more credible, but can also induce a status-quo bias, locking states into policies that may become inefficient as international conditions change. For example, the fact that the Maastricht Treaty went through a difficult and public ratification process created high stakes for states attempting to live up to its provisions on monetary union. But increasingly, economic studies of the implications of monetary union and changing economic conditions within the EU make the value of the TEU provisions questionable. However, backing out of the commitments at this stage would involve very high costs. In this instance, the EU may have sacrificed too much flexibility for the sake of credibility. In general, executives considering this trade-off may decide at times that the value of flexibility is high enough—for example, if future conditions are highly unpredictable—that they are willing to forgo the credibility benefits of legislative involvement.

These speculations about executive incentives can only appear ad hoc at this stage. But they suggest the potential for developing regular, testable expectations about the conditions under which executives will welcome legislative activity, and when they will resist it. For example, they suggest that the higher the international demand for credibility, the more the executive will work to institutionalize domestic procedures. In contrast, on international issues that are one-shot or have alternative commitment-mechanisms built in, the executive will choose to maintain a high level of discretion. In fact, we found some evidence of this pattern of variation in chapter 3, on the use of executive agreements and treaties in the United States, as the use of executive agreements varied across issues. The fact that executives do not uniformly welcome high levels of institutionalized legislative oversight is an important and intriguing empirical puzzle, but does not undermine the logic of legislatures and commitment spelled out in this book.

Modern international relations among democracies means high levels of interdependence. States can only cope with such interdependence if they are able to make credible commitments to one another. Democracies are able to do so, in spite of theories that tell us that the role of legislatures in democracies undermines the capacity for credible commitments. Legislatures have the capacity to influence processes of international cooperation, and the extent to which they do so varies systematically. But far from destroying the credibility of state commitments, institutionalized legislative influence enhances it. In international cooperation, organized legislatures are a democratic asset.

References

Adams, William James, ed. 1993. *Singular Europe: Economy and Polity of the European Community after 1992.* Ann Arbor: University of Michigan Press.

Aldrich, John H. 1995. *Why Parties? The Origin and Transformation of Political Parties in America.* Chicago: University of Chicago Press.

Allen, David. 1992. "The European Community and the New Europe." In Dennis Swann, ed., *The Single European Market and Beyond: A Study of the Wider Implications of the Single European Act.* New York: Routledge.

Alt, James, and Barry Eichengreen. 1989. "Parallel and Overlapping Games: Theory and an Application to the European Gas Trade." *Economics and Politics* 1, no. 2 (July): 119–44.

Arnold, R. Douglas. 1990. *The Logic of Congressional Action.* New Haven, Conn.: Yale University Press.

Arter, David. 1995. "The Folketing and Denmark's 'European Policy': The Case of an 'Authorizing Assembly'?" *Journal of Legislative Studies* 1, no. 3: 110–23.

Atwood, J. Brian. 1981. "Downtown Perspective: Lessons on Liaison with Congress." In Thomas M. Franck, ed., *The Tethered Presidency.* New York: New York University Press.

Audretsch, H. A. H. 1986. *Supervision in European Community Law.* 2d rev. ed. Amsterdam: North-Holland.

Axelrod, Robert. 1984. *The Evolution of Cooperation.* New York: Basic Books.

Axelrod, Robert, and Robert O. Keohane. 1986. "Achieving Cooperation under Anarchy: Strategies and Institutions." In Oye, ed.: 226–54.

Baker, Pauline H. 1989. "The United States and South Africa: The Reagan Years." *South Africa Update Series.* New York: Ford Foundation Foreign Policy Association.

Baldwin, David A. 1985. *Economic Statecraft.* Princeton, N.J.: Princeton University Press.

Baldwin, Richard E., Joseph F. Francois, and Richard Portes. 1997. "EU Enlargement: Small Costs for the West, Big Gains for the East." *Economic Policy* 24 (April): 125–76.

Banks, Jeffrey S., and Barry R. Weingast. 1992. "The Political Control of Bureaucracies under Asymmetric Information." *American Journal of Political Science* 36, no. 2 (May): 509–24.

Banks, William C., and Peter Raven-Hansen. 1994. *National Security Law and the Power of the Purse.* New York: Oxford University Press.

Baron, David P. 1991. "Majoritarian Incentives, Pork Barrel Programs, and Procedural Control." *American Journal of Political Science* 35, no. 1 (February): 57–90.

Baron, David P., and John A. Ferejohn. 1989. "Bargaining in Legislatures." *American Political Science Review* 83, no. 4 (December): 1181–1206.

Barro, Robert J., and David B. Gordon. 1983. "Rules, Discretion and Reputation in a Model of Monetary Policy." *Journal of Monetary Economics* 12 (July): 101–21.

Becker, Charles M. 1987. "Economic Sanctions Against South Africa." *World Politics* 38, no. 2 (January): 147–73.

Bergman, Torbjörn. 1997. "National Parliaments and EU Affairs Committees: Notes on Empirical Variation and Competing Explanations." *Journal of European Public Policy* 4, no. 3 (September): 373–87.

Bocquet, Dominique. 1995. "Clarifying the Relationship between the European Union and its Citizens." *How Can the EU's Voters Have Their Say?* Philip Morris Institute (December): 40–53.

Borchard, Edwin M. 1947. "Treaties and Executive Agreements." *American Political Science Review* 40, no. 4 (August): 729–39.

Borre, O. 1986. "The Danish Referendum on the EC Common Act." *Electoral Studies* 5, no. 2 (August): 189–93.

Boyce, Brigitte. 1993. "The Democratic Deficit of the European Community." *Parliamentary Affairs* 46, no. 4 (October): 458–77.

Branner, Hans. 1992. "Danish European Policy Since 1945: The Question of Sovereignty." In Kelstrup, ed.: 297–327.

Brenner, Philip, and William M. Leogrande. 1991. "Congress and Nicaragua: The Limits of Alternative Policy Making." In James A. Thurber, ed., *Divided Democracy: Cooperation and Conflict Between the President and Congress.* Washington, D.C.: Congressional Quarterly Press.

Brewer, John. 1989. *The Sinews of Power: War, Money and the English State, 1688–1783.* New York: Alfred A. Knopf.

Bronckers, Marco C. E. J. 1989. "Private Enforcement of 1992: Do Trade and Industry Stand a Chance Against the Member States?" *Common Market Law Review* 26, no. 3: 513–33.

Brzezinski, Zbigniew. 1983. *Power and Principle.* New York: Farrar, Straus, and Giroux.

Burns, William J. 1985. *Economic Aid and American Policy toward Egypt, 1955–1981.* Albany: State University of New York Press.

Calvert, Randall L., Mathew D. McCubbins, and Barry R. Weingast. 1989. "A Theory of Political Control and Agency Discretion." *American Journal of Political Science* 33, no. 3 (August): 588–611.

Carter, Barry E. 1988. *International Economic Sanctions: Improving the Haphazard U.S. Legal Regime.* Cambridge: Cambridge University Press.

Chayes, Abram, and Antonia Handler Chayes. 1993. "On Compliance." *International Organization* 47, no. 2 (Spring): 175–205.

Ciavarini Azzi, Giuseppe, ed. 1985. *The Implementation of EC Law by the Member States.* Maastricht, The Netherlands: European Institute of Public Administration.

———. 1988. "What is This New Research into the Implementation of Community Legislation Bringing Us?" In Siedentopf and Ziller, eds., 1:190–201.

Clarke, Michael. 1992. *British External Policy-Making in the 1990s.* Washington, D.C.: Brookings Institution.

Cochrane, Willard W., and Mary E. Ryan. 1976. *American Farm Policy, 1948–1973.* Minneapolis: University of Minnesota Press.

Cohen, Marc J. 1988. "'Food for War' in Southeast Asia: U.S. Food Policy, 1973–1987." *Wisconsin Papers on Southeast Asia,* no. 16. University of Wisconsin, Madison.

Colchester, Nicholas, and David Buchan. 1990. *Europe Relaunched: Truths and Illusions on the Way to 1992.* London: Economist Books.

Commission of the European Communities [Commission]. 1992. *Seventh Report of the*

Commission to the Council and the European Parliament Concerning the Implementation of the White Paper on the Completion of the Internal Market. Brussels: European Commission, 2 September.

Congressional Information Service. 1986. *Comprehensive Anti-Apartheid Act of 1986,* CIS no. 86-PL99-440 (October 2), 99th Cong., 2d Sess.

Congressional Research Service [CRS]. 1993. *Treaties and Other International Agreements: The Role of the United States Senate.* Washington, D.C.: Government Printing Office.

Congressional Research Service, Foreign Affairs and National Defense Division. 1979. *Human Rights and U.S. Foreign Assistance: Experiences and Issues in Policy Implementation (1977–1978).*

Corwin, Edward S. 1940. *The President, Office and Powers: History and Analysis of Practice and Opinion.* New York: New York University Press.

Cowhey, Peter F. 1993. "Domestic Institutions and the Credibility of International Commitments: Japan and the United States." *International Organization* 47, no. 2 (Spring): 299–326.

Cox, Gary W. 1987. *The Efficient Secret: The Cabinet and the Development of Political Parties in Victorian England.* Cambridge: Cambridge University Press.

Cox, Gary W., and Mathew D. McCubbins. 1993. *Legislative Leviathan: Party Government in the House.* Berkeley: University of California Press.

Crabb, Cecil V., Jr., and Pat M. Holt. 1992. *Invitation to Struggle: Congress, the President, and Foreign Policy.* 4th ed. Washington, D.C.: Congressional Quarterly Press.

Crone, Donald K. 1988. "State, Social Elites, and Government Capacity in Southeast Asia." *World Politics* 40, no. 2: 252–68.

Cusack, David F. 1977. *Revolution and Reaction: The Internal Dynamics of Conflict and Confrontation in Chile.* Denver: University of Denver, Graduate School of International Studies.

Dahl, Robert A. 1950. *Congress and Foreign Policy.* New York: Harcourt, Brace and Company.

Daoudi, M. S., and M. S. Dajani. 1983. "Sanctions: The Falklands Episode." *World Today* 39, no. 4 (April): 150–60.

Dassel, Kurt. 1998. "Institutions over Norms: Reevaluating the Literature on the Democratic Peace." Weatherhead Center for International Affairs Working Paper 98–12, Harvard University, Cambridge, Mass.

De Winter, Lieven, and Thierry Laurent. 1995. "The Belgian Parliament and European Integration." *Journal of Legislative Studies* 1, no. 3: 77–91.

Defalque, Lucette. 1985. "Belgique: Synthèse Nationale." In Giuseppe Ciavarini Azzi, ed., *The Implementation of EC Law by the Member States.* Maastricht, The Netherlands: European Institute of Public Administration.

Destler, I. M. 1978. "United States Food Policy 1972–1976: Reconciling Domestic and International Objectives." In Raymond F. Hopkins and Donald J. Puchala, eds., *The Global Political Economy of Food.* (Madison: University of Wisconsin Press).

———. 1980. *Making Foreign Economic Policy.* Washington, D.C.: Brookings Institution.

———. 1986. *American Trade Politics: System under Stress.* New York: Institute for International Economics.

———. 1994. "Delegating Trade Policy." In Peterson, ed.: 228–45.

Downs, George W., and David M. Rocke. 1990. *Tacit Bargaining, Arms Races, and Arms Control.* Ann Arbor: University of Michigan Press.

———. 1995. *Optimal Imperfection? Domestic Uncertainty and Institutions in International Relations.* Princeton, N.J.: Princeton University Press.

Duina, Francesco. 1997. "Explaining Legal Implementation in the European Union." *International Journal of the Sociology of Law* 25, no. 2 (June): 155–79.

Eichengreen, Barry, and Jeffry Frieden, eds. 1994. *The Political Economy of European Monetary Unification.* Boulder, Colo.: Westview Press.

Eichengreen, Barry, Jeffry Frieden, and Jürgen von Hagen, eds. 1995. *Politics and Institutions in an Integrated Europe.* Berlin: Springer-Verlag.

Elklit, Jørgen, and Nikolaj Petersen. 1973. "Denmark Enters the European Communities." *Scandinavian Political Studies* 8: 198–213.

Enelow, James M., and Melvin J. Hinich. 1984. *The Spatial Theory of Voting: An Introduction.* New York: Cambridge University Press.

Epstein, David, and Sharyn O'Halloran. 1997. "Choosing How to Decide: Efficient Policy Making Under Separate Powers." Manuscript, Columbia University, April.

European Centre for Parliamentary Research and Documentation. 1990. *Bodies within National Parliaments Specialising in European Community Affairs.* Luxembourg: Office for Official Publications of the European Communities.

European Commission, Directorate-General for Information, Communication, Culture and Audiovisual Media. 1995. *Intergovernmental Conference 1996: Commission Report for the Reflection Group.* Luxembourg: Office for Official Publications of the European Communities.

Evans, Peter B., Harold K. Jacobson, and Robert D. Putnam, eds. 1993. *Double-Edged Diplomacy: International Bargaining and Domestic Politics.* Berkeley: University of California Press.

Fearon, James D. 1990. "Deterrence and the Spiral Model: The Role of Costly Signals in Crisis Bargaining." Paper presented at the 1990 Annual Meeting of the American Political Science Association, San Francisco, Cal.

———. 1993. "Ethnic War as a Commitment Problem." Manuscript, University of Chicago.

———. 1994. "Domestic Political Audiences and the Escalation of International Disputes." *American Political Science Review* 88, no. 3 (September): 577–92.

Featherstone, Kevin. 1994. "Jean Monnet and the 'Democratic Deficit' in the European Union." *Journal of Common Market Studies* 32, no. 2 (June): 149–70.

Ferejohn, John, and Charles Shipan. 1990. "Congressional Influence on Bureaucracy." *Journal of Law, Economics, and Organization* 6 (special issue): 1–20.

Fiorina, Morris P. 1977. *Congress: Keystone of the Washington Establishment.* New Haven, Conn.: Yale University Press.

———. 1985. "Group Concentration and the Delegation of Legislative Authority." In Roger G. Noll, ed., *Regulatory Policy and the Social Sciences.* Berkeley: University of California Press.

———. 1992. *Divided Government.* New York: Macmillan.

Fitzmaurice, John. 1976. "National Parliaments and European Policy-Making: The Case of Denmark." *Parliamentary Affairs* 29, no. 1 (Winter): 281–92.

———. 1981. *Politics in Denmark.* London: C. Hurst & Company.

———. 1996. "National Parliamentary Control of EU Policy in the Three New Member States." *West European Politics* 19, no. 1 (January): 88–96.

Flood, Patrick. 1986. "U.S. Human Rights Initiatives Concerning Argentina." In David D. Newsom, ed., *The Diplomacy of Human Rights*. Lanham, Md.: University Press of America.

Forsythe, David P. 1988. *Human Rights and U.S. Foreign Policy: Congress Reconsidered*. Gainesville: University of Florida Press.

Fraenkel, Richard M., Don F. Hadwiger, and William P. Browne, eds. 1979. *The Role of U.S. Agriculture in Foreign Policy*. New York: Praeger.

Freedman, Lawrence, and Efraim Karsh. 1993. *The Gulf Conflict, 1990–1991: Diplomacy and War in the New World Order*. Princeton, N.J.: Princeton University Press.

Friedberg, Aaron L. 1991. "Is the United States Capable of Acting Strategically? Congress and the President." *Washington Quarterly* 14 (Winter): 5–23.

From, Johan, and Per Stava. 1993. "Implementation of Community Law: The Last Stronghold of National Control?" In Svein S. Andersen and Kjell A. Eliassen, eds., *Making Policy in Europe: The Europeification of National Policy-Making*. London: Sage.

Garrett, John. 1992. *Westminster: Does Parliament Work?* London: Victor Gollancz.

Garst, Rachel, and Tom Barry. 1990. *Feeding the Crisis: U.S. Food Aid and Farm Policy in Central America*. Lincoln: University of Nebraska Press.

Gasiorowski, Mark, and Solomon W. Polachek. 1982. "Conflict and Interdependence: East-West Trade and Linkages in the Era of Detente." *Journal of Conflict Resolution* 26, no. 4 (December): 709–29.

Gilligan, Thomas W., and Keith Krehbiel. 1989. "Asymmetric Information and Legislative Rules with a Heterogeneous Committee." *American Journal of Political Science* 33, no. 2 (May): 459–90.

———. 1990. "Organization of Informative Committees by a Rational Legislature." *American Journal of Political Science* 34, no. 2 (May): 531–64.

Gilmore, Richard. 1982. *A Poor Harvest: The Clash of Policies and Interests in the Grain Trade*. New York: Longman.

Gjørtler, Peter. 1993. "Ratifying the Treaty on European Union: An Interim Report." *European Law Review* 18 (August): 356–60.

Goetz, Klaus H. 1995. "National Governance and European Integration: Intergovernmental Relations in Germany." *Journal of Common Market Studies* 33, no. 1 (March): 91–116.

Govaere, Inge, and Frédérique Hélin. 1990. "Implementing the Internal Market: Problems and Perspectives." In Jürgen Schwarze, Inge Govaere, Frédérique Hélin, and Peter Van den Bossche, eds., *The 1992 Challenge at National Level*. Baden-Baden: Nomos Verlagsgesellschaft.

Gowa, Joanne. 1988. "Public Goods and Political Institutions: Trade and Monetary Policy Processes in the United States." *International Organization* 42, no. 1 (Winter): 15–32.

Granell, Francisco. 1995. "The European Union's Enlargement Negotiations with Austria, Finland, Norway and Sweden." *Journal of Common Market Studies* 33, no. 1 (March): 117–41.

Greif, Avner, Paul Milgrom, and Barry R. Weingast. 1994. "Coordination, Commitment, and Enforcement: The Case of the Merchant Guild." *Journal of Political Economy* 102, no. 4: 745–76.

Grieco, Joseph M. 1988. "Anarchy and the Limits of Cooperation: A Realist Critique of the Newest Liberal Institutionalism." *International Organization* 42, no. 3 (Summer): 485–507.

Guizzi, Vincenzo, and Umberto Leanza. 1985. "Italie: Synthèse Nationale." In Giuseppe Ciavarini Azzi, ed., *The Implementation of EC Law by the Member States*. Maastricht, The Netherlands: European Institute of Public Administration.

Haas, Ernst B. 1958. *The Uniting of Europe: Political, Economic and Social Forces, 1950–1957*. Stanford: Stanford University Press.

Hagel-Sørenson, Karsten, and Hjalte Rasmussen. 1985. "The Danish Administration and its Interaction with the Community Administration." *Common Market Law Review* 22, no. 2: 273–300.

Haggard, Stephan. 1988. "The Institutional Foundations of Hegemony," *International Organization* 42 (Winter): 91–119.

———. 1990. *Pathways from the Periphery: The Politics of Growth in the Newly Industrializing Countries*. Ithaca, N.Y.: Cornell University Press.

Hegeland, Hans, and Ingvar Mattson. 1996. "To Have a Voice in the Matter: A Comparative Study of the Swedish and Danish European Committees." *Journal of Legislative Studies* 2, no. 3 (Autumn): 198–215.

Herman, Valentine, and Rinus van Schendelen, eds. 1979. *The European Parliament and the National Parliaments*. New York: St. Martin's Press.

Hermele, Kenneth, and Bertil Odén. 1988. *Sanctions Dilemmas: Some Implications of Economic Sanctions Against South Africa*. Uppsala: Scandinavian Institute of African Studies.

Hinckley, Barbara. 1994. *Less Than Meets the Eye: Foreign Policy Making and the Myth of the Assertive Congress*. Chicago: University of Chicago Press.

Hopkins, Raymond F., and Donald J. Puchala. 1980. *Global Food Interdependence: Challenge to American Foreign Policy*. New York: Columbia University Press.

House of Commons. 1995. "The 1996 Inter-Governmental Conference: The Agenda. Democracy and Efficiency. The Role of National Parliaments." Vol. 1: Report. Select Committee on European Legislation, 24th Report.

Hrbek, Rudolf. 1992. "The German Länder and EC Integration." *Journal of European Integration* 15, nos. 2–3 (Winter/Spring): 173–93.

Huber, John D. 1992. "Restrictive Legislative Procedures in France and the United States." *American Political Science Review* 86, no. 3 (September): 675–87.

———. 1996. *Rationalizing Parliament: Legislative Institutions and Party Politics in France*. New York: Cambridge University Press.

Hufbauer, Gary Clyde, Jeffrey J. Schott, and Kimberly Ann Elliott [HSE]. 1990. *Economic Sanctions Reconsidered*. 2d ed. Washington, D.C.: Institute for International Economics.

Huntington, Samuel P. 1991. *The Third Wave: Democratization in the Late Twentieth Century*. Norman, Okla.: University of Oklahoma Press.

Ikenberry, G. John. 1986. "The Irony of State Strength: Comparative Responses to the Oil Shocks in the 1970s." *International Organization* 40, no. 1: 105–37.

Ingebritsen, Christine. 1997. "Coming Out of the Cold: Nordic Responses to European Union." In Alan W. Cafruny and Carl Lankowski, eds. *Europe's Ambiguous Unity:*

Conflict and Consensus in Post-Maastricht Europe. Boulder, Colo.: Lynne Reiner Publishers.

Jacobs, Francis, Richard Corbett, and Michael Shackleton. 1995. *The European Parliament.* 3d ed. London: Cartermill International.

Jacobson, Gary C. 1990. *The Electoral Origins of Divided Government: Competition in U.S. House Elections, 1946–1988.* Boulder, Colo.: Westview Press.

Jentleson, Bruce W. 1986. *Pipeline Politics: The Complex Political Economy of East-West Energy Trade.* Ithaca, N.Y.: Cornell University Press.

Jervis, Robert. 1978. "Cooperation under the Security Dilemma." *World Politics* 30, no. 2 (January): 167–214.

Johnson, D. Gale, and G. Edward Schuh, eds. 1983. *The Role of Markets in the World Food Economy.* Boulder, Colo.: Westview Press.

Johnson, Loch K. 1984. *The Making of International Agreements: Congress Confronts the Executive.* New York: New York University Press.

Judge, David. 1995. "The Failure of National Parliaments?" *West European Politics* 18, no. 3 (July): 79–100.

Kaiser, K. 1971. "Transnational Relations as a Threat to the Democratic Process." *International Organization* 25 no. 3 (Summer): 706–20.

Kaiser, Wolfram. 1995. "Austria in the European Union." *Journal of Common Market Studies* 33: 411–25.

Kang, David C. 1995. "South Korean and Taiwanese Development and the New Institutional Economics." *International Organization* 49, no. 3 (Summer): 555–87.

Katzenstein, Peter, ed. 1978. *Between Power and Plenty: Foreign Economic Policies of Advanced Industrialized States.* Madison, Wisc.: University of Wisconsin Press.

Kelstrup, Morten, ed. 1992. *European Integration and Denmark's Participation.* Copenhagen: Copenhagen Political Studies Press.

Keohane, Robert O. 1980. "The Theory of Hegemonic Stability and Changes in International Economic Regimes, 1967–1977." In Ole Holsti et al., *Change in the International System.* Boulder, Colo.: Westview Press, 131–62.

———. 1984. *After Hegemony: Cooperation and Discord in the World Political Economy.* Princeton, N.J.: Princeton University Press.

———. 1986. "Reciprocity in International Relations." *International Organization* 40, no. 1: 1–27.

———. "International Institutions: Two Approaches." *International Studies Quarterly* 32, no. 4 (December): 379–96.

———. 1993. "Sovereignty, Interdependence, and International Institutions." In Linda B. Miller and Michael Joseph Smith, eds., *Ideas and Ideals: Essays on Politics in Honor of Stanley Hoffmann.* Boulder, Colo.: Westview Press.

Keohane, Robert O., and Stanley Hoffmann, eds. 1991. *The New European Community: Decisionmaking and Institutional Change.* Boulder, Colo.: Westview Press.

Keohane, Robert O., and Joseph S. Nye. 1977. *Power and Interdependence: World Politics in Transition.* Boston: Little, Brown.

Kernell, Samuel. 1991. "Facing an Opposition Congress: The President's Strategic Circumstance." In Gary W. Cox and Samuel Kernell, eds., *The Politics of Divided Government.* Boulder, Colo.: Westview Press: 87–112.

Kiewiet, D. Roderick, and Mathew D. McCubbins. 1991. *The Logic of Delegation.* Chicago: University of Chicago Press.

King, Gary, and Lyn Ragsdale. 1988. *The Elusive Executive: Discovering Statistical Patterns in the Presidency.* Washington, D.C.: Congressional Quarterly Press.

King, Gary, Robert O. Keohane, and Sidney Verba. 1994. *Designing Social Inquiry: Scientific Inference in Qualitative Research.* Princeton, N.J.: Princeton University Press.

Klotz, Audie. 1995. "Norms Reconstituting Interests: Global Racial Equality and U.S. Sanctions Against South Africa." *International Organization* 49, no. 3 (Summer): 451–78.

Knight, Jack. 1992. *Institutions and Social Conflict.* New York: Cambridge University Press.

Knudsen, Tim. 1992. "A Portrait of Danish State-Culture: Why Denmark Needs Two National Anthems." In Kelstrup, ed.: 262–96.

Korn, Jessica. 1993. "Separation of Powers in Practice: The Limits of Legislative Veto and the Impact of Chadha." Ph.D. dissertation, Harvard University.

———. 1994–95. "The Legislative Veto and the Limits of Public Choice Analysis." *Political Science Quarterly* 109, no. 5: 873–94.

Krasner, Stephen D. 1976. "State Power and the Structure of International Trade." *World Politics* 28, no. 3 (April): 317–43.

———. 1978a. *Defending the National Interest: Raw Materials Investment and U.S. Foreign Policy.* Princeton, N.J.: Princeton University Press.

———. 1978b. "United States Commercial and Monetary Policy: Unravelling the Paradox of External Strength and Internal Weakness." In Katzenstein, ed.: 51–87.

———. ed. 1983. *International Regimes.* Ithaca, N.Y.: Cornell University Press.

Krehbiel, Keith. 1991. *Information and Legislative Organization.* Ann Arbor, Mich.: University of Michigan Press.

———. 1993. "Where's the Party? Political Parties in Legislative Politics." *British Journal of Political Science* 23, no. 2: 235–67.

Krupadanam, B. J. B. 1985. *Food Diplomacy (A Case Study): Indo-US Relations.* New Delhi: Lancers Books.

Laver, Michael, and Kenneth A. Shepsle, eds. 1994. *Cabinet Ministers and Parliamentary Government.* New York: Cambridge University Press.

Lenaerts, Koen, and Koen Coppenholle. 1992. "The Application of Community Law in Belgium, 1989–1992." *European Law Review* 17 (October): 447–65.

Lenman, Bruce P. 1992. *The Eclipse of Parliament: Appearance and Reality in British Politics since 1914.* London: Edward Arnold.

Lindsay, James M. 1994a. *Congress and the Politics of U.S. Foreign Policy.* Baltimore: Johns Hopkins University Press.

———. 1994b. "Congress, Foreign Policy, and the New Institutionalism." *International Studies Quarterly* 38, no. 2 (June): 281–304.

Lipton, Merle. 1988. *Sanctions and South Africa: The Dynamics of Economic Isolation.* Special Report no. 1119 (January). London: The Economist Intelligence Unit.

Lodge, Juliet. 1991. "The Democratic Deficit and the European Parliament." Fabian Society Discussion Paper no. 4, January.

———. 1994. "Transparency and Democratic Legitimacy." *Journal of Common Market Studies* 32, no. 3 (September): 343–68.

Loewenberg, Gerhard. 1971. *Modern Parliaments: Change or Decline?* Chicago: Aldine-Atherton.

Lohmann, Susanne. 1992. "Optimal Commitment in Monetary Policy: Credibility versus Flexibility." *American Economics Review* 82, no. 1 (March): 273–86.

Lohmann, Susanne, and Sharyn O'Halloran. 1994. "Divided Government and U.S. Trade Policy: Theory and Evidence." *International Organization* 48, no. 4: 595–632.

Ludlow, Peter. 1991. "The European Commission." In Keohane and Hoffmann, eds.: 85–132.

Lumsdaine, David Halloran. 1993. *Moral Vision in International Politics: The Foreign Aid Regime, 1949–1989.* Princeton, N.J.: Princeton University Press.

Lupia, Arthur, and Mathew D. McCubbins. 1992. "Designing Bureaucratic Accountability." Manuscript, University of California, San Diego.

———. 1994a. "Who Controls? Information and the Structure of Legislative Decision Making." *Legislative Studies Quarterly* 19, no. 3 (August): 361–84.

———. 1994b. "Learning From Oversight: Fire Alarms and Police Patrols Reconstructed." *Journal of Law, Economics, and Organization* 10, no. 1: 96–125.

———. 1995. "Can Democracy Work? Persuasion, Enlightenment, and Democratic Institutions." Manuscript, University of California, San Diego.

Mann, Michael. 1986. "The Autonomous Power of the State: Its Origins, Mechanisms, and Results." In John A. Hall, ed., *States in History.* Oxford: Basil Blackwell: 109–36.

Mansfield, Edward D. 1994. *Power, Trade, and War.* Princeton, N.J.: Princeton University Press.

Mansfield, Edward, Helen Milner, and B. Peter Rosendorff. 1998. "Why Democracies Cooperate More: Electoral Control and International Trade Agreements." Paper presented at the 1998 annual meeting of the American Political Science Association, Boston, Mass., September 3–6.

Margolis, Lawrence. 1986. *Executive Agreements and Presidential Power in Foreign Policy.* New York: Praeger.

Marks, Gary, Liesbet Hooghe, and Kermit Blank. 1996. "European Integration from the 1980s: State-Centric v. Multi-level Governance." *Journal of Common Market Studies* 34, no. 3: 341–78.

Marquand, David. 1981. "Parliamentary Accountability and the European Community." *Journal of Common Market Studies* 19, no. 3 (March): 221–36.

Martin, Lisa L. 1992a. *Coercive Cooperation: Explaining Multilateral Economic Sanctions.* Princeton, N.J.: Princeton University Press.

———. 1992b. "Institutions and Cooperation: Sanctions during the Falkland Islands Conflict." *International Security* 16, 4 (Spring): 143–78.

———. 1993a. "Credibility, Costs, and Institutions: Cooperation on Economic Sanctions." *World Politics* 45, no. 3: 406–32.

———. 1993b. "International and Domestic Institutions in the EMU Process." *Economics and Politics* 5, no. 2 (July): 125–44.

———. 1994. "Heterogeneity, Linkage, and Commons Problems." *Journal of Theoretical Politics* 6, no. 4 (October): 475–95.

———. 1997. "Legislative Influence and International Engagement." In Miles Kahler, ed., *Liberalization and Foreign Policy.* New York: Columbia University Press.

Martin, Lisa L., and Kathryn Sikkink. 1993. "U.S. Policy and Human Rights in Argentina and Guatemala, 1973–1980." In Evans, Jacobson, and Putnam, eds.: 330–62.

Mastanduno, Michael, David A. Lake, and G. John Ikenberry. 1989. "Toward a Realist Theory of State Action." *International Studies Quarterly* 33, no. 4: 457–74.

Mayer, Kenneth R. 1995. "Closing Military Bases (Finally): Solving Collective Dilemmas Through Delegation." *Legislative Studies Quarterly* 20, no. 3 (August): 393–412.

Mayhew, David R. 1991. *Divided We Govern: Party Control, Lawmaking, and Investigations, 1946–1990.* New Haven, Conn.: Yale University Press.

McCubbins, Mathew D. 1985. "Legislative Design of Regulatory Structure." *American Journal of Political Science* 29 no. 4 (November): 721–48.

———. 1991. "Government on Lay-Away: Federal Spending and Deficits Under Divided Party Control." In Gary W. Cox and Samuel Kernell, eds. *The Politics of Divided Government.* Boulder, Colo: Westview Press, 1991.

McCubbins, Mathew D., Roger G. Noll, and Barry R. Weingast. 1989. "Structure and Process, Politics and Policy: Administrative Arrangements and the Political Control of Agencies." *Virginia Law Review* 75: 431–82.

McCubbins, Mathew D., and Talbot Page. 1987. "A Theory of Congressional Delegation." In McCubbins and Sullivan, eds.: 409–25.

McCubbins, Mathew D., and Thomas Schwartz. 1984. "Congressional Oversight Overlooked: Police Patrols versus Fire Alarms," *American Journal of Political Science* 28, 1 (February): 165–79.

McCubbins, Mathew D., and Terry Sullivan, eds. 1987. *Congress: Structure and Policy.* New York: Cambridge University Press.

McGillivray, Fiona. 1995. "How Voters Shape the Institutional Framework of International Negotiations." Paper presented at a conference on Strategic Politicians, Institutions, and Foreign Policy, University of California, Davis (April 28–29).

Mearsheimer, John J. 1994/95. "The False Promise of International Institutions." *International Security* 19, no. 3 (Winter): 5–49.

Meernik, James. 1995. "Congress, the President, and the Commitment of the U.S. Military." *Legislative Studies Quarterly* 20, no. 3 (August): 377–92.

Mellor, John W. 1976. *The New Economics of Growth: A Strategy for India and the Developing World.* Ithaca, N.Y.: Cornell University Press.

Menges, Constantine G. 1988. "Sanctions '86: How the State Department Prevailed." *National Interest* 13 (Fall): 65–77.

Mercer, Jonathan. 1996. *Reputation and International Politics.* Ithaca, N.Y.: Cornell University Press.

Merriam, John G. 1979. "U.S. Wheat to Egypt: The Use of an Agricultural Commodity as a Foreign Policy Tool." In Fraenkel, Hadwiger, and Browne, eds.: 90–106.

Mezey, Michael L. 1995. "Parliament in the New Europe." In Jack Hayward and Edward C. Page, eds., *Governing the New Europe.* Durham, N.C.: Duke University Press.

Migdal, Joel. 1988. *Strong Societies and Weak States: State-Society Relations and State Capabilities in the Third World.* Princeton, N.J.: Princeton University Press.

Milgrom, Paul R., Douglass C. North, and Barry R. Weingast. 1990. "The Role of Institutions in the Revival of Trade: The Law Merchant, Private Judges, and the Champagne Fairs." *Economics and Politics* 2, no. 1 (March): 1–23.

Millett, Stephen M. 1990. *The Constitutionality of Executive Agreements: An Analysis of United States v. Belmont.* New York: Grand Publishing.

Milner, Helen V. 1988. *Resisting Protectionism: Global Industries and the Politics of International Trade.* Princeton, N.J.: Princeton University Press.

———. 1992. "International Theories of Cooperation Among Nations: Strengths and Weaknesses." *World Politics* 44, no. 3 (April): 466–96.

———. 1997. *Interests, Institutions, and Information: Domestic Politics and International Relations.* Princeton, N.J.: Princeton University Press.

Milner, Helen, and Peter Rosendorff. 1995. "Elections and International Trade Negotiations: Why Divided Government Makes International Cooperation More Likely but Less Efficient." Manuscript, Columbia University.

Milward, Alan S. 1992. *The European Rescue of the Nation-State.* Berkeley: University of California Press.

Moe, Terry M. 1990. "Political Institutions: The Neglected Side of the Story." *Journal of Law, Economics, and Organization* 6 (special issue): 213–53.

Møller, J. Ørstrøm. 1983. "Danish EC Decision-Making: An Insider's View." *Journal of Common Market Studies* 21, no. 3 (March): 245–60.

Moravcsik, Andrew. 1991. "Negotiating the Single European Act: National Interests and Conventional Statecraft in the European Community." *International Organization* 45, no. 1 (Winter): 19–56.

———. 1993. "Preferences and Power in the European Community: A Liberal Intergovernmentalist Approach." *Journal of Common Market Studies* 31, no. 4 (December): 473–523.

———. 1994. "Why the European Community Strengthens the State: Domestic Politics and International Institutions." *Center for European Studies Working Paper Series,* no. 52. Cambridge: Harvard University.

———. 1998. *The Choice for Europe: Social Purpose and State Power from Messina to Maastricht.* Ithaca, N.Y.: Cornell University Press.

Morrow, James D. 1994. "Modeling the Forms of International Cooperation: Distribution versus Information." *International Organization* 48, no. 3 (Summer): 387–423.

Muravchik, Joshua. 1992. *Exporting Democracy: Fulfilling America's Destiny.* Washington, D.C.: American Enterprise Institute Press.

Nathan, James A., and James K. Oliver. 1994. *Foreign Policy Making and the American Political System.* 3d ed. Baltimore: Johns Hopkins University Press.

National Academy of Sciences. 1991. *Finding Common Ground: U.S. Export Controls in a Changed Global Environment.* Washington, D.C.: National Academy Press.

Nau, Henry R. 1978. "The Diplomacy of World Food: Goals, Capabilities, Issues, and Arenas." In Raymond F. Hopkins and Donald J. Puchala, eds., *The Global Political Economy of Food.* Madison, Wisc.: University of Wisconsin Press.

Nelson, Joan M. 1968. *Aid, Influence, and Foreign Policy.* New York: Macmillan.

Nelson, Michael, ed. 1989. *Congressional Quarterly's Guide to the Presidency.* Washington, D.C.: Congressional Quarterly.

Neunreither, Karlheinz. 1994. "The Democratic Deficit of the European Union: Towards Closer Cooperation between the European Parliament and the National Parliaments." *Government and Opposition* 29, no. 3 (Summer): 299–314.

Niblock, Michael. 1971. *The EEC: National Parliaments in Community Decision-Making.* London: Chatham House.

Nielsen, Hans Jørgen. 1992. "The Danish Voters and the Referendum in June 1992 on the Treaty of Maastricht." In Kelstrup, ed.: 365–80.

Nincic, Miroslav. 1992. *Democracy and Foreign Policy: The Fallacy of Political Realism.* New York: Columbia University Press.

Nogee, Joseph L. 1981. "Congress and the Presidency: The Dilemmas of Policy-Making in a Democracy." In John Spanier and Joseph Nogee, eds., *Congress, the Presidency and American Foreign Policy.* New York: Pergamon Press.

Nordlinger, Eric. 1987. "Taking the State Seriously." In Myron Weiner and Samuel P. Huntington, eds., *Understanding Political Development.* Boston: Little, Brown, 353–90.

North, Douglass C. 1981. *Structure and Change in Economic History.* New York: W. W. Norton.

———. 1990. *Institutions, Institutional Change and Economic Performance.* New York: Cambridge University Press.

North, Douglass C., and Barry R. Weingast. 1989. "Constitutions and Commitment: The Evolution of Institutions Governing Public Choice in Seventeenth-Century England." *Journal of Economic History* 49, no. 4 (December): 803–32.

Norton, Philip, ed. 1995a. *Journal of Legislative Studies* 1, no. 3 (Autumn). Special Issue on National Parliaments and the European Union.

———. 1995b. "Introduction: Adapting to European Integration." *Journal of Legislative Studies* 1, no. 3 (Autumn): 1–12.

———. 1995c. "Conclusion: Addressing the Democratic Deficit," *Journal of Legislative Studies* 1, no. 3 (Autumn): 177–93.

Nugent, Neill. 1991. *The Government and Politics of the European Community.* 2d ed. Durham, N.C.: Duke University Press.

O'Halloran, Sharyn. 1994. *Politics, Process, and American Trade Policy.* Ann Arbor, Mich.: University of Michigan Press.

O'Leary, Michael Kent. 1967. *The Politics of American Foreign Aid.* New York: Atherton Press.

Oye, Kenneth A. 1979. "The Domain of Choice: International Constraints and Carter Administration Foreign Policy." In Kenneth A. Oye, Donald Rothchild, and Robert J. Lieber, eds. *Eagle Entangled: U.S. Foreign Policy in a Complex World.* New York: Longman.

———. ed. 1986a. *Cooperation under Anarchy.* Princeton, N.J.: Princeton University Press.

———. 1986b. "Explaining Cooperation under Anarchy: Hypotheses and Strategies." In Oye, ed.: 1–24.

Paarlberg, Robert L. 1978. "Food, Oil, and Coercive Resource Power." *International Security* 3, no. 2 (Fall): 3–19.

———. 1980. "Lessons of the Grain Embargo." *Foreign Affairs* 59, no. 1 (Fall): 144–62.

———. 1985. *Food Trade and Foreign Policy: India, the Soviet Union, and the United States.* Ithaca, N.Y.: Cornell University Press.

Paige, Joseph. 1977. *The Law Nobody Knows: Enlargement of the Constitution—Treaties and Executive Agreements.* New York: Vantage Press.

Pastor, Robert A. 1980. *Congress and the Politics of U.S. Foreign Economic Policy, 1929–1976.* Berkeley: University of California Press.

Pempel, T. J. 1978. "Japanese Foreign Economic Policy: The Domestic Bases for International Behavior." In Katzenstein, ed.: 139–190.

Peterson, Paul E., ed. 1994a. *The President, the Congress, and the Making of Foreign Policy.* Norman, Okla.: University of Oklahoma Press.

———. 1994b. "The International System and Foreign Policy." In Peterson, ed.: 3–22.

———. 1994c. "The President's Dominance in Foreign Policy Making." *Political Science Quarterly* 109, no. 2: 215–34.

Peterson, Trudy Huskamp. 1979. *Agricultural Exports, Farm Income, and the Eisenshower Administration.* Lincoln: University of Nebraska Press.

Pfiffner, James P. 1991. "Divided Government and the Problem of Governance." In James A. Thurber, ed., *Divided Democracy: Cooperation and Conflict Between the President and Congress.* Washington, D.C.: Congressional Quarterly Press.

Pierson, Paul. 1996. "The Path to European Integration: A Historical Institutionalist Analysis." *Comparative Political Studies* 29, no. 2: 123–163.

Prasad, Devki Nandan. 1980. *Food for Peace: The Story of U.S. Food Assistance to India.* Bombay: Asia Publishing House.

Przeworski, Adam, and Fernando Limongi. 1993. "Political Regimes and Economic Growth." *Journal of Economic Perspectives* 7, no. 3 (Summer): 51–69.

Putnam, Robert D. 1988. "Diplomacy and Domestic Politics: The Logic of Two-Level Games." *International Organization* 42 (Summer): 427–60.

Pyle, Christopher H., and Richard M. Pious. 1984. *The President, Congress, and the Constitution: Power and Legitimacy in American Politics.* New York: Free Press.

Rasmussen, Hjalte. 1988. "Denmark." In Siedentopf and Ziller, eds., 2:89–162.

Reinhardt, Eric. 1994. "Posturing Parliaments: Ratification, Uncertainty, and International Bargaining." Ph.D. dissertation, Columbia University.

Revel, Alain, and Christophe Riboud. 1986. *American Green Power.* Baltimore: Johns Hopkins University Press.

Rizutto, Franco. 1995. "The French Parliament and the EU: Loosening the Constitutional Straitjacket." *Journal of Legislative Studies* 1, no. 3 (Autumn): 46–59.

Rodrik, Dani. 1989. "Promises, Promises: Credible Policy Reform via Signalling." *Economic Journal* 99 (September): 756–72.

Rogoff, Kenneth. 1985. "The Optimal Degree of Commitment to an Intermediate Monetary Target." *Quarterly Journal of Economics* 100 (November): 1169–89.

Rogowski, Ronald. 1989. *Commerce and Coalitions: How Trade Affects Domestic Political Alignments.* Princeton, N.J.: Princeton University Press.

Rose, Richard. 1989. *Politics in England: Change and Persistence,* 5th ed. London: Macmillan.

Rueschemeyer, Dietrich, Evelyne Huber Stephens, and John D. Stephens. 1992. *Capitalist Development and Democracy.* Cambridge: Polity Press.

Russett, Bruce M. 1993. *Grasping the Democratic Peace: Principles for a Post–Cold War World.* Princeton, N.J.: Princeton University Press.

Ruttan, Vernon W., ed. 1993. *Why Food Aid?* Baltimore: Johns Hopkins University Press.

Saalfeld, Thomas. 1995. "The German Houses of Parliament and European Legislation." *Journal of Legislative Studies* 1, no. 3: 12–34.

Sanford, Jonathan E. 1977. *U.S. Policy and the Multilateral Banks: Politicization and Effectiveness.* Staff report to the Senate Foreign Relations Subcommittee on Foreign Assistance.

Santacruz, Marta Arpio. 1991. "Spanish Adaptation to Community Law: 1986–1988." *European Law Review* 16 (April): 149–60.

Sbragia, Alberta M., ed. 1992. *Euro-Politics: Institutions and Policymaking in the "New" European Community.* Washington, D.C.: Brookings Institution.

Schelling, Thomas C. 1960. *The Strategy of Conflict.* New York: Oxford University Press.

Schlesinger, Arthur M., Jr. 1989. *The Imperial Presidency.* Boston: Houghton Mifflin.

Schmitter, Philippe C. 1981. "Interest Intermediation and Regime Governability in Contemporary Western Europe and North America." In Suzanne Berger, ed., *Organizing Interests in Western Europe.* New York: Cambridge University Press: 285–327.

Schneider, William. 1984. "Public Opinion." In Joseph S. Nye, Jr., ed., *The Making of America's Soviet Policy.* New Haven, Conn.: Yale University Press.

Schou, Tove Lise. 1992. "The Debate in Denmark 1986–91 on European Integration and Denmark's Participation." In Kelstrup, ed.: 328–64.

Schoultz, Lars. 1980. "U.S. Economic Aid as an Instrument of Foreign Policy: The Case of Human Rights in Latin America." In Jack L. Nelson and Vera M. Green, eds., *International Human Rights: Contemporary Issues.* Stanfordville, N.Y.: Human Rights Publishing Group.

Schultz, Kenneth A. 1998. "Domestic Opposition and Signaling in International Crises." *American Political Science Review* 92, no. 4 (December): 829–44.

Sharpe, Kenneth E. 1988. "U.S. Policy toward Central America: The Post-Vietnam Formula under Siege." In Nora Hamilton et al., eds., *Crisis in Central America: Regional Dynamics and U.S. Policy in the 1980s.* Boulder, Colo.: Westview Press.

Shepsle, Kenneth A. 1986. "Institutional Equilibrium and Equilibrium Institutions." In Herbert Weisberg, ed., *Political Science: The Science of Politics.* New York: Agathon Press.

Shepsle, Kenneth A., and Barry R. Weingast, eds. 1995. *Positive Theories of Congressional Institutions.* Ann Arbor, Mich.: University of Michigan Press.

Siedentopf, Heinrich. 1988. "The Implementation of Directives in the Member States." In Siedentopf and Ziller, eds., 1:169–80.

Siedentopf, Heinrich, and Christoph Hauschild. 1988. "The Implementation of Community Legislation by the Member States: A Comparative Analysis." In Siedentopf and Ziller, eds., 1:1–87.

Siedentopf, Heinrich, and Jacques Ziller, eds. 1988. *Making European Policies Work: The Implementation of Community Legislation in the Member States.* 2 Vols. London: Sage.

Simmons, Beth A. 1994. *Who Adjusts? Domestic Sources of Foreign Economic Policy during the Interwar Years.* Princeton, N.J.: Princeton University Press.

Singer, Hans, John Wood, and Tony Jennings. 1987. *Food Aid: The Challenge and the Opportunity.* Oxford: Clarendon Press.

Smith, Steven S. 1994. "Congressional Party Leaders." In Peterson, ed.: 129–57.

Snidal, Duncan. 1986. "The Game *Theory* of International Politics." In Oye, ed.: 25–57.

Spaulding, Robert Mark, Jr. 1991. "German Trade Policy in Eastern Europe, 1890–1990: Preconditions for Applying International Trade Leverage." *International Organization* 45, no. 3 (Summer): 343–68.

Stanley, Harold W., and Richard G. Niemi. 1994. *Vital Statistics on American Politics,* 4th ed. Washington, D.C.: Congressional Quarterly Press.

Stein, Arthur A. 1980. "The Politics of Linkage." *World Politics* 33, no. 1 (October): 62–81.

Stein, Janice Gross. 1993. "The Political Economy of Security Agreements: The Linked Costs of Failure at Camp David." In Evans, Jacobson, and Putnam, eds.: 77–103.

Stern, Jonathan P. 1982. *East European Energy and East-West Trade in Energy.* British Institutes' Joint Energy Policy Programme, Energy Paper no. 1, London: Policy Studies Institute.

Stern, Paula. 1979. *Water's Edge.* Westport, Conn.: Greenwood Press.

Stevens, Charles J. 1977. "The Use and Control of Executive Agreements: Recent Congressional Initiatives." *Orbis* 20, no. 4 (Winter): 905–31.

Strom, Kaare. 1990. *Minority Government and Majority Rule.* New York: Cambridge University Press.

Sullivan, Roger W. 1992. "Discarding the China Card." *Foreign Policy* 86 (Spring): 3–24.

Sundquist, James L. 1981. *The Decline and Resurgence of Congress.* Washington, D.C.: Brookings Institution.

———. 1992. *Constitutional Reform and Effective Government.* Rev. ed. Washington, D.C.: Brookings Institution.

Tananbaum, Duane. 1988. *The Bricker Amendment Controversy: A Test of Eisenhower's Political Leadership.* Ithaca, N.Y.: Cornell University Press.

Timmer, C. Peter, Walter P. Falcon, and Scott R. Pearson. 1983. *Food Policy Analysis.* Baltimore: Johns Hopkins University Press.

Tisch, Sarah J., and Michael B. Wallace. 1994. *Dilemmas of Development Assistance: The What, Why, and Who of Foreign Aid.* Boulder, Colo.: Westview Press.

Tocqueville, Alexis de. 1945. *Democracy in America.* Vol. 1. New York: Vintage.

Toma, Peter A. 1967. *The Politics of Food for Peace: Executive-Legislative Interaction.* Tucson: University of Arizona Press.

Toonen, Theo A. J. 1992. "Europe of the Administrations: The Challenges of '92 (and Beyond)." *Public Administration Review* 52, no. 2 (March-April): 108–15.

Treverton, Gregory, ed. 1988. *Europe, America and South Africa.* Europe/America 7. New York: Council on Foreign Relations.

Tsebelis, George. 1994. "The Power of the European Parliament as a Conditional Agenda Setter." *American Political Science Review* 88, no. 1 (March): 128–42.

———. 1995a. "Conditional Agenda-Setting and Decision-Making *Inside* the European Parliament." *Journal of Legislative Studies* 1, no. 1 (Spring): 65–93.

———. 1995b. "Decision Making in Political Systems: Veto Players in Presidentialism, Parliamentarism, Multicameralism, and Multipartyism." *British Journal of Political Science* 25: 289–326.

Udell, Gilman G. 1976. *Agricultural Trade Development and Assistance Act of 1954 and Amendments.* Washington, D.C.: Government Printing Office.

U.S. Department of Agriculture [USDA]. Various years. *Food for Peace: Annual Report on Public Law 480* U.S. House. 1955. Agriculture Committee. *Activities under Public Law 480.* 84th Cong., 1st sess.

———. 1964a. Agriculture Committee. *Public Law 480 Extension Conference Report.* Report no. 1897. 88th Cong., 2d sess.

———. 1964b. Agriculture Committee. *Extension and Amendment of Public Law 480.* Report no. 1767. 88th Cong., 2d sess.

U.S. Department of Agriculture [USDA]. 1974. Appropriations Committee. *Agriculture— Environmental and Consumer Protection Appropriations for 1975*. 93d Cong., 2d sess.

———. 1976. International Relations Subcommittee on International Organizations. *Chile: The Status of Human Rights and Its Relationship to U.S. Economic Assistance Programs*. 94th Cong., 2d sess.

———. 1977. International Relations Committee. *New Directions in Development Aid: Excerpts from the Legislation (as of January 1977)*. 95th Cong., 1st sess.

———. 1978a. Committee on Standards of Official Conduct. *Korean Influence Investigation*. 95th Cong., 2d sess.

———. 1978b. Banking, Finance, and Urban Affairs Subcommittee on International Development Institutions and Finance. *U.S. Participation in Multilateral Development Institutions*. 95th Cong., 2d sess.

———. 1980. Foreign Affairs Committee. *Resolution of Inquiry concerning Human Rights Policies*. 96th Cong., 2d sess.

U.S. Senate. 1964. Agriculture and Forestry Committee. *Extension and Amendment of Public Law 480*. Report no. 1467. 88th Cong., 2d sess.

———. 1965. Agriculture and Forestry Committee. *Food and Agriculture Act of 1965*. 89th Cong., 1st sess.

———. 1966. Agriculture and Forestry Committee. *Emergency Food Relief for India*. 89th Cong., 2d sess.

———. 1973a. Agriculture and Forestry Committee, Subcommittee on Foreign Agricultural Policy. *U.S. Foreign Agricultural Trade Policy*. 93d Cong., 1st sess.

———. 1973b. Foreign Relations Committee. *Foreign Economic Assistance, 1973*. 93d Cong., 1st sess.

———. 1974a. Agriculture and Forestry Committee, Subcommittee on Foreign Agricultural Policy. *Foreign Food Assistance*. 93d Cong., 2d sess.

———. 1974b. Select Committee on Nutrition and Human Needs. *Report on Nutrition and the International Situation*. 93d Cong., 2d sess.

———. 1977. Foreign Relations Committee, Subcommittee on Foreign Assistance. *Human Rights*. 95th Cong., 1st sess.

———. 1982. Foreign Relations Committee, Subcommittee on International Economic Policy. *Soviet-European Gas Pipeline*. 97th Cong., 2d sess.

———. 1986. Foreign Relations Committee. *Hearings on the South African Situation*. 99th Cong., 2d sess.

Vaubel, Roland. 1986. "A Public Choice Approach to International Organization." *Public Choice* 51, no. 1: 39–57.

Vázquez, Carlos Manuel. 1995. "The Four Doctrines of Self-Executing Treaties." *American Journal of International Law* 89, no. 4 (October): 694–723.

Vedel, Georges. 1994. "Revisions to the French Constitution (Article 88) for French-EC Affairs." The Mentor Group Conference, Conseil D'Etat, Paris (July).

Victor, David G., Kal Raustiala, and Eugene Skolnikoff. 1998. *Implementation and Effectiveness of International Environmental Commitments: Theory and Practice*. Cambridge: MIT Press.

Vogelgesang, Sandy. 1980. *American Dream, Global Nightmare: The Dilemma of U.S. Human Rights Policy*. New York: W. W. Norton and Co.

von Amerongen, Otto Wolff. 1980. "Economic Sanctions as a Foreign Policy Tool?" *International Security* 5, no. 2 (Fall): 159–67.

Wallace, Helen. 1973. *National Governments and the European Communities*. London: Chatham House.

———. 1984. "Implementation across National Boundaries." In David Lewis and Helen Wallace, eds., *Policies Into Practice: National and International Case Studies in Implementation*. New York: St. Martin's Press.

Wallensteen, Peter. 1976. "Scarce Goods as Political Weapons: The Case of Food." *Journal of Peace Research* 13, no. 4: 277–98.

Wallerstein, Mitchel B. 1980. *Food for War—Food for Peace: United States Food Aid in a Global Context*. Cambridge: MIT Press.

Waltz, Kenneth N. 1967. *Foreign Policy and Democratic Politics: The American and British Experience*. Boston: Little, Brown.

———. 1979. *Theory of International Politics*. New York: Random House.

Weinbaum, Marvin G. 1982. *Food, Development, and Politics in the Middle East*. Boulder, Colo.: Westview Press.

———. 1986. *Egypt and the Politics of U.S. Economic Aid*. Boulder, Colo.: Westview Press.

Weingast, Barry R. 1989. "The Political Institutions of Representative Government: Legislatures." Hoover Institution Working Papers in Political Science, P-89–14.

Weingast, Barry R., and William J. Marshall. 1988. "The Industrial Organization of Congress; or, Why Legislatures, like Firms, Are Not Organized as Markets." *Journal of Political Economy* 96, no. 1: 132–63.

Weingast, Barry R., and Mark J. Moran. 1983. "Bureaucratic Discretion or Congressional Control: Regulatory Agency Policy Making at the FTC." *Journal of Political Economy* 91, no. 5: 765–800.

Williams, Shirley. 1991. "Sovereignty and Accountability in the European Community." In Keohane and Hoffmann, eds.: 155–76.

Williamson, Oliver. 1985. *The Economic Institutions of Capitalism: Firms, Markets, Relational Contracting*. New York: Free Press.

Wittman, Donald. 1989. "Why Democracies Produce Efficient Results." *Journal of Political Economy* 97, no. 6: 1395–424.

Worre, Torben. 1988. "Denmark at the Crossroads: The Danish Referendum of 28 February 1986 on the EC Reform Package." *Journal of Common Market Studies* 26, no. 4 (June): 361–88.

———. 1995. "First No, Then Yes: The Danish Referendums on the Maastricht Treaty 1992 and 1993." *Journal of Common Market Studies* 33, no. 2 (June): 235–57.

Zysman, John. 1978. "The French State in the International Economy." In Katzenstein, ed.: 255–93.

Index

Abdication Hypothesis, definition of, 49; abdication model, 148, 149, 150, 153, 168
African National Congress (ANC), 102
Agency for International Development (AID), 122, 135
Agricultural Trade Development and Assistance Act of 1954, 114. *See also* Public Law (PL) 480
Allende, Salvador, 132
Angola, 93; U.S. policy on, 93
apartheid, 81, 100; U.S. anti-apartheid groups, 101
Argentina, conflict with Britain over Falkland Islands, 84
arms-control agreements, 73
Audretsch, H. A. H., 175
Austria, 157, 160, 161, 180, 181

Badeau, John, 142
Bangladesh, 118–19, 136
Banks, Jeffrey S., 29
bargaining power, 126, 127; of Denmark, 179
beggar-thy-neighbor economic policies, 1
Belgian Congo, arms shipments to, 143
Belgium, 157, 160, 170, 173–74, 175, 179, 180, 183, 184, 185, 185n.9; Senate in, 156
Benson, Ezra Taft, 114
Bergman, Torbjörn, 160, 180–81
Borchard, Edwin M., 57
Brazil, 118–19
Brewer, John, 46
Bricker, John W., 76–77; Bricker amendment, 77; Brickerites, 76; revolt, 76
Britain, 84, 101, 160, 175, 195; conflict with Argentina over Falkland Islands, 84; policy toward the EU in, 33. *See also* United Kingdom
Brussels, 12n.3, 183, 185
Buchan, David, 172
Burma, 117
Bush, George, 105, 106, 107, 108, 109; administration of, 105, 108, 110
Butz, Earl, 135

Cambodia, 121, 134, 135; U.S. military involvement in, 28

Camp David accords, 123, 142, 144, 199, 201
Carter, Jimmy, 133, 146, 201; administration of, 100
Case, Clifford, 78; Case Act, 77, 77n.8, 78, 197
Central Intelligence Agency (CIA), 102
Chadha v. Immigration and Naturalization Service, 61n.3, 104
Chile, 38, 132
China, 23, 109–10, 137; government of, 105, 109; most-favored nation (MFN) status of, 82, 103–10; sanctions against, 23, 105
Christopher, Warren, 108, 109
Ciavarini Azzi, Giuseppe, 176, 185n.9
Clinton, Bill, 108, 109, 110; administration of, 105
Colchester, Nicholas, 172
Cold War, 6, 17, 57
collaborative control, 45
collective-action problems, 30, 35, 36, 39, 47, 92, 194
Columbia, 132
commitment dilemma(s), 4, 30, 36, 198
Commodity Credit Corporation (CCC), 115–16
Communist countries, 103, 104, 115, 121
Comprehensive Anti-Apartheid Act (CAA) of 1986, 100, 101, 102
constrained optimizers, 167
Cooley, Harold, 117; Cooley Loan program, 117
Cooperation Hypothesis, definition of, 51; empirical results of, 200
Cox, Gary W., 29, 35
Credibility Hypothesis, definition of, 23; empirical results of, 200
Crone, Donald K., 45
Cuba, 93, 121; Soviet Union support of, 83

Davis, John H., 120
decline of parliaments, 21, 24
DeConcini, Dennis, 93
Delegation Hypothesis, definition of, 48; delegation model, 32, 149, 153, 154, 155; empirical results of, 200

Denmark, 152, 157, 160, 161, 165, 170–72, 173–74, 180–81, 183–84, 189, 195, 199; constitution of, 176; Danish European Committee, 160; Danish model, 161; entry into the EU of, 177; *Folketing*, 176–78, 181, 189; interests of, 169; ministers of, 169, 177, 178; negotiators for, 175, 179; parliamentary system of, 42; TEU resistance of, 155
détente, 104
distributional models, 32
Dole, Robert, 101
Dominican Republic, 85
Downs, George W., 38n.4

Ecuador, 132
Egypt, 113, 117, 118–19, 121, 123, 133, 136, 142–45, 146, 199, 201
Eisenhower, Dwight D., 68, 70, 76, 77, 114, 142; administration of, 76, 114, 117, 132
Elliot, Kimberly Ann, 87
England, 46; cabinet government in, 29; evolution of government institutions in, 46. *See also* United Kingdom
equilibrium institutions, 11n.2
European Affairs Committee, 160, 177n.8. *See also* Market Relations Committee (MRC)
European Central Bank (ECB), 160
European Court of Justice (ECJ), 165, 170, 175, 185
European Monetary Union (EMU), 4, 160, 188
European Parliament (EP), powers of, 153
Evasion Hypothesis, definition of, 53
executive-dominance model, 8, 9, 48, 49, 80, 89, 95–96, 182
Export-Import Bank, 100

Falkland Islands, conflict between Argentina and Britain over, 84
fast-track, 11, 59, 61
Federalist Papers, 6
Federal Trade Commission (FTC), 27
Ferejohn, John, 29
Finland, 180; parliament of, 157, 161
Fitzmaurice, John, 156
food-aid programs, Food for Progress, 122; Food for Development, 122; Food for Peace, 122
Ford, Gerald, 94, 132, 134
Foreign Assistance Act (1974), 121
Foreign Relations Committee, 77
Formosa [Taiwan], 117

France, 17, 44, 156, 157, 160, 173–74, 180; complaints filed against, 175n.5; government of, 153; scrutiny procedures in, 160n.3; TEU referendum in, 155
Freeman, Orville, 139
free-trade areas, 21, 38

Galbraith, John Kenneth, 138
Gandhi, Indira, 140
George, Walter, 77; George amendment, 77
Germany, 156, 158, 166, 173–74, 179, 180, 181, 184, 185; *Bundesrat*, 156, 160; *Länder*, 181, 184, 185, 185n.9; parliament of, 160
Gilligan, Thomas W., 26
Greece, 117, 132, 156, 158, 172, 173–74, 180, 184
Greif, Avner, 46
Guyana, 132

Haiti, 34, 81, 83, 85; U.S. policy toward, 84
Hamilton, Lee, 110
Hauschild, Christoph, 179
Hegeland, Hans, 160, 161
hegemonic-stability theory, 39
Helms, Jesse, 109
hidden-hand presidency, 76
House Ways and Means Committee, 107, 109
Huber, John D., 148
Hufbauer, Gary Clyde, 87
Humphrey, Hubert, 115, 120, 124, 136

Ikenberry, G. John, 45
India, 113, 117, 118–19, 121, 132, 133, 137, 138, 139, 140, 141, 144, 199; government of, 139, 139n.5; investments of, 142; policies of, 134
Indonesia, 118–19, 132
Influence Hypothesis, definition of, 49; empirical results of, 200; legislative-influence model, 8
informational models, 26, 32
institutional equilibrium, 11n.2
Intergovernmental Conference (1996), 156
International Emergency Powers Act, 86
Interparliamentary Conference (COSAC), 156
Iran, 117, 132; government of, 117
Iraq, 81; invasion of Kuwait, 86
Ireland, 158, 170, 173–74, 180
Italy, 156, 158, 170, 172, 173–74, 177, 179, 180; *Camera Dei Deputati*, 156; parliaments of, 166

Jackson, Henry, 103
Jackson-Vanik Amendment, 103, 104, 109
Japan, 44, 113, 116–17; production in, 114
Johnson, Gary C., 76n.7
Johnson, Lyndon B., 68, 70, 121, 130, 133, 134, 138, 139, 140–41, 143, 145, 146, 199, 200; administration of, 121, 143
Judge, David, 156

Kashmir, 140
Kennedy, John F., 142; administration of, 100, 132, 143
Keohane, Robert O., 9, 13
Kiewiet, D. Roderick, 35
King, Gary, 9
Kissinger, Henry, 144
Knowland, William F., 76; Knowland amendment, 76
Korea, 117, 137; South Korea, 118–19, 132
Korean War, 114, 137
Korn, Jessica, 61n.3
Krehbiel, Keith, 26
Krugerrands, ban on import of, 101
Krupadanam, B. J. B., 141
Kuwait, Iraqi invasion of, 86

Latin America, 44; human rights practices of, 81
Laver, Michael, 33, 154, 167, 167n.1
League of Nations, 38
Lindsay, James M., 7, 36n.3
Lodge, Juliet, 150
Lord, Winston, 108
Lugar, Richard, 101
Lumsdaine, David Halloran, 123n.2
Luxembourg, 156, 159, 173–74, 179, 180

Maastricht Treaty, 151, 152, 155, 156, 196, 201. See also Treaty on European Union (TEU)
Malaysia, 132
Mann, Michael, 45
Margolis, Lawrence, 65, 72
Market Relations Committee (MRC), 177, 177n.8, 178. See also European Affairs Committee
Marshall, William J., 25
Martin, Lisa L., Coercive Cooperation, vii
Mattson, Ingvar, 160, 161
McCubbins, Mathew D., 27–28, 29, 35
Mead, Arthur, 129–30
Milgrom, Paul R., 46

Milner, Helen V., 40n.5, 43
Mitchell, George, 106–107
Møller, J. Ørstrøm, 179
Moran, Mark J., 27
Moravcsik, Andrew, 167
Morocco, 118–19
most-favored nation (MFN) status, 103–10
Moynihan, Daniel Patrick, 106

Nasser, Gamal Abdel, 142, 143, 144
Nathan, James A., 6, 57
National Commitments Resolution, 77
National Security Council (NSC), 102, 122, 135
neofunctionalism, 182–84
Netherlands, 159, 173–75, 180
Neunreither, Karlheinz, 168n.2
new institutionalism, 24n.1
Nixon, Richard, 94, 132, 134, 145; administration of, 34, 196
Noll, Roger G., 29
North American Free Trade Agreement (NAFTA), 10, 59
North Atlantic Treaty Organization (NATO), 4, 59; allies of, 116
North, Douglass C., 46

O'Leary, Michael Kent, 143n.6
Oliver, James K., 6, 57
Ordinary Least Squares (OLS), 66, 70–71

Paarlberg, Robert L., 139n.5, 141
Pakistan, 117, 118–19, 136; Kashmir settlement of, 138, 140
Pareto-improving, 13
parliamentary activism, 148
parliamentary impotence, 148
parliamentary institutions, logic of, 11
partisan-politics explanation, 96
Pastor, Robert A., 115n.1
Pelosi, Nancy, 106, 107, 108, 109; Pelosi bill, 109
Persian Gulf crisis, 83, 84
Peterson, Paul E., 6
Peterson, Trudy Huskamp, 115, 123
Poisson model, 71
Portugal, 159, 172–74, 180, 184–85; economy of, 184
power of the purse, 28, 42
presidential shirking, 95
principal-agent interactions, 22, 24; settings, 62

Prisoners' Dilemma, 35, 37, 41
Public Law (PL) 480, Title I, 116–17, 120–21, 129, 131–37, 144; Title II, 116; Title III, 116. *See also* Agricultural Trade Development and Assistance Act of 1954

Reagan, Ronald, 100, 101; administration of, 85, 101, 102, 122
Realism, 37
Reciprocal Trade Agreements Act of 1934, 59
Reinhardt, Eric, 43
Rocke, David M., 38n.4
Rosendorff, Peter, 43
Rueschemeyer, Dietrich, 9n.1
Russia, *Duma*, 166. *See also* Soviet Union
Ruttan, Vernon W., 131n.4

Sadat, Anwar, 144
Schott, Jeffrey J., 87
Schultz, George, 102
Schultz, Kenneth A., 50, 63
Schwartz, Thomas, 27–28
self-executing agreements, 42
Senate Committee on the Judiciary, 76
Senate Foreign Relations Committee, 102
Sharpe, Kenneth E., 6
Shepsle, Kenneth A., 11n.2, 33, 154, 167, 167n.1
Shipan, Charles, 29
Siberian natural-gas-pipeline-sanctions episode, 85
Siedentopf, Heinrich, 179
signaling, 63
Silva, Aníbal Cavaco, 184
Single European Act (SEA), 151, 152, 153, 154, 155, 171, 176, 188
Soares, Mário, 184
Solarz, Stephen, 106
sole-executive authority, 54, 58, 59
Solomon, Gerald, 109; Solomon bill, 110
South Africa, 81, 111; government of, 100, 101, 102; sanctions against, 78n.9, 87n.2, 93n.3, 99–101, 102, 195n.1; Sharpeville shootings in, 100; Soweto student protests in, 100
Southeast Asia, 45, 130, 135, 138, 196; economic powers of, 44; Nixon administration's policies in, 34; U.S. military commitments in, 77
Soviet Union, 81, 85, 105, 117, 138–39; support for Cuba, 83. *See also* Russia

Spain, 159, 173–74, 180, 184, 185; as alliance partner in post-Franco era, 63; court system of, 185; military bases in, 62, 63; parliament of, 179
state-owned industries, 107
states' rights, 77
state strength, 41, 44, 45, 46. *See also* strong state(s)
status-quo bias, 64
Stephens, Evelyne Huber, 9n.1
Stephens, John D., 9n.1
Strategic Politicians, Institutions, and Foreign Policy, 53
strong state(s), 6, 43–44, 45, 177. *See also* state strength
struggle for power, 4, 11, 55
subgame-perfect strategy, 14, 14n.4
Subramaniam, Chidambara, 139n.5
Suez Canal, 142
Sweden, 159, 161, 174, 180; parliament of, 160, 161
Symington, Stuart, 77; Symington subcommittee, 77

tactical issue-linkage, 84
Tananbaum, Duane, 76, 76n.7
Tanzania, 132
Tiananmen Square massacre, 104, 105
time-series effects, 66, 71
Tocqueville, Alexis de, 5
Toonen, Theo A. J., 177
Trading with the Enemy Act, 86
transaction-cost economics, 38, 46
Trans Africa, 101
Treaty on European Union (TEU), 151, 152, 153, 155, 161, 177n.8, 178, 188, 201. *See also* Maastricht Treaty
Treaty of Rome, 152, 165
Truman, Harry, 137
Turkey, 117
two-level games, 39, 41

United Kingdom, 159, 173–74, 179, 180. *See also* Britain; England
United Nations Genocide Convention, 76
U.S. Constitution, 54, 56
U.S. Supreme Court, 57, 61n.3, 104

Vázquez, Carlos Manuel, 61n.3
Verba, Sidney, 9

Vietnam, 6, 7, 134, 144; South Vietnam, 113, 118–19, 121, 134, 135, 136; South Vietnamese government, 116, 121, 134; U.S. involvement in, 28, 76, 77, 140

Wallerstein, Mitchel B., 134
Watergate, 34, 196
Weingast, Barry R., 25, 27, 29, 46

Williams, Shirley, 177
Wittman, Donald, 47

Yemen, 142
Yugoslavia, 81, 117, 118–19; succession crisis in, 83

zero-sum, 4, 11, 19
Zimbabwe, sanctions against, 87n.2